The Textbook of
TOTAL QUALITY
in
HEALTHCARE

Edited by

A.F. Al-Assaf, M.D.
Department of Health Administration and Policy
University of Oklahoma Health Sciences Center

June A. Schmele, R.N., Ph.D.
College of Nursing
University of Oklahoma Health Sciences Center

S^{t}L

St. Lucie Press
Delray Beach, Florida

Library of Congress Cataloging-in-Publication Data

The Textbook of total quality in healthcare / edited by A. F. Al-Assaf and June A. Schmele.
      p.   cm.
    Includes bibliographical references and index.
    ISBN 0-9634030-4-4
    Includes bibliographical references and index.
    1. Medical care—Quality control. 2. Total quality management.
  I. Al-Assaf, A. F., 1956– II. Schmele, June A., 1935–
    [DNLM: 1. Quality Assurance, Health Care—organization & administration—United States. W 84 AA1 T3 1993]
    RA399.A1T49   1993
    362.1'068'5—dc20
    DNLM/DLC   93-31083
    for Library of Congress   CIP

Direct all inquiries to St. Lucie Press, Inc., 100 E. Linton, Blvd., Suite 403B, Delray Beach Florida, 33483.
    Phone: (407) 274-9906
    Fax: (407) 274-9927 S_{L}^{t}

Published by
St. Lucie Press
100 E. Linton Blvd., Suite 403B
Delray Beach, FL 33483

This book is dedicated to our families:

Rehab, Ali, Alia, and General and Mrs. Al-Assaf—

Bob, Bill, my nieces and nephews
and the memory of Jimmy—

And to our mutual mentor and friend,
the late Ivan Hanson, Ph.D.

FOREWORD

Quality is an important aspect of healthcare; indeed, for most people, it is the most important aspect. Quality is defined in the dictionary as "degree of excellence" or "superiority in kind."

Quality of care must be a part of both the process and the outcome of healthcare wherever possible. The issue is how does the system develop the mechanisms to assure such quality?

This book is an excellent compilation of methods to define, implement, and monitor such mechanisms. A comprehensive discussion of Total Quality and its impact on healthcare is also presented. It is both timely and important. Developed as a textbook to educate future healthcare workers, it can also serve as a reference book for those already in the field.

Clearly, Total Quality in healthcare is very important. This book will make an essential contribution to the future of quality healthcare.

Edward N. Brandt, Jr., MD, PhD
Professor and Co-Director
Center of Health Policy Research and Development
University of Oklahoma Health Sciences Center and
Former Assistant Secretary for Health, DHHS (1981–1984)

CONTRIBUTORS

A. F. Al-Assaf, M.D., M.P.H., M.S., CQA
Assistant Professor of Health
  Administration and Policy
University of Oklahoma Health
  Sciences Center
Oklahoma City, Oklahoma

Ronna K. Baird, R.N., M.S., ARNP
Pediatric Program Consultant
Child Health and Guidance Services
Oklahoma State Department of Health
Oklahoma City, Oklahoma

Sherry Cadenhead, R.N., M.S.
Nurse Consultant
Shawnee, Oklahoma

Keith Curtis, M.B.A., Ph.D.
Associate Professor of Health
  Administration and Policy
University of Oklahoma Health
  Sciences Center
Oklahoma City, Oklahoma

Steven J. Gentling, M.H.A.
Director
VA Medical Center
Oklahoma City, Oklahoma

Carol Lee Hamilton, R.N., J.D., M.P.A.
Attorney at Law and
  Management Consultant
Southlake, Texas

Allen C. Meadors, M.B.A., Ph.D., FACHE
Professor and Dean
College of Health, Social and Public
  Services
Eastern Washington University
Cheney, Washington

John Morrison, M.P.H.
Total Quality Improvement
  Coordinator
VA Medical Center
Oklahoma City, Oklahoma

June A. Schmele, R.N., Ph.D.
Associate Professor
College of Nursing
University of Oklahoma Health
  Sciences Center
Oklahoma City, Oklahoma

Douglas W. Stewart, D.O.
Clinical Assistant Professor of
  Pediatrics
University of Oklahoma College of
  Medicine–Tulsa
Tulsa, Oklahoma

Brian S. Tindall, M.S.H.A.
Administrator
Lawton Outpatient Clinic
Lawton, Oklahoma

CONTENTS

PREFACE

Total Quality, already an established movement in many businesses and industries, has only recently been introduced into the healthcare system. This textbook is intended to provide an overview of this relatively new leadership paradigm specifically as applicable to healthcare organizations. The selection of the topics for each chapter was directed toward meeting the specific objective of providing a blend of theory and practice application. Students of TQ and healthcare professionals will find this book helpful as a practical guide to implementation of TQ as well as a learning guide that can be used for education and training in TQ. It is intended to provide the knowledge base and practical application that is essential to the implementation of this management philosophy.

The book is targeted to TQ students and healthcare professionals in management, clinical, and support services. It is also suitable for those involved in leadership and management education and training. Academic programs will find this book very useful as a major textbook for courses in TQ, quality management, general and strategic management, or leadership. This book can also serve as a reference for health administrators and others involved in the cultural transformation and coordination of a Total Quality Program.

There are several chapters that introduce the TQ philosophy as a unique leadership paradigm and these chapters include a collection of classic articles on TQ by leaders in the field. The book starts with an introduction and history of TQ and its movement from the manufacturing sector to the healthcare industry. Quality is then discussed as a major cornerstone of the healthcare delivery system. TQ is further described according to the main principles, methods of implementation, and the tools of assessing progress. Environmental elements including cost, legality, and research are presented. The book includes a section on the comparative analysis of TQ with other management principles and concludes with an annotated bibliography.

PART I

HISTORY AND OVERVIEW

1

INTRODUCTION and HISTORICAL BACKGROUND

A. F. Al-Assaf, MD, MPH

This book is about the Total Quality (TQ) philosophy as a contemporary leadership paradigm in healthcare. It focuses on the idea that healthcare has three major cornerstones: *quality, access,* and *cost.* Although they are interdependent and can impact one another, quality has a major influence on access and cost. Quality is achieved when accessible services are provided in an efficient, cost-effective, and acceptable manner. A quality service is customer oriented. It is also a service that is available, accessible, acceptable, affordable, and controllable. Quality is achieved when the needs and expectations of the customer are met. In healthcare, the patient is the most important customer. When properly implemented, TQ should ensure the quality of services rendered by an organization and the quality of the outcomes produced by those services.

TQ originated in Japan. This new management concept was introduced shortly after World War II to help the Japanese manufacturing industry improve its products and services. With major improvements in Japanese industries, U.S. industries started to search for the factors behind these improvements. However, TQ was not introduced *en masse* in U.S. industry until the early 1980s.

Let us now look at the history of this management concept and its evolution into a leadership paradigm. We will also examine the shift of emphasis in healthcare from *structure* standards to *process* standards and, more recently, to *outcome* standards.

The EARLY DAYS of QUALITY ASSURANCE

Quality assessment and control in healthcare dates back to mid-nineteenth-century England, where Florence Nightingale served as a nurse during the Crimean War (Bull, 1992). Nightingale was the first to identify a positive correlation between the introduction of adequate nursing care to wounded soldiers and the lower mortality rate among them. She attributed a positive outcome to quality of care. After the end of the war, Nightingale documented this fact in several studies that examined other components of quality as well. She studied the extent of services provided and resources utilized in relation to quality of outcome and was instrumental in preparing several quality criteria for nursing care. These concepts were tested for a period, but few clinicians continued to study the correlation between care and outcome. During the early part of the twentieth century, several U.S. physicians conducted studies on the assessment of quality in healthcare. In 1914, Ernest Codman, a surgeon at Massachusetts General Hospital, studied general surgeries and their follow-ups. He was responsible for influencing the adoption of follow-up exams one year after surgery. This prompted the American College of Surgeons, in 1918, to create the Hospital Standardization Program, which provided criteria and standards for accreditation that were later adopted by the then Joint Commission on Accreditation of Hospitals.

In the early 1900s, an interest in structure criteria began to develop. In 1910 Abraham Flexner presented a famous report documenting his study of physician education in the U.S., in which he was quick to point out deficiencies in the medical education system. He emphasized that the quality of care the patient received is directly related to physician education and that medical education needed substantial reform. As a consequence of Flexner's study, a large number of medical schools closed because of their inability to meet the reform criteria outlined in his report. The emphasis had shifted from process elements (activities) to structure elements (i.e., human and physical resources). Education, certification, and licensure became very important in qualifying a healthcare professional and an educational institution. Several professional associations were established to provide these services. State licensure and examining boards spread slowly throughout the country.

A similar interest in structure standards of healthcare organizations started taking place. This influenced the American College of Surgeons to establish the Joint Commission on Accreditation of Hospitals (JCAH) in 1952 (JCAH later changed its name to the Joint Commission on Accreditation of Healthcare Organizations or JCAHO). JCAH, as it was then called, published its first list of accreditation standards for hospitals. A hospital that met those standards was accredited and certified as a quality institution. (It is noteworthy that this first list of accreditation standards fit on a single page. Today the list is compiled in a manual consisting of a few hundred pages.) JCAH standards were structural standards that emphasized the quality of the credentialing process as well as risk management standards. The objective of the accreditation process was to ensure that care was delivered in a safe physical environment by qualified providers. Of course, the then JCAH assumed that meeting the structure criteria was equivalent to providing quality medical care.

The interest in quality measures continued in the 1950s. In clinical practice several physicians studied the quality of medical care delivered by practitioners in the U.S. Unlike the JCAH, these studies were primarily process oriented, focusing on the process of delivering care. According to Brook and Avery (1975), one study by Dr. O. L. Peterson focused on the care provided by general practitioners. Dr. Peterson reviewed the processes and procedures conducted during patient examinations and follow-ups. Another physician, Dr. M. A. Morehead, compared the ambulatory care practices of physicians. A third study was conducted by Dr. B. C. Payne. He compared the care delivered by a select group of physicians in acute care hospitals with a set of predesigned criteria. All three studies concluded that there were deficiencies in patient care and that quality of care needed to be monitored and improved continuously.

HISTORY of TQ in MANUFACTURING

Between 1948 and 1949, Japan was trying to recover from its losses from World War II and was searching for ways to revive its economy. Several Japanese engineers found that improvement in quality usually led to increased productivity (Deming, 1986). This finding was derived from Walter A. Shewhart's (1931) earlier work and literature supplied by Bell Laboratories (from General Douglas MacArthur's staff) and became the impetus for Japanese management to learn quality improvement methods. In 1950, W. Edwards Deming, an American statistician, was invited to Japan to teach methods of improving quality. Dr. Deming was instrumental in showing the Japanese engineers that improving productivity is dependent on decreasing the variability of processes in a plant. He emphasized Shewhart's Statistical Quality Control principle: production errors can be predicted and prevented. When this principle is correctly applied, a defective product is rarely produced, so the consumer rarely sees one. The Japanese learned rather quickly that, to survive, they needed to study the consumers who used their products. They understood that focusing on meeting the needs and expectations of their customers was the only way to improve their economy.

Following World War II, Japan's natural resources (i.e., oil, fuel, etc.) were depleted. The only resource Japan had was its people. In order to survive, manufactured products had to be marketed and sold successfully to an outside market. Of course, such markets were purchasing higher quality goods than the Japanese were producing. To compete, Japan

5

needed to improve the quality of the products it produced. Hence, management made quality the most important target. A defect-prevention paradigm was communicated to workers. This paradigm predicted that as quality is improved, costs will decline (the system will incur less rework, waste, and errors and will use its human and physical resources more efficiently), and productivity will improve. As productivity improves, more markets can be captured, more jobs maintained and created, and more businesses succeed. Every worker came to understand that producing affordable, reliable, defect-free, and acceptable products was important to keeping his or her job. They also recognized that this approach was important to rebuilding Japan's economy. It became obvious to the worker that improving quality was not only a requirement of his or her job, but also a personal responsibility. TQ spread throughout Japan's corporations and institutions over the next twenty years. Although American goods and products were dominant during this period, this success was detrimental in the long term. Shielded by its dominant position, American industry lacked incentive for the major improvements and developments necessary to maintain market share.

It was not until 1973, when the OPEC oil embargo took effect, that Americans began to recognize their dependence on other countries. The automobile industry finally realized that foreign cars were taking over more and more of the U.S. auto market. The same was true for other products, particularly those produced in Japan. From cameras to electronics to watches, Japanese products gained market share at the expense of American industries. Japan began to export many fine products to the U.S. and to the rest of the world. As their market share eroded, American corporations began studying Japanese companies to determine the reasons for their success. In time it became obvious to U.S. industries that quality is dependent on the worker and that utilizing this potential is critical to improving productivity. A number of American management programs were based primarily on worker participation and involvement in problem solving. Quality Circles, Employee Involvement, and Quality of Worklife were all based on participative management. These programs and others continued through the 1970s with varying degrees of success.

Those companies that understood the need for cultural change achieved improvements in quality. Those that did not change their culture were not as successful. Commitment and active involvement by management must drive any significant organizational change, particularly a radical cultural change, because these changes cannot be delegated or decreed. Without a commitment from management, quality programs that encouraged employee participation faltered and failed. Employees sensed that management did not support their work and managers were not ready to empower their employees. Overall, management in American industry was still unaware that the problems it faced were mainly system problems, not people problems. Many did not realize what was happening until June 1980, when NBC aired the landmark program entitled "If Japan Can, Why Can't We?" In an interview, Dr. W. Edwards Deming told of his experiences and successes with the manufacturing industry in Japan. He emphasized the major principles for improving quality and productivity—basic management skills and statistical process control to reduce process variability. Certain major U.S. corporations decided to test this philosophy, introducing it in their organizations. Word spread to other companies, and for the next several years the "quality movement" became a reality in a number of U.S. industries.

THE INFLUENCE OF GOVERNMENT on QUALITY in HEALTHCARE

Several events occurred before healthcare organizations started adopting TQ, or quality improvement principles. TQ did not become known in healthcare until the late 1980s. Until that time, organizations in the healthcare industry generally viewed TQ as a business management practice that was not applicable to this field. In their opinion, quality in healthcare was assured through the efforts of several quasi-regulatory agencies that demanded the application of certain standards in providing care. This was evident in the sequence of events discussed below.

In 1965, President Johnson signed into law two major amendments to the Social Security Act, namely Title 18 (Medicare) and Title 19 (Medicaid). The main objectives of these amendments were to increase access to healthcare services for certain beneficiaries—the elderly and the poor, respectively. However, the act also provided mechanisms to ensure the provision of quality healthcare services to those benefiting. These mechanisms were intended to ensure quality of care by monitoring the structure of a healthcare organization (its providers and institutions) and, to a lesser extent, its process (the way it delivers care). Medicare and Medicaid also provided certain incentives for providers to deliver quality services. During and after this time, the government encouraged the JCAH (as it was then named) to enforce its accreditation requirements and tighten its standards for certifying the quality of hospitals. Some consider this role semi-regulatory, and it has had a major influence on the establishment of quality assurance departments in healthcare organizations.

During the same period (1966), Avedis Donabedian, a university professor and physician, introduced his three approaches to assess quality: structure, process, and outcome. He urged healthcare organizations to examine all three approaches when monitoring and ensuring the quality of care. He described *structure* as including both human and physical resources associated with the delivery of healthcare to the patient. His definition of *process* included all the procedures and activities required to deliver medical care by providers and support systems. *Outcome*, on the other hand, included results and outputs of the care process, for example, morbidity and mortality rates, patient satisfaction, etc. Different players in the healthcare industry used this model without fully understanding it. Unfortunately, they used these approaches separately and independent of each other, when they should have been used together.

During the 1970s, government concern over escalating healthcare costs continued. In an attempt to control cost and preserve quality, the legislature passed two bills that had direct impact on the quality of care delivered. In 1972, one bill established Professional Standards Review Organizations (PSROs). These organizations were to review the standards for care provided to inpatient Medicare recipients, to ensure that they received adequate and appropriate treatment. PSROs, however, received several negative reactions from a number of interest groups. Because PSROs were physician oriented, other disciplines felt that they were not fairly represented in the assessment process. They argued that this situation was counterproductive to the effective evaluation of care provided. Physicians, on the other hand, felt that their work and humanitarian efforts to preserve life were being questioned. Those physicians who participated in PSROs found themselves ostracized by their peers and were viewed as "traitors" to their profession. All of these factors kept PSROs from fulfilling the function for which they were originally created. Despite the failure of PSROs in achieving their objectives, they represent a first attempt to emphasize process quality and opened the door for a new paradigm in monitoring and assessing quality.

Two years after the creation of PSROs, another bill was passed which established Health Systems Agencies (HSAs). These agencies were created to analyze the needs and requirements of healthcare and to maintain the quality of care provided. Special interest groups found ways to limit their authority, and these agencies gradually began to disappear as the need for their services diminished and funding ceased.

This trend on the part of the government continued in an effort to contain sharply rising and seemingly uncontrollable healthcare costs and at the same time maintain quality. Government was first to realize that after a decade of intervention, healthcare costs were still rising and the quality of care was not improving; thus, funding for PSROs and HSAs ceased. The legislature then passed the Tax Equity and Fiscal Responsibility Act (TEFRA) of 1982. TEFRA introduced a new ceiling on reimbursements for Medicare inpatient services. This act also mandated studies to introduce Diagnosis-Related Groups (DRGs) as the basis for reimbursement of Medicare providers (for inpatient services). Reimbursements were through a Prospective Payment System (PPS), and the Health Care Financing Administration

(HCFA) was empowered to enforce and administer this system. PPS was enacted as an amendment to the Social Security Act. President Reagan signed it into law in October of 1983. The act provided a mechanism to ensure both access to and quality of healthcare, and it included a cost reduction effort. To address the mandate to control costs, the Social Security amendment also required Peer Review Organizations (PROs) to be established by October 1984.

PROs were intended to replace PSROs, and their objective was to assess and improve the quality of care delivered. Similar to PSROs, the influence of PROs extended only to Medicare inpatient services. Though limited in its focus, the impact of PROs on quality of care has been considerable. PROs examine the process of care. Unlike PSROs, PROs are not limited to physicians, but has liberal access to them. A PRO can be a for-profit or a not-for-profit organization. Hospitals are required to contract with a PRO to review their services. PROs have the authority to enforce quality improvement measures on the provider by either an extensive evaluation process or through monetary fines. PROs also have a mandate to review other professional services rendered in a hospital and may refer to the appropriate professions for advice on specific standards of care.

QUALITY ASSURANCE DEPARTMENTS

Starting in the 1970s, Quality Assurance (QA) departments became very active, collecting and analyzing data on patient care and health risk management. Structure, rather than process, aspects were emphasized (i.e., credentialing, certification, etc.). QA professionals had new empowerment in identifying structurally deficient providers. These inferior providers felt harassed by the system. As knowledge of their shortcomings and mistakes became public, medical liability lawsuits increased. This trend had a negative effect on the providers, as well as their institutions and patients. Patient–provider relationships began to erode and providers lost the anticipated trust of their patients. Also, administration–physician relationships started to show some stress, as one blamed the other for the cause of the problem. The situation was exacerbated when physicians practiced medicine defensively. Physicians ordered more, often unnecessary, tests before making any diagnosis. This was, and continues to be, an attempt to protect themselves from a potential malpractice lawsuit. The legal system did not help alleviate this situation but, on the contrary, intensified it. Lawyers prompted patients to question their healthcare providers about any unexpected outcome of care. Attorneys offered their services to patients on a contingency basis, accepting payment only after a financial settlement or judgment was reached (usually 33–50% of the award). This trend continued to cause the misuse and misallocation of precious resources. Unfortunately, expenditures on healthcare kept rising while the level of quality did not.

Once again, the government stepped in and, as a reactionary measure to the malpractice crisis, passed the National Health Quality Improvement Act of 1986. This act had two major provisions that encouraged patients to become better informed and track providers with a record of malpractice. It called for the creation of a national clearinghouse to store the malpractice records of providers. Further, the act made it mandatory for healthcare institutions to report incidents of provider malpractice to the clearinghouse. The act encourages institutions and physicians to report these incidents and provides immunity against violation of privacy lawsuits that may be initiated by providers who have been reported. This information would become available to licensure boards and other entities inquiring about practicing providers in different states. Due to inadequate funding, however, the act was not implemented until 1989.

It is obvious that the act was passed in an attempt to improve the quality of medical care delivered, but again the emphasis was primarily on structure without involving process and outcome measures. Chapter 7 in this book provides a more detailed description of the act.

By the late 1980s, the focus of the government shifted to the process-oriented review of the PROs and away from the primarily structure-oriented review of the JCAH—with a renewed emphasis on outcome. In December 1987, the HCFA published its list of Medicare Hospital Mortality Information (HCFA, 1987). This list made headlines when it was published in the *New York Times.* Major reactions came from the hospitals, who refuted the validity and usefulness of the list. They pointed out that the list did not take the case-mix index into consideration. For example, they thought that the list should differentiate between acute care hospitals and cancer treatment hospitals. Despite the flaws associated with this list, and the annual lists thereafter, it triggered many organizations to look into patient care outcomes. JCAHO changed its name to include other healthcare organizations (in addition to hospitals) in their accreditation process. At about the same time, in an effort to maintain its reputation, JCAHO also announced their Agenda for Change (O'Leary, 1987). The agenda called for a gradual refocus of its standards toward outcomes. These events prompted several other groups to consider clinical outcomes and physician practice patterns as qualifiers for care quality (Daley, 1991).

Outcome assessments were later explored in greater detail by researchers, as the government and other sources made more funding available, particularly in the area of research into clinical outcomes (refer to Chapter 10 for a further discussion on outcome management).

TRANSITIONS

In its quest for improved outcomes with limited resources, the healthcare industry began to look outside for answers. This thinking prompted an interest in TQ in the late 1980s. Starting with hospitals, and followed by other healthcare organizations, the principles of TQ began to infiltrate the industry. Leadership paradigms that were originally designed for manufacturing were modified to make them applicable to healthcare. Quality experts were quick to realize that a tremendous amount of work was necessary to bring this giant industry into the realm of quality management. Several of these experts set up companies and subsidiaries to educate the healthcare industry in these relatively new philosophies. Healthcare professionals had a growing appetite to learn more about TQ. They started attending workshops designed for them by quality experts. This trend continues to grow as most hospitals (AHA, 1992) have either started the journey toward TQ or intend to do so. However, other healthcare organizations, such as long-term care and mental health organizations, have not been as quick to adopt TQ principles.

Clearly, TQ is new to healthcare. When it was first introduced, it received mixed reactions. Because it calls for a change in the culture of an organization, traditional bureaucrats (who unfortunately are abundant in healthcare) have fought its adoption every step of the way. At last, they are reluctantly accepting the change as an inevitable tide that is moving swiftly through levels of management, backed by support from consumer groups, regulators, and accrediting agencies. The next two chapters address the issue of the recent adoption of TQ by healthcare organizations.

REFERENCES

Brook, R. and Avery, A. (1975). *Quality Assurance Mechanism in the U.S.: From There to Where?* Santa Monica, Calif.: Rand Corporation.

Bull, M. J. (1992). "QA: Professional Accountability via CQI." in *Improving Quality: A Guide to Effective Programs,* C. G. Meisenheimer (Ed.), Gaithersburg, Md.: Aspen.

Codman, E. (1914). "The Product of a Hospital." *Surgical Gynecology and Obstetrics,* 18:491–494.

Daley, J. (1991). "Mortality and Other Outcome Data." in *Quantitative Methods in Quality Management: A Guide to Practitioners,* Longo and Bohr (Eds.), Chicago: American Hospital Association, pp. 27–43.

Deming, W. E. (1986). *Out of the Crisis,* Cambridge, Mass.: Massachusetts Institute of Technology.

Donabedian, A. (1966). "Evaluating the Quality of Medical Care." *Milbank Memorial Fund Quarterly,* 44:194–196.

Health Care Financing Administration (1987). *Medicare Hospital Mortality Information: 1986,* Vols. I–VII, GPO No. 017-060-00206-9, Washington, D.C.: U.S. Department of Health and Human Services, December 1987.

O'Leary, D. S. (1987). *The Joint Commission Agenda for Change,* Chicago: Joint Commission on Accreditation of Healthcare Organizations, pp. 1–10.

2

The UNITED STATES HEALTHCARE
SYSTEM and QUALITY of CARE

Allen C. Meadors, MBA, PhD, FACHE

Ironically, the term "U.S. healthcare system" is a misnomer. In fact, the United States has never had a *formal healthcare system*. Instead, over the years we have developed an informal collection of healthcare mini-systems and cottage industries to meet our healthcare needs. To shape our future successfully, it is important for us to know how we arrived where we are today. This chapter provides that awareness, reviewing the evolution of the U.S. healthcare system and reflecting on some of the events that have had an impact on quality of care.

The FIRST TWO HUNDRED FIFTY YEARS (1600–1850)

The first physician in the U.S., Samuel Fuller, arrived with the Pilgrims on the Mayflower at Plymouth, Massachusetts in 1620. However, the elite English physicians remained in England, and the fairly acceptable standards of training for that time became diluted in the colonies (Starr, 1982). Because we had not yet developed the germ theory, physicians knew little about sanitation, and the scope of assistance they could offer to patients was extremely limited. Mothers and other family members provided most of the care in the home. In 1765 the first medical school in the U.S. was established—the Medical School of the College of Philadelphia, which later became part of the University of Pennsylvania.

Like the humble beginnings of physician training, hospitals emerged without substantial focus or direction. The earliest hospitals were formed from either poorhouses (also called almshouses) or pesthouses. A poorhouse was an establishment much like today's homeless shelters. It provided shelter for those who had nowhere else to go and often was controlled by the local government (Jonas, 1992). Pesthouses were used to quarantine sailors coming into port with known contagious or questionable health conditions. As Starr noted, "Before the Civil War, an American doctor might contentedly spend an entire career in practice without setting foot on a hospital ward" (Starr, 1982). The level of sanitation and technology was so poor that before the mid-1800s hospitals had little to offer and much to discourage their utilization.

In 1798 Congress established the Marine Hospital Service, which is now the U.S. Public Health Service. Its broad objective was to consolidate the almshouses and pesthouses. As a result, over the next hundred years hospitals developed very distinct profiles.

As the mid-1800s approached, a couple of events occurred that significantly shaped the future of healthcare in the United States. By 1842 anesthesia had been developed, making surgery an acceptable option for physicians. Perhaps more important, the *germ theory* emerged as a respected body of knowledge.

The NEXT HUNDRED YEARS (1850–1950)

The second half of the 1800s changed the face of healthcare in the United States forever. It moved from a very individualized approach to medicine to an institutionalized approach. A number of major developments quickly followed the discoveries of anesthesia and the germ theory. Nursing became a profession, new technologies (such as radiographs, blood typing, and advanced surgery) became available, and clinical laboratories were improved. Together, these developments allowed the rise of American hospitals (Rakich et al., 1992). Between 1887 and 1915, the number of hospitals in the United States grew from fewer than 200 to over 5000. This explosive growth moved the healthcare industry from nearly nonexistent to become a major factor in American economic culture.

Where was quality during the 1700s and 1800s? It was not an issue. Medicine was viewed first and foremost as an art. In terms of quality control, it was on shaky ground at best. As a society, we trusted our instincts more than medicine. We believed faith and good thoughts were perhaps more valuable than the "healing arts." However, public health findings during the last part of this period (i.e., germ theory, sanitation, and some vaccinations) began to give credibility to medicine as a science. Eventually, these findings and developments were incorporated into medical training.

In 1910 Alexander Flexner proposed the first coherent methodology for training physicians in a report entitled *Medical Education in the United States and Canada,* which was funded by the Carnegie Foundation. At the time, there were over 130 medical schools in the United States (14 in Chicago alone), using dozens of different training approaches. This report, which became known as the "Flexner Report," demonstrated that the best physicians were those who had a university-based science curriculum followed by four years of medical school. The United States and Canada both endorsed this report and agreed to move toward affiliating all medical schools with a research-based university. The Rockefeller Foundation supported this movement to address quality issues in medical training, and by 1930 only 80 medical schools remained, each with a university affiliation.

At the same time, hospitals began to address quality issues. In 1913 the American College of Surgeons (ACS) was founded, and in 1918 it established a Hospital Standardization Program for hospitals where surgery was performed. The program was voluntary, but over the years it became the standard for hospitals. Eventually, it evolved into what is now known as the Joint Commission on Accreditation of Healthcare Organizations, or JCAHO (Kovner, 1990). Although the JCAHO has suffered a number of internal and external problems in recent years, it is still considered the key accrediting agency for hospitals.

During the early 1900s the American healthcare industry was viewed as a freestanding entity primarily composed of independent physicians and community-based voluntary hospitals. Except for a few public health programs, federal and state governments maintained an arms-length posture. During this period, however, several ideas emerged that would change the industry forever.

Health insurance was the first major conceptual development to influence the healthcare industry. In 1929, Blue Cross established the first notable model in Dallas, Texas. During the Depression, Baylor University Hospital wanted to insure its own survival. It offered Dallas schoolteachers a prepaid hospitalization plan for a set monthly premium. Later, in 1939, California-based physicians developed another model that became the prototype for future Blue Shield plans. These two models set the standard for health insurance plans. They would flourish during the wage freeze era of World War II and the rapid growth of unions and collective bargaining after the war.

The second significant conceptual development to influence healthcare was embodied in the Social Security Act of 1935. Ironically, the Social Security Act had very few healthcare provisions, and its primary objective was to provide a supplemental retirement program. It did, however, make those supplemental retirement funds available for reimbursement of nursing home care. Over the next 30 years, significant growth in the nursing home industry occurred.

Between 1900 and 1950 two other landmark events impacted the healthcare industry. First, Kaiser Permanente established its initial managed care plan in 1942. Kaiser duplicated this plan many times, and it became the prototype of the Health Maintenance Organization (HMO) movement of the 1970s and 1980s. The other significant event was the passage of the Hospital Survey and Construction Act of 1946 (better known as the Hill–Burton Act). With this act, the federal government became directly involved with the nongovernmental sector of the hospital industry (Williams and Torrens, 1993). This program enabled communities (especially rural) to renovate existing hospitals or build new ones. Over 35% of all current hospital beds were built with the support of Hill–Burton funds. These funds were also used for other types of healthcare facilities, such as nursing homes, etc.

Today there are approximately 6500 hospitals in the United States. Most are not-for-profit, with fewer than 15% for-profit. They tend to be fairly large and heavily staffed, with approximately three full-time equivalent employees (FTE) per staff bed. Occupancy rates are around 60%, but may be considerably lower in small rural hospitals. On the other hand, the nearly 16,000 nursing homes tend to be small (fewer than 80 beds) and for-profit. The average staffing ratio tends to be two thirds FTE per bed and most nursing homes average an occupancy rate of over 90%.

1950 to the 1990s

The 1950s marked the beginning of a major change in how healthcare (especially hospitalization) is financed in the United States. Table 2-1 shows the dramatic transition from a direct consumer spending pattern (49.6%) to primarily third-party payers (87%) between the 1950s and 1990s. This transition has played a significant role in escalating healthcare costs. Table 2-2 shows the rapid rise in healthcare expenditures as a percentage of the Gross National Product (GNP) since the 1950s. As we will discuss, this movement away from the direct involvement of the consumer in reimbursing healthcare providers is just one of the many factors that have brought about the present crisis—a position where all players agree that they must join forces to create a cohesive, efficient U.S. healthcare system.

As the tables reflect, the passage of the Social Security Act in 1935 was the most significant event in that era. This amendment was part of President Lyndon B. Johnson's Great Society and what then Chairman of the House Ways and Means Committee, Representative Wilbur Mills, called the "three-layer cake." The three layers were Medicare Part A, Medicare Part B, and Medicaid.

The Johnson administration believed governmental healthcare programs should provide health insurance coverage to the elderly (primarily those over age 65 and eligible for Social Security) and those eligible for Aid for Dependent Children (AFDC). On the basis of what it cost to deliver healthcare in the early 1960s, the administration estimated that this program

Table 2-1. Who Pays the Healthcare Bill?

Percentage of Cost Paid By:	1950	1960	1966	1981	1985	1991
1. Private Insurance	29.3%	52.5%	51.4%	43.5%	41.9%	35%
2. Government	21.1%	18.8%	25.5%	42.5%	42.3%	52%
3. Direct Consumer Spending	49.6%	28.7%	23.1%	14.0%	15.8%	13%

How it breaks down:
Government Spending: 40% Medicare + 12% Medicaid = 52%
Private Insurance: 35% Third Party = 35%
Direct Consumer Spending: 7% self pay + 6% other payer = 13%

Source: American Hospital Association, "Gross Patient Revenue by Source for Community Hospitals." in *AHA Hospital Statistics 1992–93*. Contact (312) 280-6000

Table 2-2. National Health Expenditures.

	Year	Health Expenses as a Percent of GNP	Health Expenses Per Capita
	1929	3.5%	$29
26 years ↓	1955	4.5%	$104
10 years ↓	1965	5.9%	$198
20 years ↓	1985	10.7%	$1728
5 years ↓	1990	12.4%	$2660
↓ ↓	1991	13.1%	$2817
10 years	2000	16.4%	$5712

would require a relatively small amount of additional money. At that time, salaries paid by health service organizations were among the lowest in the U.S.—particularly hospitals and nursing homes. Before the 1960s, working in a healthcare organization was similar to providing a community service rather than pursuing a career. For example, registered nurses accounted for the largest and one of the best paid segments of the hospital staff, yet nurses were often paid less than public school teachers (another extremely low paying profession). It was no accident that over 95% of employees in

17

hospitals and nursing homes were female. Jobs filled by women were typically low in pay.

Medicare and Medicaid rapidly became key programs in the U.S. healthcare scheme. A quick look at each will help to identify major components of current healthcare financing arrangements.

Through Medicare the federal government pays for specific healthcare costs incurred by certain disabled people and those over age 65. Medicare is financed by a combination of payroll taxes, general federal revenue, and premiums and currently covers just over 13% of the population (DeLew et al., 1992).

Medicare Part A (the first layer of the "cake") primarily provides inpatient coverage for eligible participants. After an initial deductible is met ($676 in 1993), 100% of covered services is paid for the first 60 days of qualified hospitalization. Beyond that, participants must pay co-insurance for the next 30 days (days 61 through 90). Participants are allowed a one-time lifetime reserve of 60 days. Medicare Part A also provides reimbursement for costs incurred in a Skilled Nursing Facility (SNF). An individual who requires SNF care is eligible only *after* he or she has had a hospital stay of at least 72 hours. Participants do not receive Medicare reimbursement for SNF costs incurred at home or through a lower level of care. Medicare Part A pays for the first 20 days, and then continuing days (days 21 through 100) are available with a co-insurance rate ($84.50 per day in 1993). An individual automatically becomes covered by Medicare Part A upon initiating his or her Social Security benefits.

Medicare Part B (the second layer of the "cake") provides ambulatory care coverage, which primarily consists of physician services. Individuals become eligible for Medicare Part B at the same time that they qualify for Part A, but they are not automatically enrolled. To enroll, individuals must sign up for the insurance and arrange for a monthly premium ($36 in 1993) to be withheld from their Social Security checks. By law, this premium is intended to cover 25% of the cost of the program. The remaining 75% comes from general federal revenue. Medicare Part B also requires an annual deductible of $100 and 20% co-insurance.

Providers can choose whether or not to participate in Medicare. If a provider does participate, or accept assignment, reimbursement is made by the federal government through various intermediaries. Reimbursement is based on published schedules for specific services provided. If a provider chooses not to participate, the patient may be billed directly. In this case, the intermediary reimburses the patient directly upon receipt of the appropriate forms. In either case, the amount reimbursed is minus the deductible and any co-insurance. Almost all hospitals and about 53% of physicians participate directly in the Medicare program. Physician participation varies

Table 2-3. Medicare Growth.

Year	Cost
1967	$4 Billion (19.5 million people covered)
1972	$8.5 Billion
1975	$14 Billion
1984	$62.5 Billion
1992	$118.6 Billion (34 million people covered)

greatly from state to state, however, ranging from as low as 20% participation to nearly 80% in some states.

As mentioned earlier, the Johnson administration did not expect the cost of the Medicare program to be significant. Table 2-3 shows what has occurred in reality. The table illustrates why controlling escalating costs has become a central focus for governmental healthcare programs.

While Medicare Part B had an assigned reimbursement level for various services provided by physicians, in an attempt by the federal government to be fair, Medicare Part A used a cost reimbursement system. As any student of economics will realize, this arrangement has immediate negative ramifications regarding expenditure of time and energy to be cost efficient and cost effective. The reimbursement systems used for governmental healthcare programs were another reason why the better part of the 1970s was spent attempting to bring Medicare costs under control.

The Professional Standards Review Organization (PSRO) was one of the first governmental efforts toward this end. Originally, PSROs were created to monitor the utilization and quality of healthcare services provided to Medicare recipients. However, in the end they were used more as a cost containment vehicle rather than for quality control. The government established over 200 PSROs nationwide, chartering them to review the appropriateness of several medical factors: the medical service itself, the level of service provided by the physician, and the length of stay. Despite good intentions, PSROs were ineffective and in time, were replaced by Peer Review Organizations (PROs) (Rakich et al., 1992).

Meanwhile, the costs of government healthcare programs continued to rise. In response, the government established the Tax Equity and Fiscal

19

Responsibility Act of 1982 (PL 97–248) and enacted additional amendments to the Social Security Act. These actions resulted in major transformations in the Medicare program. They also indicated a central theme in the evolution of our healthcare system—to remove healthcare utilization and reimbursement decisions from the control of physicians. Medicare Part A changed from a cost reimbursement system to a Prospective Payment System (PPS). Under this system, the government established hospital reimbursement rates prospectively, using diagnosis-related groups (DRGs). Notably, today most primary care physicians cannot afford to treat a large number of Medicare recipient patients, because current reimbursement by the government is significantly less than the actual cost of delivering care (Church Chason, 1993).

As Table 2-3 shows, the cost of Medicare has risen dramatically over the past 25 years. However, the elderly now spend considerably more of their after-tax income on health expenses than they did before the implementation of Medicare (DeLew et al., 1992).

Medicaid (the third layer of the "cake") is a joint program between the federal government and individual states that provides healthcare coverage for specific groups of impoverished individuals. The program requires all states to provide certain mandatory services, such as acute, long-term care and preventive care. Individual states are free to add to this minimum level of service. In addition, they must include specific groups as eligible, but may expand the program to include other groups. The federal government pays between 50 and 78.5% of the total cost of Medicaid, based on the per capita income of each state.

When Medicaid was established, it was projected that the program would only cost an additional $250,000. This was at a time when existing federally sponsored healthcare programs cost more than $1.3 billion. Table 2-4 provides an overview of how the Medicaid program has grown.

Constant change has characterized the Medicaid program. As state tax forecasts rise and fall, the services available and the individuals eligible for Medicaid change accordingly. It is not uncommon for a state to reduce services and/or eligibility standards during a fiscal year. These fluctuations cause extreme difficulty for covered patients as well as the providers who serve them.

Medicaid provides the largest individual segment of coverage for long-term care. Unlike Medicare, which only covers limited skilled nursing care, Medicaid provides coverage for both Intermediate Care Facilities (ICFs) and SNFs. Almost 44% of the Medicaid budget is spent on ICF and SNF levels of care. In contrast, only about 1.3% of the Medicare budget is spent on SNF care.

Table 2-4. Medicaid Expenditures.

Year	Cost
1968	$3.45 Billion (11.5 million people covered)
1974	$10 Billion
1977	$17 Billion
1984	$37 Billion
1992	$72.5 Billion (25 million people covered)

Even with the expansion of these two government programs during the 1970s, 1980s, and 1990s, there are still approximately 37 million Americans without any type of formal health insurance. A large segment of this group is composed of individuals who work in part-time and full-time jobs that do not provide affordable heath insurance. These individuals and many others often choose not to buy health insurance because the plans available to them are limited in coverage and are expensive (Church Chason, 1993). The total also includes a substantial number of children under the age of 18, as well as individuals who simply cannot afford to pay for the insurance even when employers make it available. This problem is one of two driving forces behind the health reform movement of the 1990s. The other is the rapidly increasing cost of providing healthcare.

There are two primary causes of inflation of healthcare costs—the high cost of medical technology and the modified fee-for-service model. Throughout history, fee-for-service has been the traditional method for reimbursing healthcare providers. This system allows the patient to deal directly with the provider in determining how to pay for services rendered. To a certain extent, cost control mechanisms were built into patient–provider relationships. Eventually, the insurance companies and federal and state governments attempted to build their requirements around this traditional approach to reimbursement. The result was a modified fee-for-service model, where the consumer no longer had the incentive to negotiate price, and the provider was encouraged to price services at whatever level the market would bear—what insurance companies or federal and state governments would pay. The risk of being sued for malpractice, or for failure to diagnose, provided another stimulus to physicians, encouraging them to perform extra, marginally necessary services in order to protect themselves. Thus,

21

while the original fee-for-service approach was inherently cost effective, the new modified fee-for-service model inadvertently included a strong disincentive to control fees.

The managed care movement evolved as a viable approach to control these escalating healthcare costs, and over the years its application has been encouraged and expanded. In managed care systems, a central entity controls the financial and delivery aspects of healthcare. The system itself provides incentives for effective utilization of services and cost control. Three managed care systems deserve attention: Managed Fee-for-Service, Health Maintenance Organizations, and Preferred Provider Organizations.

Managed Fee-for-Service maintains many of the features of traditional fee-for-service. From the patient's perspective, perhaps the most important feature is that he or she can choose a primary provider and referral specialists. Other features, however, limit the authority of medical providers, particularly the physicians. For example, patients must have prior approval for nonemergency hospital admissions, a second opinion on elective surgery, concurrent review during a hospital stay, and medical providers must meet strict utilization review requirements.

Health Maintenance Organizations (HMOs) consist of four basic components:

1. The HMO assumes contractual responsibility for ensuring the delivery of a stated range of healthcare services, including at least inpatient hospital and ambulatory care services.
2. The HMO serves a voluntarily enrolled population.
3. The HMO enrollee pays a fixed payment (usually monthly) for independent use of services. Some HMOs require enrollees to pay a small cost-sharing charge.
4. The HMO assumes some of the financial risk or gain in the provision of medical care services.

The federal government became interested in HMOs in the 1970s when it was noted that private insurance companies averaged approximately 800 hospital bed days per 1000 enrollees while HMOs averaged approximately 370 hospital bed days per 1000 enrollees. The difference can be accounted for by comparing the incentives to physicians in each system. A traditional fee-for-service system ties the physician's income directly to the number of services provided. Therefore, the more services a physician provides, the greater the income he or she generates. Under the umbrella of an HMO, however, physicians have an incentive to control these costs. In the above example, clearly HMO physicians have an incentive to reduce or limit hospital stays.

HMOs create these cost-saving incentives through a gatekeeper system. A gatekeeper is usually a primary care physician who coordinates and certifies an enrollee's access to all healthcare services, except emergencies. The HMO restricts the enrollee to using *only* those providers in the HMO, or other providers that have been certified for use. If the enrollee uses another provider, he or she must pay for all the charges out-of-pocket. The HMO gatekeeper system provides the physician group with a financial incentive to control costs. Besides paying physicians a set reimbursement independent of the number of services rendered, the HMO usually also pays them a portion of any profits generated over a specific period. Kaiser developed this HMO model in the 1940s, originally calling it the Prepaid Group Practice (PGP) model.

A lack of choice—being restricted to a limited set of providers—is the obvious drawback to HMOs. Still, over the past twenty years, numerous hybrids of this model have emerged. Almost all of them have given the enrollee greater flexibility. Some other common managed care models are as follows:

- Salary or Staff Model
- Individual Practice Association (IPA) Model
- Network Model
- Point of Service (POS) Model

HMOs have produced significantly less real savings than originally predicted. This may have happened because the focus of the original HMO concept was lost as other models developed.

In 1970, there were fewer than 10 million enrollees in HMOs. Today there are approximately 40 million. Originally, most HMOs were not-for-profit, but by the mid-1980s the majority had become for-profit organizations.

Preferred Provider Organizations (PPOs) emerged in the early 1980s as a less restrictive alternative to the HMO. The basic ingredients of a PPO are:

1. A limited number of providers
2. Negotiated fees
3. Utilization of claims review as a control mechanism
4. Consumer choice with financial incentives for the preferred providers
5. Faster payment of claims for preferred providers

The PPO encourages enrollees to use providers in the system. The deductible or co-payment that enrollees pay preferred providers is *less* than what they must pay nonpreferred providers. Preferred providers also discount the fee for services they provide to PPO enrollees. PPOs also provide enrollees greater flexibility than HMOs.

Table 2-5.   Health Utilization Decisions.

(What Services and Who Used)

1960	
Physician	Payer
95%	5%

1970	
Physician	Payer
90%	10%

1980	
Physician	Payer
85%	15%

1984	
Physician	Payer
70%	30%

1990	
Physician	Payer
50%	50%

Over the past 13 years, PPOs have grown from 0 to over 40 million enrollees. The majority of PPOs are for-profit organizations.

Medicare's Prospective Payment System (PPS) represents another effort to reduce healthcare expenditures in the United States. After almost 25 years of trying to control healthcare expenditures, what do we have to show for it? In 1965, we spent 5.9% of our GNP on healthcare. In 1993 we are spending more than 14%. What have we accomplished? Because of all of these efforts, today physicians have significantly less autonomy and authority. Table 2-5 shows how we have removed health utilization decisions from the control of physicians over the past 30 years.

All the previously discussed programs and mini-systems represent the essentials of the U.S. healthcare system. In addition, the U.S. government supports separate healthcare subsystems for active-duty military and their dependents, as well as retirees. These are operated by the Department of Defense (DOD). The Department of Veterans Affairs (VA) provides medical services for eligible veterans. The U.S. Public Health Service, through the Indian Health Service (IHS), provides medical services to eligible Native Americans.

Despite the presence of these numerous healthcare subsystems, the overall U.S. healthcare system is still cumbersome, expensive, and inadequate. Although the statistic can be misleading, some continue to point out that there are still approximately 37 million people in the U.S. without health coverage. Various states have initiated major reforms in an effort to make healthcare coverage available to more of their citizens. Hawaii in the 1980s and Washington and Oregon in the early 1990s are among those states trying to remedy this situation.

According to economist Victor Fuch, the U.S. spends nearly 40% more of its GNP on healthcare than any other nation. He also claims that the only real advancement we have made over other industrialized countries is greater access to expensive technology (Fuch, 1992). Moreover, the inefficiencies inherent in our current healthcare system have cost us dearly.

One of the worst backlashes to this financial crisis is that we tend to use improvements in quality of care as a cost-cutting mechanism. Certainly, the two are not without degrees of compatibility, but financial motives should not drive the choices we make when addressing quality of care issues.

REFERENCES

American Hospital Association (1993). "Gross Patient Revenue by Source for Community Hospitals." in *AHA Hospital Statistics 1992–93*, Chicago: American Hospital Association.

Church Chason, C. (1993). *Comments on Total Quality in Healthcare*, Merritt Island, Fla.: Chason Associates, Inc.

DeLew, N., Greenberg, G., and Kinchen, K. (1992). "A Layman's Guide to the U.S. Healthcare System." *Health Care Financing Review,* 14(1).

Fuch, V. R. (August 12, 1992). "The Best Healthcare System in the World?" *Journal of the American Medical Association,* 268(7).

Jonas, S. (1992). *An Introduction to the U.S. Health Care System*, 3rd edition, New York: Springer Publishing Company.

Kovner, A. R. (1990). *Health Care Delivery in the United States*, 4th edition, New York: Springer Publishing Company.

Rakich, J. S., Longest, B. B., and Darr, K. (1992). *Managing Health Services Organizations*, 3rd edition, Baltimore: Health Professions Press.

Starr, P. (1982). *The Social Transformation of American Medicine,* New York: Basic Books, p. 39.

Williams, S. J. and Torrens, P. R. (1993). *Introduction to Health Services*, 4th edition, Albany: Delmar Press.

PART II

PRINCIPLES, TOOLS, and
TECHNIQUES of TOTAL QUALITY

3

PRINCIPLES of TOTAL QUALITY in HEALTHCARE ORGANIZATIONS

A. F. Al-Assaf, MD, MPH

Total Quality (TQ) is an innovative management philosophy that has been imported to healthcare from other industries. TQ is a new way of thinking and a different way of managing organizations. It is both process driven and customer oriented. Leadership, continuous improvement, employee empowerment, teamwork, and individual responsibility all are applicable to the TQ philosophy. It is a cultural transformation and an educational experience that infiltrates throughout the organization and involves everyone—staff and management.

Three individuals have much to bring focus and understanding to the quality movement. Deming, Juran, and Crosby are quality experts who are regarded as "gurus" of TQ. A brief synopsis of their teachings follows.

According to Dr. W. Edwards Deming, TQ is a modern method of leadership by which employees are encouraged to participate in the management decision processes and where boundaries between departments are eliminated. It is this process of continuous improvement for both production and service that, according to Deming, should be constantly nurtured by top management.

Dr. Joseph M. Juran suggests that management's mission for the organization as a whole is *fitness for use* by customers, that is, the degree to which the services and products provided conform to the *needs* and *specifications* of the customer. The responsibility of individual departments in the organization is to work in accordance with those specifications to achieve fitness for use.

Juran's quality management philosophy focuses on three processes: quality control, quality improvement, and quality planning. He also provides three steps in the *universal process for quality improvement*: analyze the symptoms, identify the causes, and apply the remedies. Dr. Juran is the author of several books in quality that deal specifically with quality improvement methods and planning.

Philip B. Crosby has authored such important works as *Quality Is Free*, *Quality without Tears*, *Completeness*, and *Leading*. He developed the Zero Defect program and founded the Quality College in Winter Park, Florida.

Crosby's management philosophy is somewhat similar to the philosophies of Deming and Juran. Specifically, he introduces four *absolutes* of quality management. First, quality is conformance to requirements. Second, the system for achieving quality is prevention. Third, the performance standard is zero defect. Fourth, the measurement of quality is the price of nonconformance.

Crosby further indicates that education and awareness are key to successful quality management. Every member of the organization should have a clearly defined role in the quality management process and be provided the opportunity to be educated thoroughly in that role. Again, he emphasizes the process of corporate cultural change as well as attitudes in an organization.

Others have introduced innovative management philosophies with the objective of improving quality. The pioneering work of Taylor, Shewhart, Dodge, and Roemig has had a positive effect on quality improvement methodologies over the years. The reader is also encouraged to study the works of such scholars as Tsuda and Ishikawa, both of whom had a tremendous impact on the manufacturing industry in Japan.

This chapter presents a collection of articles that are critical to understanding the principles and guidelines of TQ and quality improvement processes in healthcare organizations. These articles have been selected because they are considered classics. The authors have been involved in their fields for years and their works are important contributions.

SOUNDING BOARD
CONTINUOUS IMPROVEMENT as an
IDEAL in HEALTH CARE

Donald M. Berwick, MD, MPP

Imagine two assembly lines, monitored by two foremen.

Foreman 1 walks the line, watching carefully. "I can see you all," he warns. "I have the means to measure your work, and I will do so. I will find those among you who are unprepared or unwilling to do your jobs, and when I do there will be consequences. There are many workers available for these jobs, and you can be replaced."

Foreman 2 walks a different line, and he too watches. "I am here to help you if I can," he says. "We are in this together for the long haul. You and I have a common interest in a job well done. I know that most of you are trying very hard, but sometimes things can go wrong. My job is to notice opportunities for improvement—skills that could be shared, lessons from the past, or experiments to try together—and to give you the means to do your work even better than you do now. I want to help the average ones among you, not just the exceptional few at either end of the spectrum of competence."

Which line works better? Which is more likely to do the job well in the long run? Where would you rather work?

In modern American health care, there are two approaches to the problem of improving quality—two theories of quality that describe the climate in which care is delivered. One will serve us well; the other probably will not.

The theory used by Foreman 1 relies on inspection to improve quality. We may call it the Theory of Bad Apples, because those who subscribe to it believe that quality is best achieved by discovering Bad Apples and removing them from the lot. The experts call this "quality by inspection," and in the thinking of activists for quality in health care it predominates under the guise of "buying right," "recertification," or "deterrence" through

Reprinted with permission from *The New England Journal of Medicine,* Vol. 320, No. 1, pp., 53–56, 1989.

litigation. Such an outlook implies or establishes thresholds for acceptability, just as the inspector at the end of an assembly line decides whether to accept or reject finished goods.

Those in health care who espouse the Theory of Bad Apples are looking hard for better tools of inspection. Such tools must have excellent measuring ability—high sensitivity and specificity, simultaneously—lest the malefactors escape or the innocent be made victims. They search for outliers— statistics far enough from the average that chance alone is unlikely to provide a good excuse. Bad Apples theorists publish mortality data, invest heavily in systems of case-mix adjustment, and fund vigilant regulators. Some measure their success by counting heads on platters.

The Theory of Bad Apples gives rise readily to what can be called the my-apple-is-just-fine-thank-you response on the part of the workers supervised by Foreman 1. The foreman has defined the rules of a game called "Prove you are acceptable," and that is what the workers play. The game is not fun, of course; the workers are afraid, angry, and sullen, but they play nonetheless. When quality is pursued in the form of a search for deficient people, those being surveyed play defense. They commonly use three tactics: kill the messenger (the foreman is not their friend, and the inspector even less so); distort the data or change the measurements (whenever possible, take control of the mechanisms that may do you harm); and if all else fails, turn somebody else in (and divert the foreman's attention).

Any good foreman knows how clever a frightened work force can be. In fact, practically no system of measurement—at least none that measures people's performance—is robust enough to survive the fear of those who are measured. Most measurement tools eventually come under the control of those studied and in their fear such people do not ask what measurement can tell them, but rather how they can make it safe. The inspector says, "I will find you out if you are deficient." The subject replies, "I will therefore prove I am not deficient"—and seeks not understanding, but escape.

The signs of this game are everywhere in health care. With determination and enormous technical resourcefulness, the Health Care Financing Administration has published voluminous data for two consecutive years about the mortality profiles of Medicare recipients in almost every hospital in the United States—profiles that are adjusted according to complex multivariate models to show many important characteristics of the patient populations.[1] Such information, though by no means flawless, could be helpful to hospitals seeking to improve their effectiveness. Yet the hundreds of pages of data are dwarfed by the thousands of pages of responses from hospitals, trying to prove whatever hospitals need to prove to build their defenses. What else should we expect?

The same game is being played between aggressive Boards of Registration in Medicine and other regulators that require hospitals and physicians to produce streams of reports on the contents of their closets. In Massachusetts, for example, merely talking with a physician about his or her involvement in a mishap may commit a hospital administrator by law to report that physician to the Board of Registration in Medicine.

The sad game played out in this theory and the predictable response to it imply a particular view of the nature of hazard and deficiency in health care, as it does in any industry playing such a game. The view is that problems of quality are caused by poor intentions. The Bad Apple is to blame. The cause of trouble is people—their venality, incompetence, or insufficient caution. According to this outlook, one can use deterrence to improve quality, because intentions need to be changed; one can use reward or punishment to control people who do not care enough to do what they can or what they know is right. The Theory of Bad Apples implies that people must be made to care; the inevitable response is the attempt to prove that one cares enough.

What a waste! The Theory of Bad Apples let American industry down for decades. It took some visionary theorists, many of them statisticians, in companies with great foresight to learn that relying on inspection to improve quality is at best inefficient, and at worst a formula for failure.[2–6] The Japanese learned first—from American theorists, ironically—that there were far better ways to improve quality, and the result is international economic history.[7] Today, no American companies make videocassette recorders or compact-disc players or single-lens-reflex cameras; we have simply given up. Xerox engineers visiting Japan in 1979 found copiers being produced at half the cost of those manufactured at Xerox's facilities, with only 1/30 the number of defects.[8]

What Japan had discovered was primarily a new, more cogent, and more valid way to focus on quality. Call it the Theory of Continuous Improvement. Its postulates are simple, but they are strangely alien to some basic assumptions of American industry—assumptions fully evident in health care today. These postulates have been codified most forcefully by two American theorists, W. Edwards Deming[5,9] and Joseph M. Juran[4,10]—heroes in Japan today, and among enlightened American companies. Juran and Deming, guided largely by a visionary group of mentors at Western Electric Laboratories (later AT&T Bell Laboratories) in the 1930s, drew on a deepened understanding of the general sources of problems in quality. They discovered that problems, and therefore opportunities to improve quality, had usually been built directly into the complex production processes they studied, and that defects in quality could only rarely be attributed to a lack of will, skill, or benign intention among the people involved with the processes. Even when people were at the root of defects, they learned, the

33

problem was generally not one of motivation or effort, but rather of poor job design, failure of leadership, or unclear purpose. Quality can be improved much more when people are assumed to be trying hard already, and are not accused of sloth. Fear of the kind engendered by the disciplinary approach poisons improvement in quality, since it inevitably leads to disaffection, distortion of information, and the loss of the chance to learn.

Real improvement in quality depends, according to the Theory of Continuous Improvement, on understanding and revising the production processes on the basis of data about the processes themselves. "Every process produces information on the basis of which the process can be improved," say these theorists. The focus is on continuous improvement throughout the organization through constant effort to reduce waste, re-work, and complexity. When one is clear and constant in one's purpose, when fear does not control the atmosphere (and thus the data), when learning is guided by accurate information and sound rules of inference, when suppliers of services remain in dialogue with those who depend on them, and when the hearts and talents of all workers are enlisted in the pursuit of better ways, the potential for improvement in quality is nearly boundless. Translated into cultural norms in production systems and made real through sound statistical techniques, these lessons are at the core of the Japanese industrial revolution.[7] They have proved their worth.

In retrospect, their success is not all that surprising. Modern theories of quality improvement in industry are persuasive largely because they focus on the average producer, not the outlier, and on learning, not defense. Like Foreman 2, the modern quality improvement expert cares far more about learning and cooperating with the typical worker than about censoring the truly deficient. The Theory of Continuous Improvement works because of the immense, irresistible quantitative power derived from shifting the entire curve of production upward even slightly, as compared with a focus on trimming the tails. The Japanese call it *kaizen*—the continuous search for opportunities for all processes to get better.[11] An epigram captures this spirit: "Every defect is a treasure." In the discovery of imperfection lies the chance for processes to improve.

How far from *kaizen* has heath care come! Not that the idea of continuous improvement is alien to medicine; self-development, continuous learning, the pursuit of completeness are all familiar themes in medical instruction and history. Yet today we find ourselves almost devoid of such thinking when we enter the debate over quality. The disciplinarians seek out Bad Apples; the profession, and its institutions by and large, try to justify themselves as satisfactory. It is the rare "customer" and "supplier" of health care today who function as partners in continuous improvement; for the most part, they are playing a different game.

34

It would be naive to counsel the total abandonment of surveillance and discipline. Even in Japan, there are police. Politically, at least, it is absolutely necessary for regulators to continue to ferret out the truly avaricious and the dangerously incompetent. But what about the rest of us? How can we best be helped to try a little *kaizen* in our medical back yards? What follows are a few small steps.

First, leaders must take the lead in quality improvement. Those who speak for the profession, for health care institutions, and for large-scale purchasers must establish and hold to a shared vision of a health care system undergoing continuous improvement. The volleys of accusation and defense badly need to be replaced by efforts to clarify the goals that producers and payers share, beginning with this assumption: "Health care is very good today; together, we intend to make it even better."

Second, investments in quality improvement must be substantial. In other industries, quality improvement has yielded high dividends in cost reductions;[12] that may occur in health care as well. For the time being, however, improvement requires additional investments in managerial time, capital, and technical expertise. With the high discount rate in health care planning today, such investment calls for steadfast long-term vision. The most important investments of all are in education and study, to understand the complex production processes used in health care; we must understand them before we can improve them.

Third, respect for the health care worker must be reestablished. Physicians, hospital employees, and health care workers, like workers anywhere, must be assumed to be trying hard, acting in good faith, and not willfully failing to do what they know to be correct. When they are caught in complex systems and performing complex tasks, of course clinicians make mistakes; these are unintentional, and the people involved cannot be frightened into doing better. In fact, if they are afraid, they will probably do worse, since they will be wasting their time in self-defense instead of learning.

Fourth, dialogue between customers and suppliers of health care must be open and carefully maintained. As an incentive to improve quality, the threat of taking one's business elsewhere is pale compared with the reminder that one is committed to a long-term relationship. Quality improves as those served (the customers) and those serving (the suppliers) take the time to listen to each other and to work out their inevitable misunderstandings. Just as marriages do not improve under the threat of divorce, neither, in general, will health care.

Fifth, modern technical, theoretically grounded tools for improving processes must be put to use in health care settings. The pioneers of quality improvement—Shewhart,[2,3] Dodge, Juran,[4,10] Deming,[5,9] Taguchi,[13] and others[14]—have left a rich heritage of theory and technique by which to analyze and improve complex production processes, yet until recently these techniques have had little use in our health care systems. The barriers have been cultural in part; physicians, for example, seem to have difficulty seeing themselves as participants in processes, rather than as lone agents of success or failure. The techniques of process flow analysis, control charts, cause-and-effect diagrams, design experimentation, and quality-function deployment, to name a few, are neither arcane nor obvious;[14,15] they require study, but they can be learned. Many will be as useful in health care as they have been in other industries. Processes that can be improved by means of systematic techniques abound in medicine. Those within institutions are obvious, such as the ways in which hospitals dispense medication, transfer information, or equip and schedule operating rooms. But even individual doctors create and use "production process." In this sense, the way a physician schedules patients constitutes a process, as does the way he or she prescribes medicines, gives a patient instructions, organizes office records, issues bills, or ensures that high-risk patients receive influenza vaccine.

Sixth, health care institutions must "organize for quality." When other types of companies have invested in quality improvement, they have discovered and refined managerial techniques requiring new structures, such as are not currently found in the American hospital or health maintenance organization. Quality engineers occupy a central place in such structures, as quality is brought to center stage in the managerial agenda, on a par with finance. Flexible project teams must be created, trained, and competently led to tackle complex processes that cross customary departmental boundaries. Throughout the organization, a renewed investment must be made in training, since all staff members must become partners in the central mission of quality improvement.

Furthermore, health care regulators must become more sensitive to the cost and ineffectiveness of relying on inspection to improve quality. In some regulatory functions, inspection and discipline must continue, but when such activities dominate, they have an unfavorable effect on the quality of care provided by the average worker. This is not to argue against measuring quality and developing tools to do so; without them, artisans could not improve their craft. The danger lies in a naive and atheoretical belief, rampant today in the orgy of measurement involved in health care regulation, that the assessment and publication of performance data will somehow induce otherwise indolent care givers to improve the level of their care and efficiency. In other industries, reliance on inspection as the agent of change has instead more commonly added cost and slowed progress toward improvement. So it will be in health care. Without doubt, regulators who willingly learn and respect modern principles of quality improvement can have a helpful role. They can do so as the partners of care givers in developing sound measurement tools that represent common values and are for use primarily by the producers themselves; by aggregating data centrally to help care givers learn from each other; by providing technical support and training in methods of quality improvement; and by encouraging and funding studies of the efficacy of technologies and procedures and thus expanding the scientific basis for specifying rational processes of care.

In addition, professionals must take part in specifying preferred methods of care, but must avoid minimalist "standards" of care. Linked closely to the reliance on inspection to improve quality is the search for standards of care, which usually implies minimal thresholds of structure, process, or outcome above which one is safe from being labeled a Bad Apple. Quality-control engineers know that such floors rapidly become ceilings, and that a company that seeks merely to meet standards cannot achieve excellence. Specifications of process (clear, scientifically grounded, continuously reviewed statements of how one intends to behave) are essential to quality improvement, on the other hand, and are widely lacking in medical care. Health care producers who commit themselves to improvement will invest energy in developing specific statements of purpose and algorithms for the clinical processes by which they intend to achieve those purposes. For example, they will specify rules both for routine procedures (e.g., "What is our system for dispensing medications correctly?") and for the content and evaluation of clinical practices (e.g., "What is our best current guess about the proper sequence of tests and therapies for back pain, and how well are they working?"). Ideally, such specifications are guidelines that are appropriate locally and are subject to ongoing assessment and revision.

Finally, individual physicians must join in the effort for continuous improvement. It may seem at first that the Theory of Continuous Improvement, coming as it does from experience in large manufacturing companies, has little relevance to individual physicians, at least those not involved in managed care organizations. But the opposite is true. At the very least, quality improvement has little chance of success in heath care organizations without the understanding, the participation, and in many cases the leadership of individual doctors. In hospitals, physicians both rely on and help shape almost every process pertaining to patients' experience, from support services (such as dietary and housekeeping functions) to clinical care services (such as laboratories and nursing). Few can improve without the help of the medical staff.

Furthermore, the theory of quality improvement applies almost as well to small systems (such as a doctor's office) as it does to large ones. Individual physicians caring for individual patients know that defects in the care they provide do not usually stem from inattention or uniformed decisions. Yet hazards and defects do occur. Often they originate in the small but complex sequences on which every doctor depends, even sole practitioners. A test result lost, a specialist who cannot be reached, a missing requisition, a misinterpreted order, duplicate paperwork, a vanished record, a long wait for the CT scan, an unreliable on-call system—these are all-too-familiar examples of waste, rework, complexity, and error in the doctor's daily life. Flawless care requires not just sound decisions but also sound supports for those decisions. For the average doctor, quality fails when systems fail. Without the insights and techniques of quality improvement embedded in their medical practice, physicians are like anyone else who depends on others to get a complicated job done. They can remain trapped by defects they do not create but will nonetheless be held accountable for. The solo doctor who embodies every process needed to ensure highest-quality care is now nearly a myth. All physicians depend on systems, from the local ones in their private offices to the gargantuan ones of national health care.

Physicians who doubt that methods designed to improve quality can help them in daily practice may consider several questions. When quality fails in your own work, why does it fail? Do you ever waste time waiting, when you should not have to? Do you ever redo your work because something failed the first time? Do the procedures you use waste steps, duplicate efforts, or frustrate you through their unpredictability? Is information that you need ever lost? Does communication ever fail? If the answer to any of these questions is yes, then ask why. How can it be changed? What can be improved, and how? Must you be a mere observer of problems, or can you lead toward their solution? Physicians and health care managers who study and apply the principles of continuous improvement daily will probably come to know better efficiency, greater effectiveness, lower cost, and the gratitude and loyalty of more satisfied patients. They will be able to make better decisions and carry them out more faithfully.

We are wasting our time with the Theory of Bad Apples and our defensive response to it in health care today, and we can best begin by freeing ourselves from the fear, accusation, defensiveness, and naiveté of an empty search for improvement through inspection and discipline. The Theory of Continuous Improvement proved better in Japan; it is proving itself again in American industries willing to embrace it, and it holds some badly needed answers for American health care.

REFERENCES

1. Health Care Financing Administration. Medicare hospital mortality information. Washington, D.C.: Government Printing Office, 1988. (GPO publication no. 1987 O-196860).
2. Shewhart WA. The application of statistics as an aid in maintaining quality of manufactured product. J Am Stat Assoc 1925; 20:546–8.
3. *Idem*. Economic control of quality of a manufactured product. New York: D. Van Nostrand, 1931.
4. Juran JM, Gryna FM Jr, Bingham RS Jr, eds. Quality control handbook. New York: McGraw-Hill, 1979.
5. Deming WE. Quality, productivity and competitive position. Cambridge, Mass.: Massachusetts Institute of Technology, Center for Advanced Engineering Study, 1982.
6. Feigenbaum AV. Total quality control. 3rd ed. New York: McGraw-Hill, 1983.
7. Garvin DA. Managing quality: the strategic and competitive edge. New York: Free Press, 1988.
8. Abelson PH. Competitiveness: a long-enduring problem. Science 1988; 240:865
9. Deming WE. Out of the crisis. Cambridge, Mass.: Massachusetts Institute of Technology, Center for Advanced Engineering Study, 1986.
10. Juran JM. Managerial breakthrough. New York: McGraw-Hill, 1964.
11. Imai M. Kaizen: the key to Japanese competitive success. New York: Random House, 1986.
12. Crosby PB. Quality is free: the art of making quality certain. New York: McGraw-Hill, 1979.
13. Kackar RN. Off-line quality control, parameter design and the Taguchi method. J Qual Technol 1985; 17:176-88.
14. Wadsworth HM, Stephens KS, Godfrey AB. Modern methods for quality control and improvement. New York: John Wiley, 1986.
15. Ishikawa K, ed. Guide to quality control. White Plains, N.Y.: Kraus International Publications, 1986.

The CASE for USING INDUSTRIAL QUALITY MANAGEMENT SCIENCE in HEALTH CARE ORGANIZATIONS

Glenn Laffel, MD

David Blumenthal, MD

In an effort to provide health care of optimal quality, providers traditionally assess or measure performance and then assure that it conforms to standards. In cases where performance fails to conform, providers attempt to modify or improve physician behavior. The analytic scope of this traditional paradigm may not be broad enough to allow modern health care organizations to provide optimal care. At a theoretical and practical level, many conceptual limitations inherent in the traditional approach are addressed in modern industrial quality science. A fundamental principle of industrial quality control is the recognition, analysis, and elimination of variation. Based on rigorous analysis of variation in outcomes and processes, industrial quality experts have developed principles and techniques for quality improvement. Health care organizations may well make important advances in the quality of care and service through the application of these principles and techniques.

(*JAMA.* 1989;262:2869-2873)

Since Codman[1] first systematically audited medical records at the Massachusetts General Hospital (Boston) in 1915, scholars and practitioners have made considerable progress in defining and assessing the quality of medical care.[2,3] Nevertheless, it is argued herein that current theory and practice have limitations that must be remedied before complex, modern health care organizations will be able to develop effective quality improvement programs. It is further argued that industrial quality science appears to address some of these deficiencies and thus might enhance the ability of health care facilities to provide care of optimal quality.

QUALITY of CARE:
CURRENT THEORY and PRACTICE

Donabedian,[4] the leading thinker in modern medical quality assurance, formulated the classic definition of quality of care in medicine: it is "that kind of care which is expected to maximize an inclusive measure of patient welfare, after one has taken account of the balance of expected gains and losses that attend the process of care in all its parts." High-quality medical care is traditionally thought to consist of a scientific or technical component and an interpersonal component that together enable the patient to attain the highest possible functional state and psychosocial result.[2]

Consistent with this definition, health care organizations' quality programs generally have three major foci: assessing or measuring performance, determining whether performance conforms to standards, and improving performance when standards are not met.[5-10]

This traditional approach to quality has several important limitations. To begin with, the classic definition of quality of care seems too narrow to meet the needs of modern health care providers. Donabedian's formulation emphasizes quite appropriately the extent to which health care providers improve the physical and psychological health of individual patients. The needs of patients should always be paramount, but health care organizations are increasingly called on to meet the needs of other individuals and groups, such as patients' families, referring physicians, and third parties. For example, teaching hospitals can achieve high-quality care in part by meeting the educational needs of interns.

Second, traditional medical quality assurance features a static approach to quality. Its goal is conformance to standards. This can be distinguished from the professional ethic of physicians to continuously improve on existing practices. The approach implicitly assumes that some rate of poor outcomes is acceptable and that little information can be obtained from the analysis of cases in which prevailing standards are met. Furthermore, should standards be set too low, quality assurance programs may breed complacency and thus contribute to poor quality. Should they be set unrealistically high, they may alienate or frustrate providers.

A third limitation of the current approach is that it tends to focus on physician performance and to underemphasize the contributions of nonphysicians and organizational processes generally. For example, consider what happens when a physician concludes that his patient has bacterial sepsis. The physician must choose an appropriate antibiotic and communicate this decision appropriately. These activities trigger subsequent processes by which the pharmacy department dispenses and nurses administer the antibiotic (Figure 1).

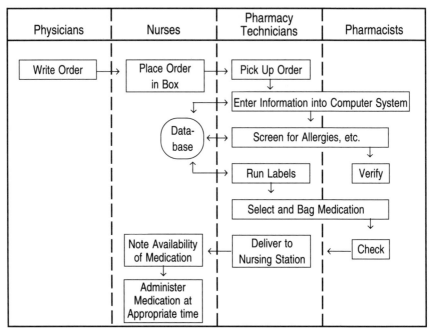

Figure 1. Flowchart: dispensing medications at Brigham and Women's Hospital, Boston, Mass.

As it relates to this example, a traditional quality program might evaluate the physician's diagnostic skills and choice of antibiotic. However, errors may occur at any step in the subsequent processes and they, too, may cause the patient to receive suboptimal care. Unfortunately, most health care organizations do not routinely analyze the performance of such critical processes. In those that do, the data may be perceived to be less important than evaluations of physician performance.

Traditional techniques for quality improvement in health care also tend to focus on physicians and changing physician behavior.[11-15] However, it is likely that quality improvement in modern health care organizations will require complex, simultaneous changes involving employees and professionals in many departments. In many industries, the transformation of the production process from one dominated by artisans to one involving complex interactions among many specialized divisions has necessitated the development of new methods for quality improvement. Health care delivery, which is undergoing similar transformation, may require similar reform in its approach to quality improvement.

The fourth limitation of the current approach is that it tends to emphasize certain aspects of physician performance: technical expertise and interpersonal relations. Other aspects of physician performance have a bearing on quality. One of the most important is the physician's ability to mobilize an organization's resources so as to meet the needs of individual patients and the goals of the organization.

Consider a physician who has expertly diagnosed and treated a patient with chest pain. On the first hospital day, the physician fails to properly specify the roentgenogram he wants, so the patient must return to radiology. On the second day, he forgets to sign his verbal orders for pain medication. This delays pharmacy and nursing and, of course, prolongs his patient's discomfort. On the day of discharge, he decides to evaluate an ancillary problem. This delays the patient and his family and prevents the hospital from accepting a patient awaiting transfer from another hospital. Has high-quality care been given?

A NEW APPROACH to QUALITY

Problems with traditional approaches to medical quality have led recently to a search for alternative methods and strategies. Modern quality science, a discipline in which statistical techniques are used to assist decision making concerning product quality and production processes, is one such alternative. Modern quality science has been adopted on a large scale outside health care, and it has led to demonstrable improvements in the quality of products and services, improved productivity and efficiency, and, in many cases, improved profitability as well.

Redefining Quality

Industrial quality experts suggest that quality be defined as a continuous effort by all members of an organization to meet the needs and expectations of the customer. For health care purposes, this definition might be modified to substitute "patients and other customers" for the word "customer."

The advantages of this definition are several. The reference to "continuous effort" emphasizes the value of striving to exceed prevailing standards, rather than accepting them even temporarily as limits on performance. The term "all members of an organization" suggests an imperative to study the organizational processes by which health care is produced and provided. The reference to "expectations" recognizes that patients' reports of their experiences and their assessments of results are valid indicators of quality, including some of its technical aspects.[16,17]

By singling out the patient from other customers, this definition acknowledges the ethical primacy of the individual patient's needs and expectations. However, one advantage of acknowledging openly the existence of other customers is that this may encourage frank discussion within health care organizations of the reality that they are constantly engaged in complex efforts to satisfy many parties. The needs and expectations of differing clients sometimes conflict, and such conflicts must always be resolved in the patient's favor.

Measuring Quality

The recognition and analysis of *variation* is fundamental to modern industrial thinking about quality measurement. All aspects of medical care display variation. For example, in a series of patients with sepsis, the etiologic agent and its antibiotic sensitivities vary. Patients themselves have unique combinations of coexisting conditions, clinical presentations, and expectations. The particular mix of physicians, nurses, and support personnel varies, as does the availability of diagnostic tests and the accuracy with which they are performed. Antibiotic batches vary in potency and bioavailability

Furthermore, all these sources of variation combine at random during the care of each patient with sepsis. It is thus not surprising that the outcomes of a sequence of seemingly similar clinical encounters can themselves display variation.

When multiple sources of variation are present, isolated observations provide insufficient information on which to base objective decision making.[18] Optimal decision making requires the application of some basic statistics to a series of observations so that recognizable and predictable patterns can be appreciated. The control chart (Figure 2) can be used to accomplish this. Control charts have been used in industrial settings for 60 years to understand patterns and types of variation and to provide a rational framework on which to formulate and evaluate quality improvement efforts. They are particularly effective when used to evaluate an unusual observation or sequence of observations. In such settings, control charts are used to determine the probability that these observations have a truly unique cause.

This fundamental thinking about multiple sources of variation and their combined impact on the measures of quality is not commonly applied in traditional medical quality programs. Instead, it is common to attribute poor outcomes to an individual or some other isolated cause. For example, an "unanticipated" death may be attributed to physician negligence, or a high rate of wound infections may be attributed to a particular technique.

Improving Quality

Having used control charts and other statistical tools for decades to study production and service provision, quality experts have more recently begun

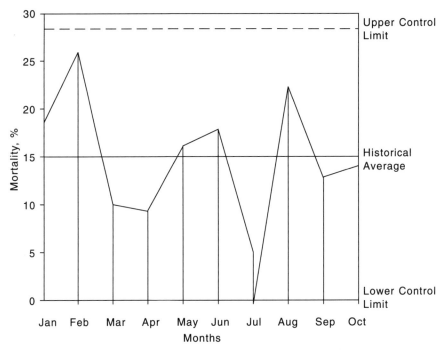

Figure 2.   Control chart demonstrating mortality rates in bacterial sepsis.

to suggest a set of managerial principles directed at quality improvement. They include (1) active, visible support from clinical and managerial leadership for the continuous improvement of quality; (2) a focus on processes as the objects of improvement; (3) the elimination of unnecessary variation; and (4) revised strategies for personnel management.

As it applies to health care organizations, quality experts' central principle of quality improvement is that *senior administrative and clinical leaders should explicitly and actively pursue an ethic of continuous improvement in the quality of care and service.* This is deceptively difficult to achieve. The very issues that have thrust quality to the top of health care leaders' agenda—cost containment, the nursing shortage, malpractice, and others—all beg for short-term solutions at the expense of a long-term commitment toward quality improvement. A most salient example of this occurs in health care organizations that face serious financial crises. In this setting, many leaders are unwilling to commit the resources and time to initiate quality improvement efforts.

In addition to committing resources, quality experts suggest that leadership must direct the effort, evaluate it, implement the process changes where indicated, provide training, and recognize those who participate. This would require uncommon leadership in health care settings, because quality management principles have yet to be empirically proved in health care as they have in industry.

As a second fundamental principle of quality improvement, quality experts suggest that *processes, not individuals, should be the objects of quality improvement.* In industry, the word "process" refers to a sequence of activities that transforms inputs into final products, or outputs. This definition should be distinguished from the definition used in the medical quality assurance literature. In the latter, "process" refers to the "set of activities that go on within and between practitioners and patients."[4,6] This traditional medical definition of process has become an important conceptual link in the analytic framework that supports traditional medical quality assurance, and it has been of great value for many years.

It is also readily apparent, however, that modern health care organizations provide medical care and ancillary services by implementing processes of the type described by industrial quality experts. There are processes by which we admit and discharge patients. There is a process by which pharmacy dispenses medications (Figure 1). And, to be sure, there are clinical decision-making processes as well.

Industrial quality experts have made several observations about process that can assist quality improvement efforts. The first is that processes are complex. During a recent demonstration project at Brigham and Women's Hospital (Boston, Mass) for example, we observed that the process by which cardiac catheterization laboratories are "turned over" between cases includes four individuals who carry out over 50 separate activities. The activities of each individual are linked to those of the other three through an exquisitely timed series of interactions, handoffs, and dependencies. This process is repeated 10 times each day at our hospital, but it is only one of dozens that take place in the catheterization laboratory, and it is only one of hundreds that a patient might be part of during even the most routine hospitalization. This suggests that health care organizations could benefit from a systematic approach to the analysis and improvement of process, as outlined in the industrial quality science literature.

Second, industrial quality experts have observed that processes are frequently characterized by unnecessary rework and waste, and process modifications that reduce these features may simultaneously improve quality and reduce cost. These observations would seem applicable to health care organizations as well. We repeat tests because they are not performed correctly the first time. We rewrite requisitions because they are lost or filled out incorrectly. We look for lost charts and reschedule appointments.

Because the time required for such activities reduces that available for direct patient care, there is a strong rationale to improve the execution of such processes.

Quality experts' third observation is that organizations can substantially improve their final products or service by training personnel at all levels to use simple analytic techniques and graphical methods[19–22] for the study of process. The implication for health care organizations is that with proper training in quality improvement methods, physicians, nurses, technicians, and other hospital employees are well positioned to contribute to quality improvement. All have important perspectives on the processes involved in health care delivery, and all can identify sources of variation in these processes.

The Elimination of Unnecessary Variation. Many sources of variation in medical care should not be controlled. For example, it is often necessary to develop treatment plans that are customized to meet the needs and expectations of individual patients. Nevertheless, quality experts suggest that substantial quality improvement can be achieved by eliminating unnecessary variation in the execution of the processes by which these treatment plans are implemented.

In the management of all patients with sepsis, for example, quality may be improved if technicians use the same techniques for obtaining, handling, and interpreting blood cultures and if nurses use the same techniques and equipment for measuring patients' temperature and applying wound dressings. The benefits of eliminating unnecessary variation in this way include rapid acquisition of technical skills through frequent repetition and consequent reduction in procedural errors. They include improved turnaround times on diagnostic information and improved reliability of this information.

The elimination of unnecessary variation in clinical practice may similarly improve the quality of care. In the above example, for instance, should physicians choose to follow similar procedures for determining the source of infection and for selecting and then modifying antibiotic coverage, it is likely that the hospital would be able to implement their care plans more efficiently and accurately. This is because allied health personnel would become familiar with the procedures and protocols physicians expect them to perform. These potential improvements in the quality of care need to be balanced against the physician's need to preserve discretion in many aspects of clinical practice.

The proposition that unnecessary variation in clinical practice causes poor quality provides an important justification to develop consensus about "best practices" and to encourage adherence to these practices. "Best practices" might be developed at the institutional level based on the medical literature and local need and constraints, and they should be updated as necessary. They are to be distinguished from mandatory adherence to externally imposed, static guidelines or standards.

The elimination of variation in clinical practice is highly desirable even in the common circumstance where physicians must make treatment decisions without clear guidance from the results of clinical trials. In such settings, widespread uncontrolled variation may inhibit the advancement of medical knowledge by confounding the interpretation of outcomes. In fact, research and development are best accomplished in circumstances where sources of variation have been identified and controlled. When this is the case, differences between control and treatment groups can more accurately be attributed to the treatment.

Industrial quality management science's intense focus on process and its improvement effectively complements current trends in medical quality assurance that increasingly rely on outcome measures. Outcome measures will always have a role in medical quality programs because there will always be a need to know when poor outcomes are occurring. However, because outcome measures do not generally provide insight into the causes of defects, they may be most useful when used in conjunction with process technology as described above.

Personnel Management. Quality experts recommend a personnel management strategy that centers around the treatment of employees and professionals as valuable resources with a central role in quality improvement. The strategy features increased training, the elimination of work standards and numerical goals, and new approaches to employee evaluation.

Quality experts suggest greatly intensified training for all hospital professionals and employees. They suggest that training be directed at the acquisition and perfection of job-specific skills and at the principles and techniques of quality improvement. Consider, for example, how new physicians learn to perform invasive procedures such as lumbar puncture and thoracentesis. When a patient develops an indication for such a procedure, the resident demonstrates his technique to the intern. The next time a patient on that intern's service requires that procedure, the intern does it himself. As the year goes on, interns continue to gain unsupervised experience with these techniques. For their part, each resident had learned his technique from a different resident the year before. This paradigm considerably increases variation in technique and increases the chance for procedural error and complications. If the training program emphasized supervision and if it formulated optimal approaches for the performance of such procedures, negative outcomes might well be reduced.

In industrial settings, employee training programs also frequently include clear statements of organizational commitment to quality improvement. Employees are shown how the organization defines and measures quality, and *how they can participate in its improvement.* This generally requires several days of instruction in communication skills, elementary statistics, and graphical techniques. Such training has become increasingly common outside health care, and it appears to be effective despite variations in employee educational levels.[19-22]

As part of their new personnel management strategy, quality experts also recommend the elimination of work standards and numerical goals. Standards and goals stimulate behavior narrowly directed at their achievement, and this may lead to impaired performance in other areas. In addition, standards may be perceived as maximal attainable levels of performance. Such perceptions may discourage creativity and risk taking, which are required to substantially improve quality.

Quality experts also suggest alternatives for employee evaluation. These are based on the assumption that employees and professionals generally want to do their best, and that variations in input should not routinely be attributed to their behavior, as there are many equally plausible explanations for such variation.

CONCLUSIONS

The focus of most quality assurance programs in health care remains the technical expertise and interpersonal skills of physicians. Their ability to mobilize the resources of complex health care organizations remains unassessed. Health care organizations themselves contribute to overall quality in ways that have yet to be measured. In addition, regulatory and legal demands to define standards of care encourage or force physicians to pursue conformance rather than the possibility that continuous improvement is possible.

Modern industrial quality science appears to offer solutions to these conceptual problems. It includes the use of statistics to analyze production and service provision processes. It is based on the assumption that employees and top leadership should continuously strive to improve these processes. It stresses interdepartmental cooperation, training, and experimentation.

These techniques have been associated with improved product quality in many Japanese and American industries, but they have yet to be widely implemented in health care. It is an appropriate time for the health care industry to begin experimentation with these techniques.

REFERENCES

1. Codman EA. The product of a hospital. *Surg Gynecol Obstet.* 1914;18:491–496.
2. Sanazuro PJ. Quality assessment and quality assurance in medical care. *Annu Rev Public Health.* 1980;1:37–68.
3. Lohr KN, Brook RH. Quality assurance in medicine. *Am Behav Sci.* 1984;27:583–607.
4. Donabedian A. *Explorations in Quality Assessment and Monitoring: The Definition of Quality and Approaches to Its Assessment.* Ann Arbor, Mich: Health Administration Press; 1980;1.
5. Donabedian A. The quality of medical care. *Science.* 1978;200:856–864.
6. Donabedian A. The quality of care: how can it be assessed? *JAMA.* 1988;260:1743–1748.
7. Siu AL, Sonnenberg FA, Manning WG, et al. Inappropriate use of hospitals in a randomized trial of health insurance plans. *N Engl J Med.* 1986;315:1259–1266.
8. Chassin MR, Kosecoff J, Park RE, et al. Does inappropriate use explain variations in the use of health care services? a study of three procedures. *JAMA.* 1987;258:2533–2537.
9. Medicare Program. Selected performance information on hospitals providing care to Medicare beneficiaries. *Federal Register.* August 17, 1987;12:30742–30745.
10. Dubois RW, Rogers WH, Moxley JH, Draper D, Brook RH. Hospital inpatient mortality...is it a predictor of quality? *N Engl J Med.* 1987;317:1674–1680.
11. Dombaugh KA, Koch S. *Practical Methods to Modify the Use of Diagnostic Tests.* Burlington: Massachusetts Hospital Association; 1987;1–59
12. Marton KI. Modifying test-ordering behavior in the outpatient clinic: a controlled trial of two educational interventions. *Arch Intern Med.* 1985;145:816–821.
13. Berwick DM, Coltin KL. Feedback reduces test use in a health maintenance organization. *JAMA.* 1985;255:1450–1454.
14. Wong ET. Cost-effective use of laboratory tests: a joint responsibility of clinicians and laboratorians. *Clin Lab Med.* 1985;5:665–672.
15. Martin AR, Ware M. A trial of two strategies to modify the test ordering behavior of medical residents. *N Engl J Med.* 1980;303:1330–1336.
16. Davies AR, Ware JE. Involving consumers in quality of care assessment. *Health Aff.* 1988;7:33–48.
17. Gerbert B, Hargreaves WA. Measuring physician behavior. *Med Care.* 1987;24:838–847.
18. Wadsworth HM, Stephens KS, Godfrey AB. *Modern Methods for Quality Control and Improvement.* New York, NY: John Wiley & Sons Inc; 1986:4–12.
19. Deming WE. *Out of the Crisis.* Cambridge: Massachusetts Institute of Technology Center for Advanced Engineering Study; 1986.
20. Tribus M. *Deming's Way.* Cambridge: Massachusetts Institute of Technology Center for Advanced Engineering Study; 1985:1–6.
21. Juran JM. *Managerial Breakthrough.* New York, NY: McGraw-Hill International Book Co; 1964:43–54.
22. Ishikawa K. *What Is Total Quality Control? The Japanese Way.* Englewood Cliffs, NJ: Prentice Hall International Inc; 1987:63–64.

TOTAL QUALITY MANAGEMENT for PHYSICIANS: TRANSLATING the NEW PARADIGM

Martin D. Merry, MD

Besieged simultaneously on all sides by demands to control costs while maintaining and improving quality, forward-thinking health care leaders are generating an unprecedented interest in exploring the relevance and possible application of industrial quality process techniques to health care. We assume that they will find much of value and will wish to implement such proven concepts as total quality management (TQM).[1] But we also warn that they can expect the same resistance in their organizations that has been experienced outside the health care field.

Physicians in particular, with their historic quasi independence of the structure and accountability of the traditional hospital and with their keen sensitivity to power and control within the health delivery system, are likely to prove an especially problematic challenge to leaders who wish to introduce industrial techniques into their institutions.

If they start from an insightful understanding of their physicians' own perceptual "starting point," however, and build a program within the framework of, rather than antithetical to, what motivates many physicians today, health care leaders have a good chance of being more successful and encountering less resistance than their forerunners in other fields.

QUALITY MANAGEMENT THEN and NOW: The DIFFERENCE IS REAL

If it were merely a matter of communicating to physicians that the new quality paradigm is only a slight shift from previous models, the task of developing medical staff support might be relatively simple. But while it is based on principles known in traditional quality assurance, the industrial quality process really *is* different. One should emphasize genuine connections between earlier methodology and modern quality process, but physicians will not respond to a "soft sell" of quality process, and it would be misleading to take that tack. Quality process encompasses major departures from traditional practices.

In the place of retrospective review of individual patient charts, analysis of statistical data is now the primary focus of review. Case review is not unimportant, but the focus is now epidemiologic. In other words, the question now is less "What went wrong with this individual *case?*" and more "What might be the common denominator of this high infection *rate?*" (or *location, organism, anatomical site of infection, physician,* etc.).

The fundamental analytic tool of "quality review"—subjective review of questioned cases by individual physicians—is augmented by an array of methodologies imported from the original quality process in industry: brainstorming, Pareto charts, scatter diagrams, "fishbone" diagrams, histograms, run charts, control charts and many others.[1-5] (See Figures 1–3.) In place of what was a largely subjective process totally controlled by physicians emerges an objective, statistically based discipline *not* controlled by clinicians.

Traditional health care quality review is built on an implicit assumption that clinical personnel generally, and physicians most centrally, are the sole determinants of patient care quality. This assumption, combined with the accreditation practice of focusing on the medical staff as a distinct entity, perpetuates the isolation of physicians as all-important in determining quality.

The traditional way of doing medical quality review has thus been blind to what has been know in industry for decades: that quality is the end result of a complex interaction of people and support systems. Quality pioneer W. Edwards Deming estimates that only 15% of quality improvement opportunity lies in focusing on the performance of people, with the remaining 85% of impediments to quality coming from systemic factors that are optimally addressed by involving everyone in the system in quality improvement activities.[5]

Both industrial quality process and current organizational effectiveness practice emphasize the enormous value of all personnel, working as a coordinated team, as essential to high-level quality process and institutional performance.[6] In contrast, the relative isolation of physicians and virtually all clinical personnel, heretofore characteristic of health care quality review, is antithetical to this team approach.

It is now evident that quality management is just that—a management, not clinical, function. While physicians and other clinical professionals remain vital to the review process, quality is no longer defined by an arcane

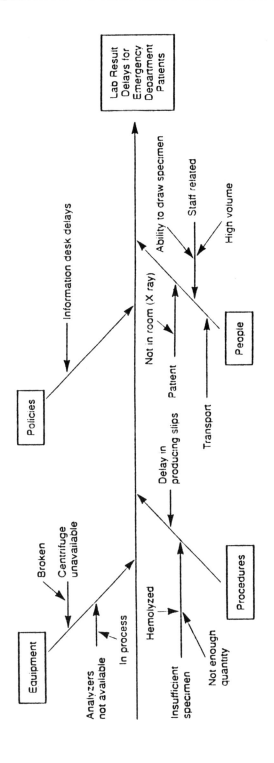

Fishbone Diagram*

Figure 1. The fishbone, or cause and effect, diagram (sometimes called an Ishikawa diagram, named after the Japanese quality control leader) is drawn during a brainstorming session. The central problem is visualized as the head of the fish, with the skeleton divided into branches showing contributing causes of different parts of the problem.

*Adapted from M. Brassard: *The Memory Jogger.* Methuen, MA: GOAL/QPC. 1988.

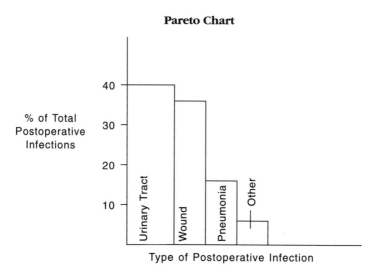

Pareto Chart

Figure 2.   The Pareto chart is drawn to show the results of prioritizing problems. Vertical bars display which components of problems account for most of the total volume of problems.

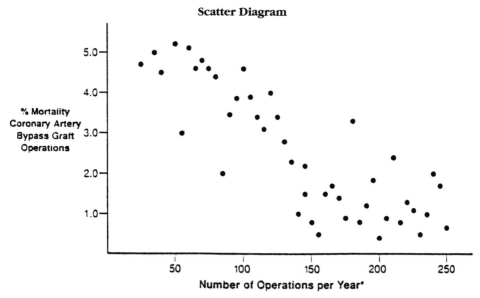

Scatter Diagram

Figure 3.   The scatter diagram is used to determine a possible relationship between two variables. The dots in this figure show a correlation between the mortality rate for a surgical procedure and the number of times the procedure is performed during a 12-month period. Each dot represents one surgical team.

54

process (retrospective case review) totally controlled by physicians. Quality can and will be defined, at least partially, by analysis of aggregate patient outcomes—that is, by how patients are actually faring within the health care system—and the data base of this analysis will be available to virtually all interested parties.

In sum, modern quality management implies no minor evolution from previous modes. It encompasses a complex paradigm shift in institutional quality culture and practice. To elicit from physicians both acceptance of and participation in modern quality management will require extraordinary leadership—clear vision, solid institutional values, a depth of understanding, careful planning and patience. And perceptive and ultimately successful leaders will start at the beginning—exactly where physicians are now.

A WORLD ACCORDING to the MEDICAL STAFF

Balancing the pressures felt by health care institutional chief executive officers, physicians have their own view of environmental chaos and suboptimal control.

It should be understood that both the process and the implicit higher level of institutional accountability bring a true culture shock to physicians. As members of an ancient and respected profession, they have come to expect autonomy and accountability only to themselves as the norm. Heretofore, the complexity of medical care and practice of focusing on individual cases to define quality kept physicians essentially immune from outside challenge. Further, the essential concept of professionalism as a special status granted by society, earned through a long period of dedicated study and service, has traditionally guaranteed relative autonomy to those who have been able to attain professional status. The "TQM generation" of physicians, however, is the first to be exposed to the "microscopic power" of modern quality process tools and techniques. It should not be surprising that their reaction to such perceived intrusion and exposure would be initially less than enthusiastic.

In fact, while there are many individual and even group exceptions, physicians in general often express themselves as a depressed and sometimes vocally angry group. They perceive that they are steadily losing power and influence, not only in large organizational settings, but even in their own office practice. Regulation progressively restricts their ability to protect both their income and their professional freedom.

Not only does paperwork mount as income and freedom are restricted, but physicians continue to get bad press from both the regulatory process and the public. The charges include insensitivity and poor communication with patients, excessive focus on money, and inadequate control of quality,

55

among others. (Substituting the word *customers* for *patients*, these charges are not dissimilar to those leveled against American industry, as it adopts TQM techniques in an attempt to regain the competitive edge over foreign-made products of reputed higher quality.) Many have likened physicians' current state of mind to Kubler-Ross's denial and anger stages of the death and dying process.

In keeping with this mental state, physicians tend to view new programs, especially if they are perceived as somehow connected with "management" or "the regulators," with suspicion. It is well known that all of us resist change, even change that is regarded as favorable. There is no reason to doubt that physicians will reflexively see new programs such as TQM as further intrusions into their power and freedom. While a growing cadre of physician leaders is publicly granting legitimacy to the introduction of industrial quality process into health care,[8] most physicians will (correctly) see this movement as coming from outside the profession and will oppose it even if it is articulated and supported by respected leaders from within their own ranks. Quality leader Joseph M. Juran describes an "immune reaction" to quality process even in "normal" organizations.[9] Physicians may well prove to be the "killer lymphocytes" opposing quality process in health care organizations.

Patient care is a very individual and private affair, with ultimate responsibility for an idiosyncratic clinical decision-making process, featuring "artistic" mixtures of inductive and deductive reasoning, resting with each physician. Further, neither by training nor experience are physicians likely to have exposure to the concepts of teamwork so essential to integrated quality improvement.[6]

Understandably, the specific tools of TQM, both old and new, given their origins in group process, are largely unfamiliar to physicians. The whole territory of brainstorming, Pareto charts, fishbone diagrams, and so forth, seems arcane, abstract, and irrelevant to their problems of individual patient care. In fact, these powerful tools can just as well be learned and incorporated into their practices, as physician pioneers utilizing TQM techniques are now demonstrating. Once over the initial resistance hump, physicians are finding that these techniques significantly enhance their problem-solving and quality improvement capability.* An important educational challenge, as well as a strategy for gaining more physician support, is demonstrating to physicians that systemic organizational weaknesses have a real and very direct effect on their ability to practice optimally. Physicians will become

---

*Personal communication with Sue Weinstein, MD, who is applying some of the most advanced TQM concepts available at a major experimental project being conducted at Bethesda Hospital, Cincinnati.

more accepting when they see their tools in action, actually solving problems high on their own priority lists.

Ironically, while patient care is an inherently complex process, physicians frequently tend to oversimplify institutional problem solving and systems improvement. For example, they believe that many patient care problems impeding their practice are due to inadequate staffing. In fact, however, systems deficiencies—poor information transfer between support services and patient floors, lack of coordination between the various diagnostic and therapeutic services, and so forth—are likely to be more basic, "root" causes of the inadequate bedside care they observe. Nonetheless, physicians' sense of time urgency typically precludes being willing to become involved in what they are likely to see as the overly rigorous and time-consuming task of team brainstorming around a fishbone diagram, tracing all the causal factors contributing to a patient care problem.

It is hard to overestimate how much a lack of trust between management and physicians, combined with what Elliot Jaques[10] would call the "nonrequisite organization" of the prototypical hospital, contributes to producing a highly unstable organizational structure. Specifically, physician members of the hospital medical staff, exercising enormous influence over hospital resource allocation, are actually part of an association within the overall hospital structure, without direct accountability to the chief executive officer. This situation creates ambiguity about authority and responsibility within the hospital that makes it a wonder that the hospital operates at all. An important literature addresses constructive approaches to the historical conflict between the medical and management professions,[11,12] and anyone attempting to introduce modern quality process to health care organizations should pay heed to this valuable experience.

TOWARD QUALITY COMMITMENT: A SHARED VENTURE

Another way of looking at the medical profession at the dawn of the 1990s is to see it as operating at relatively low levels of Maslow's hierarchy of needs.*[13] Where once the educational achievement, economic security, independence, and public esteem of physicians made them likely candidates for self-actualization (the highest level of this hierarchy), the profession as a whole now seems to be seized with fear and insecurity and preoccupied with basic needs, the lowest level of the hierarchy, as it views

---

*Abraham Maslow, a noted mid-twentieth-century American psychologist (1908–1970), formulated a hierarchy of human needs, with physiologic needs (hunger, thirst, etc.) at the base, and above it security and safety needs, belonging (friendship, affection), self-esteem, and finally self-actualization (opportunity, growth) at the top.

the future. The medical profession's "Maslovian fall" to a stance unthinkable 20 years ago provides an ample basis for the death-and-dying analogy.

Any new paradigm—and industrial quality process represents nothing less than a new paradigm for health care—must be carefully framed in terms and metaphors that are supportive of, rather than threatening to, physicians' current perceptions of their needs. If physicians are to be "part of the solution" rather than "part of the problem," they must be able to see how they can be active participants in the quality process and how they can be empowered to

- gain greater certainty over economic stability,
- maintain sufficient clinical freedom to deal with the uncertainties of patient care,
- gain a greater sense of participation and proactive influence in institutional development in the future, and
- restore a lost sense of social value of physicians' work.

Leaders who wish to assist the transition of physicians from resistance to acceptance and support of TQM must pay heed to these four essential needs and would be wise to structure early projects around the dual goals of improving patient care quality and appropriately empowering physician participants. For example, a cardiology group in a Middle Atlantic state became a proactive supporter when its members learned that they were able not only to improve patient results through careful outcome analysis, feedback and planning but also to increase their regional referrals by sharing their data with locally influential managed care plans.

Those leaders who wish to explore and implement some or all of the precepts of TQM in their institutions will need much more specific information on structure and process. Quality process is a complex undertaking that requires years to accomplish under the best of circumstances. Some of the references at the end of this commentary will give leaders a good start in preparing themselves to pursue the quality concept further.

It is unrealistic for the medical profession to expect to return to its old pedestal, which probably was unrealistically high and ultimately self-defeating anyway. But the profession's current depressed state creates a real opportunity to frame modern quality process in a way that offers realistic hope for regaining some ground lost in the past 20 years. It is equally important to abandon the "zero sum" concept of power as well. Physicians' improved status cannot be seen as coming at the expense of other legitimate "players"— managers, patients, third parties, and so forth. "Win" strategies embracing all these players are likely to characterize the truly excellent organizations of the future.

REFERENCES

1. Ishikawa K: *What Is Total Quality Control? The Japanese Way.* Englewood Cliffs, NJ: Prentice-Hall, 1985.
2. King B: *Better Designs in Half the Time: Implementing Quality Function Deployment.* Methuen, MA: GOAL/QPC, 1987, 1989 rev ed.
3. King B: *Hoshin Planning: The Developmental Approach.* Methuen, MA: GOAL/QPC, 1989.
4. Mizuno S: *Managing for Quality: The Seven New QC Tools.* Cambridge, MA: Productivity Press, 1988.
5. Walton M: *The Deming Management Method.* New York: The Putnam Publishing Group, 1986.
6. Weisbord M: *Productive Workplaces: Organizing and Managing for Dignity, Meaning and Community.* San Francisco: Jossey-Bass, 1987.
7. Ellwood P: Shattuck Lecture—Outcomes management: A technology of patient experience. *N Engl J Med* 318:1549–1556, 1988.
8. Berwick D: Continuous improvement as an ideal in health care. *N Engl J Med* 320:53-56, 1989.
9. Address to Summative Conference, National Demonstration Project on Industrial Quality Control and Health Care Quality, Boston, June 22-24, 1988.
10. Jaques E: *Requisite Organization: The CEO's Guide to Creative Structure and Leadership.* Arlington, VA: Cason Hall and Co, 1989.
11. Brown B: The profession of hospital administration. *Southern Hospitals,* Feb 1969.
12. Gill S: Can doctors and administrators work together? *Physician Executive* 3:11-16, Sep-Oct 1987.
13. Maslow A: *Toward a Psychology of Being,* 2nd ed. New York: Van Nostrand Co, 1968.

ORGANIZATIONWIDE QUALITY IMPROVEMENT in HEALTH CARE

Paul B. Batalden, MD

Organizationwide quality improvement (OQI) is a different way of thinking about and performing the job of organizational leadership. Over the last three fourths of the twentieth century, a body of knowledge and theory has developed and been applied in many different settings around the world to refine this model. This article will introduce the reader to the OQI model and what it might mean when applied to health care organizations, particularly hospitals.

INTRODUCTION

Though all knowledge is connected, most date the modern beginning of OQI thinking to the work of Walter Shewhart, the director of Bell Laboratories in the mid-1920s. Shewhart is given credit by his students, W. Edwards Deming and Joseph Juran, for the concept of the "cycle of continuous improvement." This concept suggests that quality improvement should be thought of as a continuous effort, linked to customers and led by management (see Figure 1).

After World War II, Gen. Douglas Mac Arthur invited W. Edwards Deming, a quality teacher during the wartime production effort, to Japan to teach quality improvement principles. Deming elaborated on Dr. Shewart's thoughts and offered a comprehensive theory of management grounded on the cycle of continuous improvement and on Shewhart's concern for using the study of variation as a guide to taking wise and economic management actions. The systematic implementation of these ideas is underway through-

W. A. Deming's "14 Points" reprinted from Deming, W. A., *Out of the Crisis.* Cambridge, Mass.: Massachusetts Institute of Technology Center for Advanced Engineering Study, 1986.

Reprinted from Batalden, P. B., Organizationwide Quality Improvement in Health Care, in *Topics in Health Record Management,* Vol. 11:3, pp. 1–12, with permission of Aspen Publishers, Inc., ©1991.

Figure 1.   The Shewhart cycle for continuous improvement.
Source: Deming, W.E. *Elementary Principles of the Statistical Control of Quality.* Nippon Kagaku
Gijutsu Remmei. Japanese Union of Scientists and Engineers, 1951.

out the world today. Among Deming's contributions are his 14 management
guidelines.[1]

1.   Create and publish to all employees a statement of the aims and
purposes of the company or other organization. The management must
demonstrate constantly their commitment to this statement.
2.   Learn the new philosophy, top management and everybody.
3.   Understand the purpose of inspection, for improvement of processes
and reduction of cost.
4.   End the practice of awarding business of the basis of price tag alone.
5.   Improve constantly and forever the system of production and service.
6.   Institute training.
7.   Teach and institute leadership.
8.   Drive out fear. Create trust. Create a climate of innovation.
9.   Optimize toward the aims and purposes of the company the efforts of
teams, groups and staff areas.
10.   Eliminate exhortations for the workforce.
11a.   Eliminate numerical quotas for production. Instead, learn and institute
methods for improvement.
11b.   Eliminate management by objective. Instead, learn the capabilities of
processes and how to improve them.
12.   Remove barriers that rob people of pride of workmanship.
13.   Encourage education and self-improvement for everyone.
14.   Take action to accomplish the transformation.

While straightforward and not too difficult to apply consistently, these
guidelines form a view of the worker, the work place, the work, the work
product, and the customer that significantly challenges our current thinking.

Nothing short of an organizationwide focus can be a sufficient response to these guidelines.

Shortly after Deming began teaching in Japan, Joseph Juran was invited to teach there as well. He focused on the tools and methods of applying these new insights to managing and leading organizations. A few years later, Armand Feigenbaum of General Electric and then General Systems Company was also invited to teach there. Many credit him with the term "Total quality control," which means that the concern for quality has to permeate the entire organization. A student and later long-term colleague of these Americans was Kaoru Ishikawa who, until his recent death, served as the dean of the modern Japanese quality improvement pioneers. He made a major contribution by simplifying and standardizing specific tools and methods so that front line workers as well as high school students could lean them. For example, he simplified the scientific method and cycle for continuous improvement that Deming taught by creating the Plan-Do-Check-Act cycle as a means of teaching scientific improvement of work.[2] Much more could be said about each of these pioneers in OQI, but the reader is encouraged to engage the primary sources.[3-7]

It is significant that the thoughts and teachings of these leaders are now being studied and applied in health care and other service settings. Connections can be made between their work and more familiar historic and contemporary names in health care quality-making circles such as Florence Nightingale, E.A. Codman, and Avedis Donabedian. For example, Nightingale's use of graphical data display to teach and mobilize resources for improvement, in addition to her own personal example of hospital quality leadership during the Crimean War, provides a glimpse of the role of leaders in organizationwide quality improvement in hospitals and health care settings.[8]

Moreover, Codman's focus on organizational accountability for quality and the need for senior leadership and governance units to assume their proper duties in the measurement and improvement of quality also recognizes that the responsibility for improving quality cannot be delegated to some department or voluntary committee within a hospital. Codman also encourages us to focus on the antecedent reasons for inadequate end of care results—inviting us to explore the process and the failures in that process that contribute to the result. Further, he suggests that efficiency and cost management are essential elements of organizationwide concern for the improvement of value and quality.[9]

Donabedian, the father of contemporary health care quality assessment, teaches that there is a comprehensive framework for studying the delivery of medical services. Quality assessment requires a clear understanding of that framework before attempts are made to improve the everyday operations of hospitals and other care-giving organizations.[10-13]

In the transition to the new OQI model, three words that have been used in quality improvement in the health care arena in the past take on a new meaning and some new connotations. These words are: customer, process, and result. The term *customer* is used to signify the role that a person or unit plays when receiving the service or product produced. The customer applies prior expectations to the service or product and judges the benefit or value (when cost is included) of the service or product. Unfortunately, the commerce related connotation included in the new usage pattern for this word represents a barrier to understanding for some health care professionals. Examples of the term include: patients, physicians, employees, and communities. Customers are often external to the organization and hence are referred to as external customers. There are also internal customers in health care organizations, for example, nursing units are customers of the pharmacy, medical record departments are customers of the nursing units, and so forth. Thus, the term customer is used in a particular way.

Process refers to the activities or actions that repeatedly come together to transform inputs—provided by suppliers—into the outputs received by customers. For example, a patient may "supply" a fractured wrist to the emergency department in a hospital. The patient is also a "customer" of whatever is done to produce an immobilized, aligned, less painful wrist. All that goes on between the delivery of the fractured wrist by the patient–supplier and the receipt of the splinted wrist by the patient–customer can be thought of as the process involved in care giving. Note that use of the term process is broader than some of the current usage patterns and includes some elements of structure as well.

Results commonly include both the technical output of a process as well as the judgment of benefit by the customer who receives that output. The term outcome, though widely referred to, has no precise relationship to the terms result, output of the process, or benefit from the process as assigned by the patient (or other customer of the process) to the service or product produced. (The assignment of benefit includes both the expectations and value set of the customer.) For purposes of this article, *result* is used to denote both the technical output of the process *and* the benefit assigned by the customer. *Output* refers to the service or product that is produced by the process; it can be easily measured by the producer. *Benefit* is a judgment that is made in relation to the values and expectations of the customer relative to whatever was produced. Thus, any study of benefits requires an understanding of and knowledge about the customer's needs and expectations.

With this brief introduction to quality improvement, let us now direct our attention to the core ingredients of organizationwide quality improvement.

ORGANIZATIONWIDE
QUALITY IMPROVEMENT FUNDAMENTALS

It is helpful to think about the basic elements of organizationwide quality improvement in response to four simple questions:

1. What is the basic assumption of OQI in health care?
2. What are the basic understandings being sought in health care OQI?
3. What are the basic means of gaining these understandings?
4. What are the results that might be expected?

The basic assumption of OQI is that leaders of health care organizations seek to link the organizations that they lead to the underlying social need for those organizations. While disarmingly simple at one level, the discernment of the social need for an organization is built on an understanding of the segment of society that the organization seeks to serve.[14] For hospitals and health care organizations in the United States today, social need means providing services at better value. If the vision is clear and well connected to the need society has for the organization, the task of leadership is to guide the efforts of the organization toward the realization of that vision.

The basic understandings being sought in health care OQI today are (1) knowledge of the customer and (2) knowledge of the work health care professionals do as a process. Relative to knowledge of the customer, Barbara McClintock's biography reveals that this Nobel prize-winning botanist could not do meaningful work on corn until she could "learn to think like corn," which her biographer termed "a feeling for the organism."[15] Often health care professionals do not really know their customers—patients, physicians, employees, payors, communities. Knowledge and understanding of health care customers must be drawn from a much more active and sensitive dialogue with them, and this information must pervade all levels of those organizations who seek to better meet their customers' needs. Relative to knowledge of work as a process, health care professionals typically perform work activities with a limited understanding of what the steps are and how those steps vary over time. If results are to be improved, health care professionals must better understand what produced those results. Thus, knowledge of the processes of work enables health care professionals to improve those processes—the only predictable way to improve the results of work.

The basic means of gaining these two understandings is through study and application of scientific and statistical thinking. Deming refers to this as "profound knowledge" (Deming, W.E.; "A System of Profound Knowledge;"

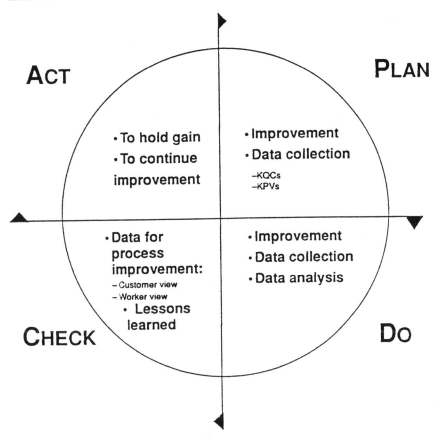

Figure 2.   The Plan-Do-Check-Act cycle.

unpublished data). Applying statistical thinking to ongoing work processes invites the use of analytic statistics rather than enumerative statistics.[16-20] The focus of this statistical thinking is the future performance of ongoing processes and systems—not describing or comparing fixed populations of the past. That is, how can we understand the process so that we can predict its performance and improve it in the future? This concept introduces a new set of data display and analysis tools such as run charts, control charts, and many others. In fact, the application of this knowledge using the scientific method is what Ishikawa's Plan-Do-Check-Act (PDCA) cycle is all about (see Figure 2).

Finally, the results health care professionals might expect fall into three major categories: (1) the reduction of leader-directed waste; (2) the satisfaction and, hopefully, the delighting of customers; and (3) the involvement and, hopefully, the eager participation of all workers.

Leaders in health care organizations own the processes whereby work is performed in their organizations every day. As owners of these work processes, leaders are not always mindful of their simultaneous responsibility to lead the improvement of these processes as well as to monitor the work done in them. Through lack of attention or misdirected attention, work processes, systems, and methods in hospitals and health care organizations still result in sizeable amounts of waste, rework, and needless complexity. Reductions can occur through the application of OQI, if the lessons learned in every other industry are applicable to the health care industry. This process, however, forces a radical reexamination of the customers—both internal and external to the organization—and of what is done every day. In so doing, greater congruence between the customers' needs and the work of the organization will occur.

Process knowledge and improvement require the insight of all who are involved in the "stuff of work," not because participation is nice but because, across-the-board participation means that gains will be made as expeditiously as possible. The effect of asking workers to work on and improve what they do is both powerful and motivating. To be meaningful, however, these fundamentals must be connected in practical strategies of organizational behavior and change.

LINKING OQI METHODS and ORGANIZATIONAL ENVIRONMENT

At the beginning of this article it was suggested that organizationwide quality improvement was a new way of thinking about performing the job of leadership. The basic elements of OQI described above come together in an organization when OQI methods and approaches are coupled with the creation of an organizational environment that fosters this new and better way. Simple put:

OQI = OQI methods + organizational environment

Quality improvement methods can be thought of in three major categories: group process, statistical and scientific thinking, and graphical methods. *Group process* methods refer to those approaches used to facilitate the effective functioning of people when working together. Group process skills include knowledge of basic meeting skills, idea generation and reduction, and management of fundamental group processes such as listening, participation, and conflict. (Note that the term process is used in a broad sense and relates to those activities that characterize the interactions of people working together.)

Statistical and scientific thinking methods address the study of variation and cause and effect. These methods include flow charts, Ishikawa dia-

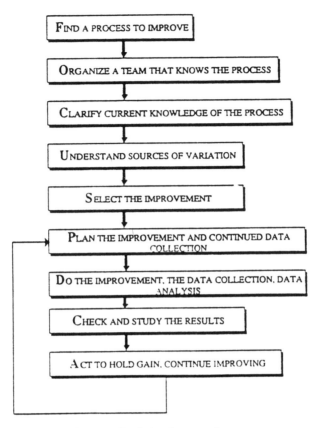

Figure 3.   The FOCUS Plan-Do-Check-Act framework.

grams, run charts, and control charts. With the help and initial leadership of David Hardison, the Hospital Corporation of America (HCA) Quality Resource Group has developed a simple framework—FOCUS PDCA—for thinking about and applying some of these tools to systematic process improvement (see Figure 3).[21]

Graphical methods refers to the importance of creating visual pictures of data and information. Hence, graphs of data over time are used rather than point-in-time tables of numbers. This category of methods includes the use of storyboards or posters that teach and make visible the steps and thought process used in the systematic improvement of work processes.[22]

Organizational environment refers to the formal design of the organization and the method of deploying that intention throughout the organization. It begins with: (1) a clear and simple statement of mission that answers the questions who and what are we, (2) a concise statement of

67

vision that answers the questions who and what do we seek to become, (3) a clear definition and understanding of what the term quality means in the context of the organization, and (4) an explicit statement of the guidelines for management that make clear the expectations of the organization for the leaders and managers within the organization. The goal is not to simply create these statements on paper. Rather it is to connect the knowledge of this policy and the activities of daily work for each worker. This task is difficult and requires the active participation of senior leaders.

Beyond the creation of quality policy framework, the formal organizational structure for the implementation of this new way of working must be developed. Most successful organizations have realized that this necessitates a change in the way that line leaders do things rather than the creation of a new QI department or shadow organization for quality. Accordingly, this process begins with the chief executive officer (CEO) and senior management who function to guide or steer the process throughout the organization. Often constituting them as a Quality Improvement Council or steering group for some portion of the time helps to give structure to the process.

The development of internal technical resources requires the identification of individuals who are prepared to learn, teach, and apply these new methods throughout the organization. These internal technical resources are coordinated in HCA by the coach, a person who is drawn from one of the areas within the hospital and who may be an existing quality assurance (QA) professional, a nursing department worker, a materiels manager, a business office person, or anyone from a number of other entry disciplines. Others who serve as specified facilitators of the work improvement effort are skilled in group process, statistical and scientific methods, and graphical methods.

The policy framework and organizational structure come together in a plan for the progression and deployment of this process throughout the organization. The QI plan should recognize the various dimensions of the change process as well as the sequencing of the change over time. One way of describing the dimensions of the change process is found in the eight steps identified by HCA as a part of its Hospitalwide Quality Improvement Process:[23]

1. Provide leadership constancy—the singlemindedness necessary for change.
2. Develop employee mindedness—the elements of change that permit all employees to contribute, develop, learn, and be treated as valuable resources.
3. Develop customer mindedness—the transitional elements that permit a clear definition of the customer, the definition of quality as driven by the customer, and the clarification and assurance of a proper linkage

among need, customer judgment, and quality improvement.

4. Become process focused—understand the way work is performed in the hospital.
5. Use statistical thinking—the application of statistical principles and techniques in all phases of operations to understand and reduce variation.
6. Become PDCA driven—the ways in which the organization applies the scientific method to initiate and manage change in all that it does.
7. Practice innovativeness—create an environment that stimulates creative thinking and encourages taking actions that yield breakthroughs in the ability to meet present and future needs of customers.
8. Foster regulatory proactiveness—identification and promotion of changes to regulatory and accreditation processes and traditional professional development that influence and limit improvement.

As can be seen, these steps involve ongoing learning and integration. Together they form a view of an organization continuously involved in learning—about its organizational intent, about its work processes, about its customers, and about the organization as a system.

Having described the fundamentals of QI and the way in which they might come together in a health care organization, let us try to apply this way of thinking to the construction of a model of patient care and the sources of variation found in daily clinical practice.

A QI MODEL of DAILY PATIENT CARE

Ackoff[24] suggests that creating a model of daily patient care necessitates thinking "up" and "down" and "again." He urges us to understand the context and then move to the specific and back again—rather than engaging in a reductionist thought process alone. This way of thinking invites the optimization of the whole, not just one of the parts.

According to Donabedian, the provider's knowledge, technical skill, and interpersonal interactions are at the heart of the health care process.[13] They are always applied in a place or locus of care giving. This locus adds support personnel, governing policies, procedures and methods of getting things done, and equipment and physical facilities to the actual delivery of care. The social context within which the provider and locus of care giving exist adds additional sources of variation to the event of providing care to a patient such as financing and economic policy, social policy, professional role and development, and regulation. The patient travels through the action and interaction of all these elements with a need to receive a specific service or result. Identification and measurement of these sources of variation in process and variation in result require a level of understanding that moves

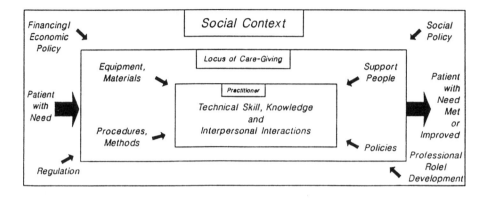

Figure 4.   Health care delivery model: Sources of variation.

us beyond our present ways of thinking about health care quality and makes the obligations of leadership for quality improvement even more real.

This model can be represented as shown in Figure 4.[25] Systematic application of organizationwide quality improvement to this model yields a significant agenda for change as organizational leaders seek to drive up the value of the social investment made in health.[26] What are the implications of all this for the existing QA professionals in health care organizations?

QA PROFESSIONALS and QUALITY IMPROVEMENT

First, resist the impulse to assume that QI is somehow what QA is *really* all about; they are different.[27] Berwick has provided a concise statement of some of the differences between QA and QI:

- QA is a specialized staff function. QI is the primary job of every manager.
- QA examines the physician and others who provide care. QI studies the processes of production.
- QA asks Who does what here? QI asks How is the hospital's work accomplished?
- QA looks for deviations from the norm to correct unacceptable variations. QI also looks at deviations, but is much more interested in improving the average. QA asks Why is this different? QI asks How can we make this continuously better?

- QA's annual report might note that the hospital's operative mortality is 4.2 percent below the national rate and that no significant problems were detected. QI's report would set an objective for the next two years to reduce the rate to less than 3 percent.
- QA uses performance standards. When performance is not met, managers are expected to respond with action plans. QI has little use for performance standards. QI tries to continuously improve the capability of processes to better meet the requirements of patients, employees, and other hospital stakeholders.
- QA's activities involve physicians, nurses, and other professionals. QI is based on the premise that a wide range of job functions and hierarchical levels must be involved in analyzing problems and formulating solutions.
- QA's quality reports use judgmental terms such as excellent or needs improvement. QI's reports are less judgmental and more analytical. QI uses process flow diagrams and control charts.
- QA's quality reports are prepared by staff members. QI's reports are written by team members from every hospital department.
- QA's reports ask for specific management actions such as setting up task forces. QI's reports give managers the information they requested to improve quality.[28]

Another way of understanding the relationships between inspection, regulation, public safety, improvement, management, design, redesign, and research and development can be seen in Figure 5. There is a clear and important role for inspection and regulation in support of the social need for accountability over public safety. Sanctions can and should be a part of this process. Further, the focal point for our formal efforts at health care research and development should be explicitly connected to an assessment of the quality of the developer's care giving. The vast majority of providers fall into the middle of the distribution, however. To assume that the methods useful for discharging the inspection, regulation, and public safety functions, or the methods helpful in research and development are the same that will be sufficient to achieve the movement of the entire curve toward improved quality is to expect more than has been achievable in any other industry. Here (in the mainstream) we need the full energies of organizations and their leaders.

How might QA professionals begin to apply some of these insights to the management of their duties? You may wish to begin by asking yourself the following questions.

- What is the actual social and organizational need for the QA work that I do?

71

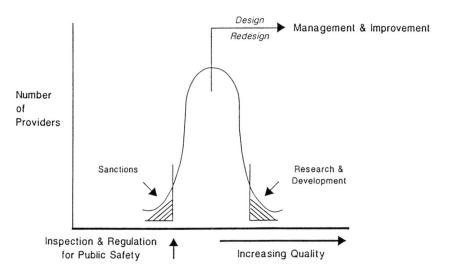

Figure 5.   The relationships between quality inspection, regulation, management, and improvement.

- Who are the customers of what I do? Who is the immediate recipient of what I produce? Who ultimately benefits from what I produce?
- What are the major work processes that I work in to produce what I produce for my customers?
- What are the steps involved in those processes? And how do those processes vary currently?
- How might I improve those processes to reduce the waste, needless complexity, and rework that may be involved in them? (You will find that you can apply process, customer, and statistical thinking and improvement just the way everyone else can.)
- Based on what I now know about the methods and the results of what I do, are there others who do what I do—in health care settings or not—who might have a process for doing what I do, but who do it with even greater value for their customers? (This process of simultaneous comparison of process and results has been developed to a fine degree by the Xerox Corporation.[29]) Note that this method of comparison begins with a clear and simultaneous understanding of process and results of your own work—a step often overlooked when rushing to compare results from one setting to another.

When QA professionals understand their work in this new way, they can become a valuable resource for others as they together study and improve what is done every day in the care of patients. This is best achieved in an environment that is undertaking the organizationwide transformation around quality.

Organizationwide quality improvement has offered many organizations in many different industries a new approach to work and leadership. The lessons learned can be applied to the health care setting. QA professionals can play an important role in this change by leading through example—first in their own departments and the work they currently perform and then throughout the entire organization.

REFERENCES

1. *The Deming Library Videotape Series: The Quality Leader.* Vol. 16. Washington, D.C.: CCM Productions, 1990. Videotape.
2. Ishikawa, K. *What Is Total Quality Control?* Englewood Cliffs, N.J.: Prentice Hall, 1985.
3. Deming, W.E. *Out of the Crisis.* Cambridge, Mass.: Massachusetts Institute of Technology Center for Advanced Engineering Study, 1986.
4. Juran, J.M. *Juran on Planning for Quality.* New York, N.Y.: Free Press, 1988.
5. Juran, J.M. *Juran's Quality Control Handbook.* New York, N.Y.: McGraw-Hill, 1988.
6. Feigenbaum, A.V. *Total Quality Control.* New York, N.Y.: McGraw-Hill, 1983.
7. Ishikawa, K. *Guide to Quality Control.* White Plains, N.Y.: UNIPUB/Quality Resources, 1988.
8. Cohen, I.B. "Florence Nightengale." *Scientific American* 250 (1984): 128-37.
9. Codman, E.A. *A Study in Hospital Efficiency: As Demonstrated by the Case Report of the First Five Years of a Private Hospital.* Boston, Mass.: Privately published, circa 1917.
10. Donabedian, A. *Explorations in Quality Assessment and Monitoring.* Vol. 1, *The Definition of Quality and Approaches to Its Assessment.* Ann Arbor, Mich.: Health Administration Press, 1980.
11. Donabedian, A. *Explorations in Quality Assessment and Monitoring.* Vol. 2, *The Criteria and Standards of Quality.* Ann Arbor, Mich.: Health Administration Press, 1982.
12. Donabedian, A. *Explorations in Quality Assessment and Monitoring.* Vol. 3, *The Methods and Findings of Quality Assessment and Monitoring: An Illustrated Analysis.* Ann Arbor, Mich.: Health Administration Press, 1985.
13. Donabedian, A. "The Quality of Care: How Can It Be Assessed?" *JAMA* 260 (1988): 1743-48.
14. Nolan, T.W. "Quality as an Organizational Strategy." Paper presented at Philadelphia Annual Quality Conference: Philadelphia Area Council for Excellence, May 1990.
15. Keller, E.F. *A Feeling for the Organism: The Life and Work of Barbara McClintock.* New York, N.Y.: W.H. Freeman, 1983.
16. Deming, W.E. *Some Theory of Sampling.* New York, N.Y.: Dover, 1966.
17. Deming, W.E. "On the Distinction between Enumerative and Analytic Surveys." *Journal of American Statistics Association* 48 (1953): 244-55.
18. Nolan, T.W. "Estimation and Prediction in Statistical Studies." Paper presented at the Michigan Conference on Teaching and Use of Statistical Theory and Methods, Michigan State University, East Lansing, Michigan, October 1990.
19. Gitlow, H., Gitlow, S., Oppenheim, A., and Oppenheim, R. *Tools and Methods for the Improvement of Quality.* Boston, Mass.: Richard D. Irwin, 1989.

20. Wheeler, D.J., and Chambers, D.S. *Understanding Statistical Process Control.* Knoxville, Tenn.: Statistical Process Controls, 1986.

21. Quality Resource Group of Hospital Corporation of America. "FOCUS PDCA." Nashville, Tenn.: Hospital Corporation of America, 1988. Pamphlet.

22. Batalden, P.B., and Gillem, T. *Hospitalwide Quality Improvement Storytelling.* Nashville, Tenn.: Quality Resource Group of Hospital Corporation of America, 1989. Monograph.

23. Hospital Corporation of America, HCA Management Company, Inc., and Executive Learning, Inc. *"Q101 Leader Workbook."* Nashville, Tenn.: Quality Resource Group of Hospital Corporation of America, 1990.

24. Ackoff, T.L. "The Second Industrial Revolution." Washington, D.C.: Alban Institute Publications, 1975.

25. Batalden, P.B., and Nelson, E.C. "Health Care Work and Its Improvement: The Role of Hospitalwide Quality Improvement and Patient, Physician and Employee Judgements of Quality." *International Journal of Health Care Quality Assurance.* In press.

26. Batalden, P.B., and Buchanan, E.D. "Industrial Models of Quality Improvement." In *Providing Quality Care: The Challenge to Clinicians,* edited by N. Goldfield and D.B. Nash. Philadelphia, Pa.: The American College of Physicians, 1989.

27. Roberts, J.S., and Schyve, P.M. "From QA to QI: The Views and Role of the Joint Commission." *The Quality Letter for Health Care Leaders* 5 (1990): 2.

28. "Quality: How Do QI and QA Differ? Expert Illustrates the Answer." *Hospital Management Review* 9 (1990): 2.

29. Camp, R.C. *Benchmarking: The Search for Industry Best Practices That Lead to Superior Performance.* Milwaukee, Wis.: ASQC Quality Press, 1989.

ARTICLES MISCONSTRUE JOINT COMMISSION'S POSITION on QUALITY IMPROVEMENT

Dennis S. O'Leary, MD

As a veteran grocery shopper, I regularly come upon America's tabloid newspapers at the checkout stand. Trapped as I often am in a slow-moving line, it is difficult to avoid the titillating headlines that invite potential readers into a netherworld of sensational portrayals that are unimpeded by the constraining moralities of accuracy and truth. That's entertainment, or a form thereof, I guess.

Of course, this genre of reportage or entertainment does have its following. People buy, read, and maybe even believe this stuff. There's a message here: If you traffic in newsprint, spicy headlines and some elastic truth can do wonders for your circulation.

Still, all this is well removed from the realm of health care and certainly far from the mundane and sometimes technical domain of an accrediting body. Or so I once believed—that is, until an October morning when I received a special bulletin of *QI/TQM* with the boldprint headline "Joint Commission backs off CQI; QA back in favor." *QI/TQM* "has learned the Joint Commission on Accreditation of Healthcare Organizations is making an abrupt turn away from its emphasis on CQI and back toward more traditional quality assurance," began the story. "Surprise Move" read the caption over the headline. Indeed! Surprise news to me too. Where did this come from? Who are these guys? Maybe *The Globe* was right; maybe aliens have landed.

Of course, this is no laughing matter. This special bulletin and a corresponding special bulletin of a companion publication, *Hospital Peer Review,* were widely distributed, reaching an apparent specialty market penetration that would make most publishers salivate. We do not know the intent of American Health Consultants, which publishes the two newsletters, but there is nothing to indicate that it was lighthearted. However, we do know the product—misinformation—and the result—confusion. These are both most unfortunate.

I would be the first to admit that the Joint Commission has not always been a beacon of crystalline communication, but we try. We have responded to the two special bulletins. However, like most letters to the editor this one is unlikely to see the light of day in its full flavor unless we share it with you ourselves.

Even if you did not receive your own copy of one of the special bulletins, you may be interested in what Paul Schyve, our vice-president for research and standards, has to say about CQI/TQM and performance measurements, assessment, and improvement. The letter that was addressed to the editor of *QI/TQM* follows:

"I wish to express the deep concern and displeasure of the Joint Commission regarding the recent special bulletins published by *QI/TQM* and *Hospital Peer Review,* which grossly mischaracterize the Joint Commission's continuing directions with respect to assessing and improving organizational performance. This mischaracterization has created unnecessary confusion among hospitals and other health care organizations with regard to future Joint Commission expectations of accredited organizations.

"The additional articles published in the November issue of *QI/TQM* and *Hospital Peer Review* continue this mischaracterization, and thereby add to the confusion generated by the special bulletins.

"The articles allege that the Joint Commission has changed direction by returning to 'quality assurance' (QA). This is patently false, and no Joint Commission staff has indicated otherwise to you, your publications' staff, or others. Indeed, there has been no change in the basic concepts and objectives of the Joint Commission's Agenda for Change since 1987. What we said then—and continue to say now—is that the bottom line is *performance.* Good performance yields good results, which in turn lead to positive judgments about quality. We have also said—from the beginning— that we have not and will not require an organization to adopt wholesale continuous quality improvement (CQI) or total quality management (TQM) to be accredited. There is an important difference between what we require in standards and what we encourage organizations to do.

"The mission of the Joint Commission is to improve the quality of care provided to the public. Because quality is, ultimately, a judgment made by patients and others, based on their perceptions of an organization's care and its outcomes, the Joint Commission has focused its attention on the organization's performance of the activities that most affect the nature of care and its outcomes. Thus, accreditation becomes a catalyst for better quality by stimulating continuous improvement in organizational performance.

"By focusing on performance, the Joint Commission is drawing organizational attention to the activities that will strongly influence outcomes and costs and therefore shape the judgments of quality that are made by providers, patients, and others. The Joint Commission's focus on performance is not new. The Agenda for Change is (and always has been) centered on organizational performance.

"By 'performance' we simply mean doing the right things and doing them well. The standards identify many of the functions an organization should undertake ('the right things') and the key features of performing these functions ('doing them well'). The survey process will assess whether and how well these functions are being performed. The planned Indicator Monitoring System will provide process and outcome data that reflect the level of an organization's performance of important functions. Education seminars and publications will be redesigned to assist organizations in continuously improving their performance.

"We believe that CQI/TQM provides the health care field with many helpful concepts (many of which are common-sense management principles) and methods. While the Joint Commission has borrowed some of these concepts for incorporation into its standards, most CQI/TQM concepts will not appear in the standards. This approach follows a long-standing Joint Commission practice of including in standards only the core concepts of a relevant field (e.g., infection control, information management). We leave the details of implementation to each accredited organization.

"It is also important to recognize that there is a large and growing number of approaches that have been labeled CQI/TQM by their creators—approaches that vary significantly in their validity and effectiveness. If the Joint Commission were to 'adopt' CQI/TQM, we would be perceived as endorsing them all.

"Examples of CQI/TQM principles that are being incorporated into Joint Commission standards include the key role leaders (individually and collectively) play in enabling the systematic assessment and improvement of performance, the fact that most problems/opportunities for improvement derive from process weaknesses not from individual competence, the need for careful coordination of work across departments and professional groups, the importance of seeking judgments about quality from patients and other 'customers' and using such judgments to identify areas for improvement, the importance of carefully setting priorities for improvement, and the need for both systematic improvement of the performance of important functions and the maintenance of the stability of these functions.

"We do not, however, intend to dictate a particular management style, nor will we be prescriptive about the manner in which an organization conducts its performance assessment and improvement activities (e.g., we will not mandate the use of the ten-step model for systematic assessment and improvement).

"The mischaracterization of the Joint Commission's direction in the articles also reflects several misconceptions about the nature of CQI/TQM, specifically about elements of QA that the articles portray (incorrectly) as not being a part of CQI/TQM. These misconceptions include:

"a. *Misconception*: Ongoing monitoring is not a part of CQI/TQM. Therefore, the Joint Commission's requirement of such reflects a reversion to QA.

"*Fact:* Ongoing monitoring is a fundamental part of CQI/TQM. It is the continuous measurement component of 'quality control.'

"b. *Misconception:* Attention to patient outcomes amounts to 'inspection' and therefore is not acceptable in CQI/TQM.

"*Fact:* Measuring the outcomes of a manufacturing or service system (e.g., by collecting data on product defects, recalls, repair rates, customer complaints/satisfaction) has always been a cornerstone of CQI/TQM. These 'downstream' measures can help an organization to focus its attention on 'upstream' processes that may be improved. Outcomes should not be the only measures an organization uses; as noted above, ongoing collection of key process information is also important.

"c. *Misconception*: Individual competence should not be addressed under CQI/TQM and the Joint Commission's attention to this in the standards (e.g., in privilege delineation standards and in requirements for 'criteria-based' performance review) indicates a reversion to QA.

"*Fact*: Individual competence is an essential ingredient of organizational performance (e.g., not everyone can do neurosurgery, lead an organization, or provide physical therapy). Good results are achieved when competent people work in effective systems and poor results most often are the product of ineffective systems. When individual weaknesses do exist, they are not usually a justification for sanctions, rather they are cause for more education/training and for reexamination of the processes that allowed the individual to be placed in systems that required more skills than the individual possesses.

"d. *Misconception*: Peer review is not necessary under CQI/TQM.

"*Fact*: The Joint Commission's continuing reference to peer review reflects the ongoing need for professional judgments in the review of both processes and individual performance. Because health care is still an incomplete science, an organization requires the specialized knowledge, skills, and experience of peers to make the best possible judgments about individual competence based on the performance information available.

"Because of what we believe to be the *QI/TQM* and *Hospital Peer Review* articles' mischaracterization of the Joint Commission's directions, the further erroneous characterizations of the nature of CQI/TQM, and the confusion these articles have created in the hospital field, I must resign from the editorial board of *QI/TQM*. I wish thereby to make clear that I do not, in any fashion, endorse the mischaracterizations or misconceptions in the *QI/TQM* and *Hospital Peer Review* articles.

"In an effort to reduce the confusion among hospitals created by these articles, I request that this letter be published in the next issue of both of these publications."

A NEW LOOK for QUALITY in HOME CARE

Donna A. Peters, PhD, RN, FAAN

The management of quality is being transformed in healthcare. Continuous improvement is a cornerstone to this new look at quality. However, no continuous quality program will succeed without incorporating the values and wants of the consumer of care and the end point they want to reach. This article presents an overview of the values to consider and the ways to define outcomes.

The overwhelming public and political interest in healthcare today, combined with extraordinary economic pressures in the industry, make quality a timely topic—what is quality and how is it measured? Witness the huge audiences at any seminar with the word "quality" in the title. Healthcare professionals are intently seeking new answers and assurances that they are on the cutting edge of quality.

Many unique factors exist in the home care industry that make quality even more relevant. First, most consumers served by home care organizations are elderly, many of them frail, and therefore, acutely vulnerable to fraud and abuse in an unsupervised setting. Second, the in-home location, unlike healthcare provided in hospitals, nursing homes or other institutions, makes the care essentially invisible to scrutiny by others, thereby creating an even more important need for measures of quality. Last, the nature of these services is that there is minimal professional supervision of direct care at the same time there is a heavy reliance on nonlicensed care givers.[1]

According to the National Association of Home Care (NAHC), there are approximately 11,300 organizations that provide home-delivered healthcare services in this country, plus 1,200 free-standing hospices that provide terminal care to their clients in their own homes. Of these 12,500 agencies, however, 5,500 of them do not participate in Medicare.[2] Theses agencies have no requirement to comply with any federal Medicare certification standards, thereby leaving the consumer unprotected by uniform standards and more susceptible to inadequate care.

Reprinted with permission from *Journal of Nursing Administration*, Vol. 22, No. 11, pp. 21–26, November 1992.

This article describes a new perspective on quality in home care resulting in a different approach to the assessing and measuring of quality. This journey to discover the level of excellence in home care service delivery is being led by the "In Search of Excellence in Home Care" project, currently in progress at the Community Health Accreditation Program (CHAP). CHAP, a subsidiary of the National League for Nursing (NLN), has been accrediting community health organizations since 1965. Its program for accreditation has been recommended for "deemed status" by the Department of Health and Human Services (HHS), meaning that home care agencies that meet CHAP's accreditation standards will be considered to have met the federal conditions for participation in the Medicare program.

The "In Search of Excellence" project is funded by the W.K. Kellogg Foundation to strengthen the home care industry by: 1) defining quality outcomes using consumer input; 2) developing a system to assess quality using these outcomes; and 3) incorporating the process into CHAP's accreditation process. Developing meaningful outcomes for the industry at large will provide for interagency comparisons and thus allow the industry and individual agencies to assess the areas that need improvement.

The project began by soliciting as many people as possible to get involved—advisory groups, expert consultants, nine agencies to act as primary data collection sites, and most importantly, consumers. These groups contributed to defining the important values in home care. These values are contained in a mission statement developed for the industry and accompanying belief statements. The values identified are similar to the "trillitrends" defined by Mike Vance,[3] former dean of Disney University and one of the nation's foremost management experts. The values that he believes will become important in the 21st century are: empowering the individual; caring for the individual; and cooperating with the individual. Thus, as the home care industry looks for quality in the 21st century, these values need to be considered.

QUALITY ASSURANCE

Traditionally, the approach to quality has been to attempt to assure its presence at some point in time, usually in the past. The process has been to constantly look for negative factors, such as mistakes, incompetence, or harmful outcomes and to implement corrective action(s) when they were found. These negative factors were believed to be caused by imperfect caregivers, so that the solutions focused on improving staff's ability or removing them from the situation. Little attention has been paid to the environment, situation, or other circumstances that may have caused the person to act inappropriately.

The primary means for finding the negative factors has been through the collection and measurement of data against defined standards. In this way, problems could be detected and the nurse or other caregivers could be made aware of the areas that needed improvement. Assuring quality required the establishment of extensive, routine systematic data collection systems typically in the form of retrospective audits. These audits included setting and measuring standards for each element of care provided by the organization. Quality was assured if all the standards were met, i.e., if no negative factors were found.[4]

Although the pursuit of quality assurance is valuable, certain built-in limitations exist: 1) quality is only defined through the absence of negative factors, never for what it represents; 2) data are usually incomplete or inaccurate as people hide or distort information to protect themselves against being found incompetent, therefore the real picture is never seen; and 3) people spend their energy defending their ability or competence rather than improving their performance. Thus, quality measurement is repeated over and over. Audits are continually conducted in an attempt to surpass the incomplete and inaccurate information. Even when the audits are successful and the deficient areas are defined and addressed, it is usually old data, so it is still not known what is happening today. At a time when the healthcare consumer is becoming more involved and informed and asking more questions about their healthcare services, outdated data will no longer suffice. It is time for another approach.

QUALITY MANAGEMENT

Current approaches to quality come under different labels, such as Total Quality Management (TQM) or Continuous Quality Improvement (CQI). The focus is not on assuring quality, but rather, improving it. The concept is that there is always room for improvement, like peeling layers from an onion looking for the next layer only to find another one, and so on. As mistakes are found they are used as opportunities to improve the situation, and move to the next layer. Mistakes are usually system inadequacies, not people inadequacies. Problems often focus around insufficient information sharing or inadequate communication. Quality management, then, is simply finding these situations and correcting them.

Finding the situations is everyone's business—not just the prerogative of management or the quality assurance department. No employee is exempt. Quality management is enforced by all people, all of the time. Quality monitoring becomes concurrent, not retroactive and is based on reality, what is actually being done, not what was supposed to be done.

Data collection is also concurrent. Data are collected to learn rather than to find evidence of poor performance. Therefore, people no longer have to hide information or defend their competence, and are more open to use their energy for finding creative solutions to the situation at hand.

ADDING VALUES TO QUALITY

Once the concept of quality improvement has been accepted, the next step in the journey to excellence is to determine what values are important in providing services, in this case home care services. Covey states that these values serve as maps and enable us to know where we are going. Every person and every organization has values that mark their way through life.[5] People see the world through their values, the motivators for their beliefs and actions, and the energy source for their accomplishments. Managing by values is rendering services with those personal and organizational values clearly defined. Decisions about what future direction to take or about what to do in a given situation can then be based on those values.

The place to search for the values that are important to an organization is in their mission statement. Belief statements often accompany mission statements to further delineate important values that support and supplement the mission. Quality is determined by the degree to which the organization adheres to their mission and those values, i.e., how well the agency is doing what it set out to do as defined in its mission or purpose.

An organization's mission establishes its territory and the direction for growth and achievement. It provides the image of the organization's desired state of affairs to inspire action and determine behavior.[6] It encompasses what the organization cares about and therefore, holds the values that are important to the organization. For example, a mission statement could focus on promoting health or it could concentrate on maintaining financial viability.

A mission statement for the home care industry was developed by those involved in the "In Search of Excellence in Home Care" project. It states that the mission of home care is "to provide services in the home using a caring approach that empowers people to optimize and access achievable and desired health outcomes." This mission statement encompasses two of three "trillitrends" or important values identified by Vance,[3] empowering and caring for the consumer. His third trillitrend—cooperating with the consumer—can be found in the project's list of beliefs. Let's examine these "trillitrend" values more closely from the perspective of quality.

Empowerment

The first trillitrend is empowerment. The industrial world has successfully empowered its customers to define what they want; products are developed using marketing studies and evaluated through the number of customer purchases or comments. In the healthcare arena it has been different. Quality measurements, although client-centered, have been defined and proposed by professionals and payers. If empowerment is a value, then quality home care needs to be determined by the consumer or client. What does the consumer want, and are their expectations met during the time of service, i.e., did they attain the outcomes they wanted?

This concept of meeting the consumer's expectations is especially important in home care where the outcome is usually related to quality of life issues rather than a "cure" issue. Who better to determine the kind of life one wants to lead than the person who will be living it? No one else has the same insights to their culture, beliefs, aspirations, family situation and living conditions, and their pain, than the consumers themselves. However, the consumer may not have the required medical knowledge or expertise to establish realistic outcomes. Furthermore, the consumer probably lacks knowledge of the regulations and limitations of the healthcare system. These are the purview of the professional home care provider. Therefore, for "quality" care to exist, the client's outcomes need to be determined with the assistance of staff. The role of staff is to educate the consumer so that informed choices can be made and realistic outcomes can be established. The more consumers progress toward the accomplishment of their outcomes, the better the staff is doing their job and the higher the quality.[7]

Staff can only empower their clients to establish and move toward realistic, attainable outcomes if they themselves are empowered. Empowerment in this context means having the authority to do what needs to be done to get the job done at that time. In this case, staff is an organization's internal customer bringing power from the agency to pass on to the ultimate customer—the client. The more an organization empowers its internal customers, the more they empower their clients.[7] It makes sense that staff will treat their clients similarly to the way they are treated, i.e., if a nurse has to ask her supervisor about what to do in a given case, she is more likely to have her clients call her to ask what to do rather than empowering them with information to make their own choices.

Caring

Caring, the second "trillitrend," is usually thought of as warm fuzzies, with lots of tender loving care, as in taking care of. Indeed, showing respect and empathy for our consumers is an important element of caring. However, quality caring is more than that. Caring encompasses the personal accountability that accompanies empowerment—accountability to our employer, coworkers, and clients. For example, it is our professional accountability to our clients to provide them with all the information they need to make informed choices, presented so that the client has the best chance to understand it. Furthermore, once the client has made a choice, it is the staff's duty to assess, manage, teach, and provide the care necessary for the client to reach the desired outcomes. Quality, then, focuses on people, particularly the development of excellence in caregivers. One of the challenges in quality is to move past the "I gotcha" process to one designed for peer support and improvement; to move past the threat of "You did it wrong" to "How can we do it more effectively?" This requires a focus on the positive, starting with what has happened and moving forward in a positive direction. Focusing on the positive is not to be confused with positive thinking. Positive thinking imagines any wonderful thing at all, regardless of how unrelated it may be to any actual events.[8] An example of how to focus on the positive would be to reconsider peer review (finding what you did wrong) as peer praise (acknowledging what you do well and what could be done better).

Cooperation

The third trillitrend is working together, or cooperating. When empowered and caring people work together toward a common goal in such a way that all are recognized and growth is encouraged, collaboration occurs. Research indicates that collaboration potentially enhances client outcomes. Collaboration requires a collegial relationship with other peers, employees, clients, people at all organizational levels—not a hierarchical one. Establishing a collegial environment, however is not as easy as changing an organizational chart. It requires the time and commitment of everyone to establish new lines of communication and new ways of relating with each other with honesty, trust, and respect.

Cooperation can be fostered in the following ways:

- Involve staff and clients more in making choices together about the care being rendered;
- Provide the opportunity and encourage frequent informal communication among different positions within the organization that typically do not collaborate, i.e., for example, administrative support staff such as accounting clerks or data enterers and professional caregivers;
- Create a safe environment that allows staff to admit their mistakes for the purpose of quality care without recrimination or fear of losing their job;

85

- Inspire creativity by holding contests and offering other rewards;
- Honestly and frequently praise people for jobs well done.

MEASURING QUALITY

The first step in measuring quality is to define it. Quality involves the integration of values between the user and provider of the services or product. Thus, quality is composed of three parts; the user of the service or client, the producer of the service or staff member, and the organization that provides the structure in which the staff operate. The "In Search of Excellence in Home Care" project incorporated these aspects of quality into the following definition of quality: "The degree to which consumers progress toward desired outcomes, which they have established with the guidance and support of healthcare providers. These providers are part of an administratively and financially sound organization that monitors competent staff and an environment encouraging personal excellence." This definition also aligns with the mission of the home care industry.

In further examining the measurement of quality, many of the measurements associated with managing quality are seen as similar to those used in assuring quality, such as the use of quality indicators and surveys. However, there are important differences, the most fundamental being the underlying philosophy that quality is measured to improve it through support, innovation, and creativity, not to assure it through threats and "I gotchas." Quality management uses the skills of quality assurance but not the finger pointing.

The traditional approach to measuring quality has been given to us by Donabedian and his concept of structure, process, and outcome.[9] Currently, the movement is away from structure and process toward outcomes. Outcomes provide a description of the destination—the picture on the puzzle box. This picture is what the client and provider see as a result of the structure (the pieces) and process (putting the pieces together). Three levels of outcomes are used in the measurement of quality:[10] individual, intra-agency, and interagency.

Individual

Individual consumer outcomes are used by the professionals who directly care for clients. These outcomes provide benchmarks for measuring client progress. They are composed of a who—the client and/or significant other; a what—the measurable behavior; and a when—the time frame in either visits or days within which the outcome is to be accomplished. An example of an individual client outcome is: Mr. Jones will be free of pain within two visits.

These outcomes are determined in collaboration with the client, based on what is important to the client, i.e., his values. Studies have shown that an external caregiver cannot accurately assess a client's quality of life, therefore, it is crucial that clients have input into what they expect the outcome of their care to be.[11]

Intra-Agency

Intra-agency outcomes are home care organization outcomes used as part of a quality management plan at the agency level. These outcomes are the desired end results of the crucial areas (defined as pulse points in the In Search of Excellence project) that the organization has defined as essential to monitor consistently to assess quality. Taken together, they represent a picture of the broad spectrum of the services offered by the agency and the expected results of those services from an agency perspective. Two broad categories of pulse points and associated outcomes exist: administrative or those pertaining to the management of the agency and clinical or those pertaining to client results (Table 1).

The pulse points and outcomes that an agency chooses for the quality management plan are determined in many ways. First, the mission of the agency and its associated values are considered. What is the purpose of the organization and what values are important as the organization promotes its purpose? Other sources of pulse points are those programs or activities that are costly or are a high-risk potential. New programs should always be included in the pulse points for at least 1 year to determine whether they produce the desired outcomes. Finally, areas for which there is concern or anecdotal evidence that there may be a problem should be a designated pulse point. These pulse points may each have one or more associated outcomes that are being monitored. What is important is that the outcomes are specific and meaningful so that if a problem is detected (the outcome is not met), then the interventions necessary to correct the situation will be self-evident. The agency's quality management plan should be reviewed annually to add or delete pulse points or outcomes that are no longer significant to monitor.

Once these agency outcomes have been defined, the next step is to ascertain how the data that determine the level of compliance to the outcome will be collected. Traditionally, this has been done through retrospective chart review. However, it is known that it is more efficient to collect data concurrently as part of someone's everyday job, such as logging the data as the chart passes through a supervisor's or clerk's hands. So, in addition to the data source, it is necessary to determine who will be responsible for getting the data, as well as how often that person will change the data to information.

Table 1. Agency Quality Management Plan.

Mission Statement:	To provide quality home health care services that promote the health of all people in the community			
Agency Pulse Points	**Outcomes**	**Source**	**Reviewer**	**Frequency**
Administrative				
Agency admissions	Referrals for services will have visit within 24 hours	Log	Supervisor	Monthly
Clinical				
Physical therapy care	Patients admitted for gait training exhibit increase in ambulation within 2 weeks of referral	Chart	Clerk	Monthly

Often, changing the data to information can be done by adding a denominator to it. For example, assume that the agency had to monitor the outcome "Referrals for services will have a visit within 24 hours" (Table 1). If supervisors had a log that they checked as each patient was admitted (visit within 24 hours/visit not within 24 hours), at the end of each month they would tally the number of admissions and the number that had a visit within 24 hours to get the percentage compliance to the outcome. If the percentage was less than 100%, the supervisor could review the noncompliant cases for similar criteria or trends. For example, if they were all assigned to the same geographical area, the intervention would be to examine the staffing in that area to determine whether there were too many cases per staff member, or if the cases were more complex requiring longer visits. Then corrective actions could be taken.

Interagency

Interagency outcomes are common outcomes shared among agencies. Collection of these common outcomes allows agencies to compare their percentage compliance with others. This is helpful in determining what is an acceptable level of compliance. Otherwise, except in those cases where 100% compliance with an outcome is required by law, it is difficult for an agency to determine what level constitutes quality. For example, if 80% of the total consumers in an agency who were admitted with wounds are infection-free 4 weeks after admission, is that quality? Should the agency be expected to have 100% of these consumers infection-free, or is that unrealistic given the health status and age of the clientele? To date, these questions have gone unanswered. However, the In Search of Excellence Project has devised a framework for gathering data on common outcomes.

Using the mission statement for home care and the definition of quality, the project developed a home care industry quality management plan. There are 11 pulse points for quality, divided into three categories: the consumer, clinical, and organizational. The five consumer pulse points are: consumer, empowerment, caregiver relationship, knowledge/information needs, family support, and consumer expectations. The two clinical pulse points are: functional ability and physiological functioning. The four organizational pulse points are: team building, commitment to quality, coordination of care, and financial viability. For each pulse point, an outcome, data collection instrument to measure that outcome, an accountable person, and a time frame was defined. The consumer data are being collected through Likert-type scale surveys sent to each consumer on the study shortly after admission and again at discharge. The clinical data is collected through nurse assessments on 18 functional items and 16 physiological items at admission, at 45 days and at discharge, with negotiated consumer-expected outcomes included for each assessment item. Finally, the organizational data are collected though Likert-type scale surveys sent to agency staff and management and through an agency statistical and financial information report submitted by the agency every 6 months.

SUMMARY

The approach to quality care is moving from assuring its presence to continually improving current situations. Instrumental to the direction that improvements take are the values that are held by the organization and the outcomes they want to achieve.

The In Search of Excellence Project is involving the consumer in defining values and outcomes for the home care industry. Information from this project will provide beginning industry norms that will enable agencies to measure their levels of performance with others. Ultimately, this will strengthen the industry by encouraging those agencies below the norm to address their problem areas and those agencies with excellent performance outcomes to market themselves as such. And, everyone, including the consumer, will have a better sense of this elusive concept of quality—what it is, rather than what it is not.

REFERENCES

1. Donaldson MS, Lohr KN. A quality assurance sampler. Methods, data and resources. In: Lohr KN. Medicare. A *Strategy for Quality Assurance. Vol. II.* Washington, DC: National Academy Press, 1990.
2. National Association for Home Care. *Basic Statistics About Home Care.* Washington, DC: NAHC, 1991.
3. Vance M. Management by Values Seminar, National Association Home Care 10th Annual Meeting, Boston, MA: October 30, 1991.
4. Peters DA. Measuring quality: Inspection or opportunity? *Holistic Nursing Practice.* 1991; 5(3):1-7.
5. Covey SR. *The Seven Habits of Highly Effective People.* New York: Simon & Schuster, Inc., 1990.
6. Garfield C. *Peak Performers.* New York: Avon Books, 1987.
7. Peters DA, Eigsti DM. In Search of Excellence: The Personnel Issue of the Future. *Caring.* 1991; 10(4):12-15
8. John-Rogers, McWilliams P. *Do It.* Los Angeles, CA: Prelude Press, 1990.
9. Donabedian A. The Quality of Care. *Journal of the American Medical Association.* 1988; 260(12):1743-1748.
10. Peters DA, Eigsti DM. Utilizing Outcomes in Home Care. *Caring.* 1991; 10(10):44-45.
11. Slevin ML, Plant H, Lynch D, Drinkwater J, Gregory WM. Who should measure quality of life, the doctor or patient? *Br J Cancer.* 1988; 57:109-112.

4

The IMPLEMENTATION of TOTAL QUALITY

Ronna Baird, RN, MS
Sherry Cadenhead, RN, MS
June A. Schmele, RN, PhD

Total Quality (TQ) is a management philosophy and an organizational culture that encourages people to strive for continuous quality improvement. Kaluzny et al. (1992) conceptually define TQ as a participative approach to assess, plan, implement, and evaluate a continuous improvement process systematically. Successful implementation of this new leadership paradigm requires a thoughtfully derived plan for the systematic implementation of the entire TQ culture and process.

Within the healthcare field, there are a number of TQ implementation models and methods that embody this systematic approach. The following models are examples:

1. Einstein Consulting Group's Customer-Driven Management Model (Leebov and Ersoz, 1991)
2. The Ten-Step Model for Monitoring and Evaluation (Joint Commission on Accreditation of Healthcare Organizations, 1992)
3. The FOCUS-PDCA Model (Hospital Corporation of America, 1991)
4. The Ten Key Lessons for Quality Improvement (Berwick et al., 1991)
5. The Quality Improvement Framework (Omachonu, 1991)

Based on these models, the authors have developed an eclectic model that incorporates many of their key components. A conceptual TQ process model (Figure 4-1) was developed by Baird and Cadenhead in 1993 to help clarify and provide a guide to operationalize the implementation process. This model contains the following step-by-step and overlapping processes:

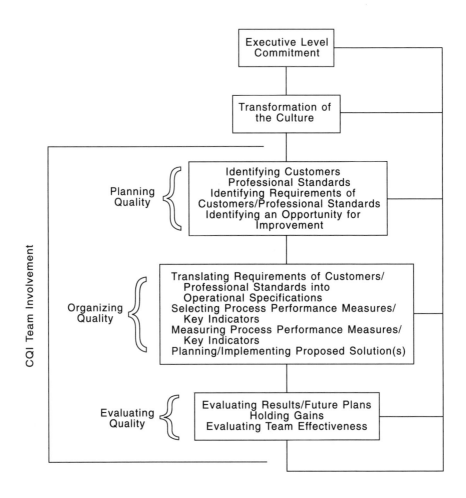

Figure 4-1. Total quality management process model.
(Source: R. Baird and S. Cadenhead, Oklahoma City, © 1993.)

(1) executive level commitment, (2) transformation of the culture, (3) planning quality, (4) organizing quality, and (5) evaluating quality. The individual components are not intended to be self-contained or mutually exclusive, but rather represent the critical elements of the process as continuous, ongoing, and overlapping building blocks to the next step. There is no precise road map that applies to all organizations. For this reason, each organization must customize its own plan for TQ. The sections that follow will cover these five elements in greater detail.

EXECUTIVE LEVEL COMMITMENT

Regardless of where the idea of implementing TQ originates, executive level commitment is crucial to its success. Once the executive level is committed to the success of TQ, education becomes the cornerstone to empowering middle management and other employees within an organization. Before implementing TQ throughout the organization, an initial task force is organized by the Chief Executive Officer (CEO) or the executive board to research various TQ philosophies. This task force is a temporary committee that is made up of individuals chosen by the CEO. This may include top executives, middle management, and grass roots employees. Task force members have the responsibility to actively seek input from various TQ consultants and organizations that have a well-established program. After the task force has explored the groundwork, synthesized information, and made subsequent recommendations for implementation, a presentation is made to the CEO and other executive board members. After the executive level has committed to implementing TQ, the CEO initiates the educational process.

The TQ concept must be established firmly at the top before structurally empowering and educating other levels within an organization. As previously discussed, education is essential to the success of TQ within an organization. This educational process is slow and has no shortcuts. An essential early step is the establishment of a glossary of terms that will result in common usage throughout the organization. All levels of management must attain a thorough knowledge of TQ principles. These principles include basic knowledge and understanding of the concept of TQ, quality tools, processes, and methodologies for quality improvement. It is imperative that executive level administrators and managers philosophically commit to and practice these quality principles on a day-to-day basis. Seminars, readings, and various levels of formal TQ training are a part of the learning process. The development of an educational plan, including time frames, is a valuable device to formulate at this time. TQ consultants may be used to assist in planning and/or training executive level managers and other individuals within an organization. It is important to explore various consulting services carefully before selection in order to choose a consultant that is supportive of the vision, culture, and goals of the organization.

In summary, executive level commitment is crucial to the success of TQ within an organization. In addition, education is the key to managers and staff understanding the relevance of TQ, quality tools, processes, and methodologies for improving quality. Education and executive level commitment to TQ are the beginning seeds to transform an organizational mindset to continuous quality improvement.

TRANSFORMATION of the CULTURE

Cultural change begins once the executive board and CEO make the commitment to TQ. This cultural transformation may take from 5 to 10 years. During this transformation process, key changes occur in the organizational climate, such as trust building, clear communication, increased employee participation, and employee performance improvements. These changes are marked by the ability and the commitment to communicate among various levels within the organization. The movement away from a unidisciplinary focus to an interdisciplinary focus is extremely important in the transformation of the culture.

There is little, if anything, in the care of patients that requires the contribution of only one discipline. Further, the system-oriented processes are seldom within the control of a single discipline. Thus it is essential that the efforts of a variety of disciplines be integrated to make sound decisions and effectively implement a plan for TQ. The movement from unidisciplinarity to interdisciplinarity is not sudden and rapid, but rather is an evolutionary growth process. The first step is multidisciplinarity, which may be defined as several distinct disciplines working together, with each representing its own professional areas. The contribution made by each discipline will represent only its own disciplinary interest. At the next level, a richer interaction takes place, where members of several disciplines interact as a team and all members contribute toward the accomplishment of a common goal. This can best be represented by the expression, "The whole is greater than the sum of the parts." In most process improvement activities, group and team interdisciplinary actions are desirable and essential. Team-building processes will facilitate breaking down interdepartmental barriers and will minimize territorial issues. One of the most effective strategies to accomplish this is to have group ownership of a common goal, such as the TQ program and its quality improvement processes. A prerequisite for this common ownership, of course, is staff empowerment by management.

Managers empower their employees through the use of positive feedback and reinforcement of positive attitudes and behaviors that support quality improvement. Team building and effectiveness result from participation in mutual goal setting and consensual problem solving. It is vital that managers lead and coach, rather than direct and order. Employees will become more involved if they begin to see greater quality improvement initiatives within the organization. Strong employee motivation toward the improvement of quality is essential in order for the cultural transformation to occur. As empowerment is experienced within individual units, pride and morale are boosted, barriers and turfs are broken down, and fear is driven out as individuals begin to take ownership of their daily work.

Communication, empowerment, building trust, and working to improve work processes is continuous. Cultural transformation is not a one-time event, but rather an ongoing organizational growth process. Employee knowledge and ownership of the TQ philosophy will result in continuous quality improvements by using an ongoing scientifically based systematic approach.

After the executive level has committed to TQ and education has become the cornerstone for training all individuals within an organization, the CEO should clarify the organization's overall quality mission. The CEO remains the pivotal driving force in implementing organizational change. Before implementing the educational process, an organizational assessment may be initiated by the CEO. This assessment will provide a baseline concerning the knowledge, attitude, and behaviors of the organization regarding quality.

Prior to planning quality, a quality council is formed. The quality council, which is chosen by the CEO, initially consists of top executives, middle managers, and grass roots employees. This council reflects the cultural make-up of the organization. The council is referred to as a cross-functional group that is representative of the entire institution. Individuals within the council possess overall knowledge and understanding of the organization as a whole. The members must have the power to initiate organizational change. Membership includes both administrative and clinical management. Because power and authority are needed to initiate change, there may be a lesser number of nonmanagement personnel on this particular council. The quality council is responsible for a number of activities within an organization. These responsibilities include the following: (1) providing guidance and overall direction in implementing the process of TQ; (2) developing the mission and vision statements of the organization; (3) developing the goals and objectives, guidelines, definitions, and value statements of the organization; (4) coordinating employee and leadership development; (5) initiating continuous quality improvement (CQI) teams; (6) ensuring that organizational policies and procedures are consistent with TQ principles; and (7) demonstrating a top-down commitment to the TQ process.

In summary, transformation of the culture involves open communication among various levels within an organization, breaking down barriers and territories, eliminating fear, and empowering employees. In addition, the CEO remains the pivotal point in implementing organizationwide change. During this process, a quality council is formed. To facilitate mastering the process of TQ, this council is instrumental in providing direction to all individuals, including CQI teams within the organization.

PLANNING QUALITY

Once executive level management has committed to the concept of TQ and transformation of the culture has begun, quality planning directly follows. Juran (1988), one of the leaders in TQ, has focused much of his efforts on the importance of planning for the implementation of quality improvement systems. During this phase, CQI teams become the focal point in guiding the TQ process. All individuals will receive formal training in team dynamics and processes. As a part of this formalized training, individuals are educated regarding the roles and responsibilities of various team members, as well as their own, and their importance to the TQ process. Initially, the quality council appoints team members who in turn select other team members who have completed adequate TQ team training. According to Scholtes (1991), roles within the team include: (1) team leader, (2) team facilitator, (3) team recorder, and (4) team member. The team leader is the content expert who is often the manager or supervisor responsible for the department where changes are likely to occur. This individual is responsible for providing knowledge and expertise in the content area under consideration. The facilitator or coach is the expert on the group process and functions as the group facilitator; thus the facilitator's area of expertise and emphasis is group and team dynamics. Inclusive in this responsibility is the ability to keep team members focused. This person acts as a process facilitator to the team and is objective and nonpartisan during discussions. The team recorder's responsibilities may be rotated among various team members; however, the facilitator may choose to serve in both capacities. The recorder is responsible for such things as documenting the flip charts, recording minutes, and assisting the team leader in preparing meeting agendas. Team member responsibilities include: (1) understanding the team's mission, (2) participating in the group process, (3) listening to each other, and (4) sharing ideas.

Ground rules and the size of the teams are also important to the functioning of a successful team. An ideal team consists of six to eight individuals. A team is ineffective if it becomes too large. Ground rules include establishing time frames for meetings and specifying acceptable and unacceptable behavioral interactions. Group norms will quickly develop and help the group to regulate itself.

Upon receiving direction from the organization's quality council, teams can begin focusing on the identification of internal and external customers and their professional standards and requirements. Leebov and Ersoz (1991) define customers as those individuals whose satisfaction with the services or products provided by the organization affects the ability of the organization to achieve its objectives. Internal customers are those individuals who provide a service within a particular organization. For example, physicians or nurses may be defined as internal customers to a health department where they are employed. External customers are those individuals who are not employed by a particular organization but who receive some type of service. Patients are an example of external customers.

Professional standards are defined as internal or external quality mechanisms set in place for the purposes of maintaining and/or improving certain aspects of quality. For example, the Joint Commission on Accreditation of Healthcare Organizations has established a set of standards for accrediting healthcare organizations. In addition, most disciplines have professional standards to which they commit. It is important to note the relevance of identifying customer requirements, professional standards, and accreditation requirements.

Healthcare providers often consider standards of care to be the answer to customer needs. However, professional standards should not replace addressing customer requirements. Various measurement tools can be used to identify these requirements. (See Chapter 5 for a detailed explanation of these tools.) For example, it may be helpful to develop some type of customer survey or interview process to identify the needs of internal and external customers. Factual data provide a basis for identifying problems and/or opportunities for improvement without making assumptions. Once this information is obtained, it is important to establish priorities, develop a problem statement, and set a goal for addressing the concern.

The following example will be used to illustrate this process. Health department personnel experienced a high rate of patient complaints regarding prolonged turnaround time (the time entering versus the time leaving the facility). In addition, public health nurses, nurse practitioners, and physicians were complaining about the backlog that was occurring before patients were seen in the clinic. As a result, a project team developed a customer (patient) survey to validate concerns and invalidate assumptions. A log was developed to record the amount of time patients spent in the health department, from the time they entered the facility to the time they exited. Once information was obtained from the customer survey, the team identified waiting time as a major customer concern. In addition, information from the log, which was visually presented by means of a histogram, revealed that patients' turnaround time averaged two hours. After identifying the problem as excessive patient turnaround time, the team developed a goal that addressed improving patient flow. Thus, the team provided valid feedback that led to decreased patient turnaround time.

In summary, quality planning emphasizes team formation and building. Planning encompasses the following key elements: (1) identification of customer requirements and professional standards, (2) data-based identification of deviation from standards and requirements (problem), and (3) identification of opportunities for improvement (goal).

ORGANIZING QUALITY

After the completion of quality planning, organizing quality becomes the second major task for the CQI team. During the initial phase of this process, the team is responsible for translating customer requirements into operational specifications. Leebov and Ersoz (1991) define operational specifications as those key work processes that consist of a chain of events that a department performs to meet customer requirements or professional standards. To flow through this process, the team focuses on analyzing the current situation by examining the step-by-step work processes that were used in meeting or not meeting customer requirements. For example, in the above case history, the expectation of the customer was to obtain service within the health department in a timely manner. To understand the work process completely, it is essential to follow the chain of activities involved in facilitating patient flow through the health department. A flowchart would probably be most helpful in documenting this process. (See Chapter 5 for a description of a flowchart.) Once a flowchart has been developed, team members can study it for possible bottlenecks in the process. The identification of these potential bottlenecks assists the team in selecting process performance measures or key indicators, which are those causes that most likely have the greatest impact on meeting customer requirements. At this stage, team members may wish to use brainstorming to help develop a cause-and-effect diagram for identifying all possible causes. To validate the findings obtained from the cause-and-effect diagram, it may be helpful to develop a checklist for observing how many times the particular event occurs, as well as its causes. During this phase, process performance measures or key indicators are measured through observation. For the purpose of developing a checklist of process performance measures or key indicators, potential causes that were noted during the development of the cause-and-effect diagram may also be documented on the checklist, to be evaluated by observation. It may also be helpful to leave two or more columns of the checklist open for documenting other causes that may have been overlooked during the preliminary stages of developing the cause-and-effect diagram. After obtaining observational data from the checklist, the team can rank order the number of occurrences under each particular cause. This information can then be documented on a Pareto chart. The Pareto chart provides a visual means for identifying the most prevalent causes. Once prevalent causes are validated, a proposed solution can be planned and implemented.

During the planning phase of developing a solution, it is important to generate as many alternatives as possible before identifying the best solution(s). Brainstorming and affinity charts may be helpful during this process (Joint Commission on Accreditation of Healthcare Organizations, 1992). A decision matrix or tree diagram may be used to identify the best solution. After the team has identified the best solution(s) for addressing the problem statement, a recommendation is made to the quality council. The purpose of this communication is to gain the sanction of executive level management so that they may demonstrate their commitment to the overall TQ process. In addition, executive level management provides support mechanisms for securing various resources (i.e., finances, staff, time). Following executive level management involvement, the solution chosen can be implemented in a pilot study or trial run. The purpose of a pilot study is to obtain necessary information for improving a project and/or for evaluating its practicality (Polit and Hungler, 1987). During this time, team members and other key players are closely attuned to observing and documenting the entire process of the pilot. The purpose of this activity is to guarantee that the solution implemented is congruent with the overall TQ plan.

In summary, organizing quality is a vital link in the improvement process. During this phase, four key elements are emphasized: (1) translating the requirements of customers and/or professional standards into operational specifications, (2) selecting process performance measures or key indicators, (3) measuring process performance measures or key indicators, and (4) planning and implementing the proposed solution(s). All of these elements provide a scientific basis for making decisions based on facts.

EVALUATING QUALITY

It is important to consider structure (resources), process (activities), and outcome (results) as key elements of evaluation. The quality improvement process itself deals with structure and process, while the ultimate improvement hopefully will be reflected in the outcome. Two key questions are vital when evaluating any quality improvement processes: (1) How did this improve organizational performance? and (2) How did this improve the quality of care? (For a more detailed discussion of outcome management, see Chapter 10.)

During the preliminary phase of evaluation, team members evaluate results of the implemented solution in order to make future plans. At this time, it is essential to monitor both process and outcome indicators to validate the success of the pilot study. This may be done using various tools. For example, in the above case history, it may be helpful to use a trend or run chart to document patient satisfaction before and after implementing the pilot study. In addition, a flowchart may be used to track individual data points regarding the total time it takes for each patient to enter and exit the facility. After evaluating the results of the implemented solution, it is important to use the findings to make future plans. For example, if the pilot study was successful, it would be important to make the needed changes as part of the routine for providing the service. On the other hand, if the pilot study was unsuccessful, further investigation would be warranted. Once a decision is made to make successful changes a part of the routine, a monitoring system should be incorporated as a means to maintain the gains. It is desirable that a routine schedule be utilized for measuring performance and ensuring that these gains continue. Again, a variety of tools may be used during this process.

Finally, as another element to evaluating quality, it is necessary that the team members evaluate their overall effectiveness in group dynamics. It is desirable that team members evaluate both their successes and areas needing further improvement. For example, it may be useful for the team to identify two factors that positively impacted the overall success of the group. This activity reinforces positive interaction among the group members. Team members may also wish to identify at least two factors that inhibited group functioning. This activity assists in eliminating or reducing future problems among group members. This information provides an effective basis for building future team successes.

In summary, evaluating quality includes the following key elements: (1) evaluating results of the implemented solution(s), (2) holding gains, (3) and evaluating team effectiveness. Once the evaluation process is in place, it is essential that teams use a cyclic approach in sharing information with key players while at the same time continuously planning and organizing quality.

SUMMARY

Leadership commitment and strong employee motivation are vital driving forces for implementing and maintaining an effective TQ system. In this chapter, the authors have suggested using the Total Quality Process Model as a framework for implementing all dimensions of the TQ concept. This model includes the following key elements: (1) executive level commitment, (2) transformation of the culture, (3) planning quality, (4) organizing quality, and (5) evaluating quality. When using a top-down participative management approach that includes CQI team involvement, all of these elements work hand in hand. The authors suggest that the elements of this process overlap with each other and also work concurrently and continuously to build an organizational commitment to quality. It is important that each organization customize the chosen implementation model to fit its own unique needs.

The next few pages contain an article by McEachern et al. (1992) that describes team building—a most important element in TQ implementation. Process improvement teams are pivotal to the process of TQ. Team planning, designing, membership, and action are crucial to their success. This article presents a model for such a process.

REFERENCES

Berwick, D., Godfrey, A., and, Roessner, J. (1991). *Curing Healthcare: New Strategies for Quality Improvement,* San Francisco: Jossey-Bass Publishers.

Hospital Corporation of America (1991). *Hospital Quality Technology Network,* Nashville: Hospital Corporation of America.

Joint Commission on Accreditation of Healthcare Organizations (1992). *Using Quality Improvement Tools in a Healthcare Setting,* Oakbrook Terrace, Ill.: Joint Commission.

Juran, J. M. (1988). *Juran on Planning for Quality,* New York: The Free Press.

Kaluzny, A. D., McLaughlin, C. P., and Simpson, K. (1992). "Applying Total Quality Management Concepts to Public Health Organizations." *Management Practices,* 107(3):257–264.

Leebov, W. and Ersoz, C. J. (1991). *The Healthcare Manager's Guide to Continuous Quality Improvement,* Chicago: American Hospital Publishing, Inc.

Omachonu, V. K. (1991). *Total Quality and Productivity Management in Healthcare Organizations,* Norcross, Ga.: Industrial Engineering and Management Press, Institute of Industrial Engineers.

Polit, D. F. and Hungler, B. P. (1987). *Nursing Research: Principles and Methods,* 3rd edition, Philadelphia: J.B. Lippincott Company.

Scholtes, P. (1991). *The Team Handbook,* Madison, Wis.: Joiner Associates, Inc.

HOW to START a
DIRECT PATIENT CARE TEAM

J. Edward McEachern, MD

Lorraine Schiff, RN, MBA

Oscar Cogan, MD

Continuous quality improvement (CQI) was first applied to health care organizations approximately six years ago,[1] primarily—and with some success—to the operations and managerial structure of hospitals.[2] However, only recently has CQI been applied to clinical processes.[3] As CQI in hospitals matures, teams will address increasingly complex (cross-functional) systems. Eventually, as CQI becomes part of the organizational fabric of hospitals, teams will become involved in improving the processes that affect one very important customer group directly—the patient. All hospital processes affect patients' care. Direct patient care processes are those that involve clinicians' direct contact with patients.

At least several current paradigms of clinicians (Table 1) make the application of CQI teams to direct patient care processes tricky. First, health care production processes, unlike those of most other industries, are more intimately connected to the welfare of the customer. Throughout history, the relationship between health care providers and patients has been viewed as a special, almost sacred relationship. Second, team members are professionals with long training in what makes the "best" health care decisions. Those involved on teams that handle patient care issues are steeped in the rich, but often burdensome, tradition of the medical profession. The status afforded to providers of care accords to the treatment process a special and somewhat unclear place in society. To some providers and even some customers, the suggestion that providers can learn from their customers or from the study of processes of care is met with much skepticism—and even regarded as taboo. The high status of providers in this society carries fixed paradigms about what is and can be "right." Often these paradigms must be

Table 1.   Comparisons Commonly Made between Direct Patient Care Teams and Administrative Cross-Functional Teams.

Direct Patient Care Teams	Administrative Cross-Functional Teams
1) Long training in "best" decisions about care processes that can and do improve care.	1) Long training in "best" decisions about administrative processes that can and do improve the efficiency of the organization.

    — How have your processes worked best?
    — What evidence is there that the "best" training leads to the best care?

2) Intimacy of the worker (the clinician) with the most important customer (the patient) precludes objective and measurable improvement in the quality of services.	2) Intimacy of the worker (the administrator) with the most important customer (the manager and the customer) precludes objective and measurable improvement in the quality of services.

    — What evidence is there that your most important customers know little about your thought, action, and communication processes?

3) Customers (patients, payers, other managers, lawyers,...) know very little about hospital processes and therefore can contribute very little information that will help the hospital improve.	3) Customers (patients, payers, administrators, lawyers,...) know very little about the process of care and can therefore contribute little information that will help us improve.

    — What evidence is there that customers have little information about the process of care?
    — How does our perception of the value of customer data change if we consider as valid outcomes of care health status, patient satisfaction, and the total cost of an episode of care

4) The decision-making processes in clinical medicine have the greatest effect on outcomes. The action and communication processes in the delivery of care are less important.	4) The decision-making processes in the administration of a health care organization have the greatest effect on outcomes. The action and communication processes in running a health care organization are less important.

    — What evidence is there that outcomes are affected more by thought processes than by communication and action processes?
    — What evidence is there that you make decisions about care without knowledge of the communication and action processes that occur at the site of care?

5) Some clinicians regularly and energetically debate their thought processes, and this leads to demonstrably better care.	5) Some administrators regularly and energetically debate their thought processes, and this leads to a demonstrably better health care organization.

    — What evidence is there that debating your thoughts about how a system functions adds value in the absence of explicit knowledge of processes and communications that take place in the system?
    — How could you know if regular and energetic debate actually improves care?

6) Facilitators of teams must be administrators.	6) Facilitators of teams must be clinicians.

    — What evidence is there that people who work in the process of care do not have working knowledge of the process of care?
    — What evidence is there that clinicians and administrators alone are qualified to describe and improve the process of care?

significantly shaken before a team of direct care providers can be established. Further, the paradigms of clinical medicine certainly need to be examined in order for clinicians to develop profound customer and process knowledge.

Finally, these current paradigms would have us assume that the patient knows very little about care—about the decision processes and about the pathophysiology of his or her condition. Yet, the paradigms that have served us well for so long can prevent us from seeing old problems in new ways. In direct patient care teams, members squarely confront several paradigms about the delivery of care that are not as apparent as they are in other cross-functional teams:

1. Providers' thoughts, actions, and communications are quite intimate to the patient's mind and body; and
2. The status afforded to the providers of the service has heretofore been viewed as somewhat mystical and sacred, allowing their work processes total respite from scrutiny.

Therefore, handling these teams seems to require a bit more finesse than other teams and may frighten a facilitator who is not aware of these commonly shared paradigms of clinicians.

Providers can learn much about health care and its delivery from the lessons hard won by industries that have undergone the quality transformation.[4] As the health care industry matures in its application of CQI to direct patient care, we may be amazed at how well the principles of CQI—customer knowledge, process focus, and statistical mindedness—work in improving the delivery and cost effectiveness of care. Along with this maturation will come a growth in the need for more direct patient care teams. After all, improvement of direct patient care is the goal of continual improvement of the process.

The similarities between direct patient care teams and other cross-functional teams far exceed the differences. The purpose of this article is to describe the differences so that facilitators can make direct patient care teams part of their "tool bag" in helping hospitals carry out the transition to CQI.

MATERIALS and METHODS

Direct patient care team deployment in an organization can be generalized in a flowchart. West Paces Ferry Hospital, a 294-bed community hospital in suburban Atlanta, uses a generic team rollout map (Figure 1), which provides structure to our deployment strategy. The deployment strategy was developed on the basis of a literature review from other

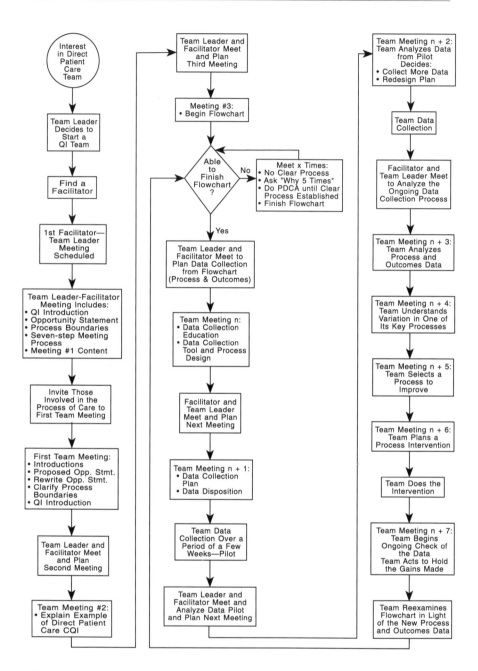

Figure 1. Flowchart of direct patient care team deployment. The direct patient care team deployment uses a generic map to provide structure to team development and a framework for analyzing improvement strategies.

industries as well as our own experience. The flowchart also provides a framework to analyze what went well in the direct patient care deployment and what could be improved and why. For the purposes of this article, the map gives the reader a structure for following the case studies, as well as a plan that may be adapted to one's own organization.

Direct patient care teams can be chosen in a number of ways. At West Paces Ferry Hospital, interest in such teams grows out of an environment rich in information and one in which all seek to learn.[5] Early in the direct patient care rollout, teams were started following the interest of an individual, usually the team leader. In each case, the team leader had an idea or a willingness to learn about his or her work processes in order to make them function better. Sometimes the team leader contacted the authors with an interest; other times the authors were referred to the team leader. This method worked well in the initial development of direct patient care teams.

As the deployment of direct patient care teams became more common in the organization, direct patient care teams were regarded as an effective way for clinicians to organize their daily activities. As clinicians became more willing to work in teams, the hospital developed a second method for choosing direct patient care teams—teams organized by body system or major functional process. The hospital's top 25 diagnosis-related groups (DRGs: by volume) were examined (Figure 2) and organized into functional body systems (Figure 3). By use of Figure 3, the hospital could determine the most efficient way to allocate its resources to better serve the patient.

In a third team deployment method (described here by means of case studies), direct patient care teams are developed by clinicians themselves as a more efficient way to help them reorganize their daily work activities. Of the three methods, this method has been found at West Paces Ferry to be the most effective in establishing ongoing, effective direct patient care teams. However, no matter how the team was selected, the deployment of the team has followed a similar path.

A meeting is scheduled between the team leader and the facilitator (J.E.M. and/or L.S.) to establish an agenda for the first team meeting and to help the team leader deepen his or her understanding of CQI tools (Figure 4). This agenda-setting meeting usually takes place at a time and place convenient for the team leader: for example, at breakfast or lunch or at a time when the leader has an hour blocked off on the calendar. Sometimes this means that the facilitator has to travel to the team leader's site of care.

At the meeting between the facilitator and the team leader, the content and process of the first team meeting is discussed and the agenda items—introduction to CQI, the seven-step meeting process,[6] and drafting an opportunity statement for the team to work with—for the first team meeting are set (Figure 5). The facilitator and team leader decide who will be invited

107

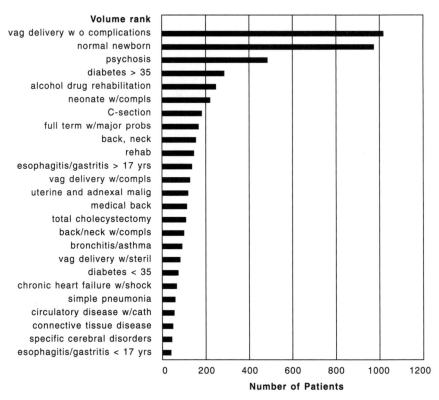

Figure 2. Top 25 diagnosis-related groups (DRGs) by patient volume (1990, HCA West Paces Ferry Hospital). One method of choosing teams is by categorizing body systems or functional processes using DRGs.

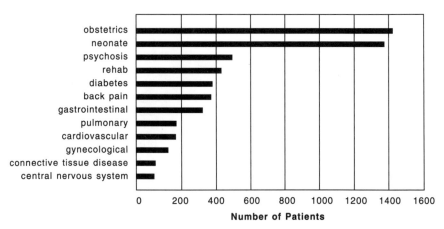

Figure 3. Direct patient care teams by patient volume (1990 DRG volume data, HCA West Paces Ferry Hospital). These teams, developed from DRG data, represent 91% of top 25 DRGs.

108

First Meeting Agenda

Objective: Further the understanding of CQI tools for the team leader. To develop the team's first meeting agenda.

Agenda

  I.   QI introduction
  II. How to create an opportunity statement
  III. Process boundaries
  IV. The 7-step meeting process
  V.   Team meeting #1 content

Figure 4.   The team leader and facilitator meet to establish the agenda for the first team meeting.

HIV Team's First Opportunity Statement

There is an opportunity to study and create a cost-effective system to provide HIV routine surveillance, prophylaxis for opportunistic infections, and use of experimental antivirals within a managed care setting. The team's process starts with an HIV-positive diagnosis and ends with terminal care.

HIV Team's Rank-Ordered List

Team member						Item #	Item	Totals
A	B	C	D	E	F			
1	5	7	4	6	1	A	Prophylaxis for *Pneumocystis carinii* pneumonia	24
6	6	8	5	7	6	B	Prophylaxis for toxoplasmosis and other opportunistic infections	38
7	2	5	1	3	3	C	ddC, ddi and other antivirals	21
8	7	6	2	9	7	D	New antiretrovirals and vaccines	39
9	3	4	8	4	5	E	Home management	33
2	1	2	6	1	2	F	Routine surveillance and laboratory follow-up	14
5	8	3	3	8	8	G	Costs of inpatient versus outpatient management	35
3	9	1	7	2	9	H	Assessing educational level of physicians	31
4	9	9	5	4	4	I	Drug interactions	35

1 = highest importance

ddC, dideoxycytidine; ddi, didanosine

Figure 5.   The team developed an opportunity statement and then rank-ordered the list (created from the CQI technique of brainstorming) to determine the group's greatest instructional needs.

109

to the first meeting (all who work in the process) and when and where the meeting will take place. All meetings are approximately one hour long. The team leader is responsible for contacting team members and arranging a convenient time to meet.

At the first team meeting, members are introduced to each other (although this is usually unnecessary). The team is oriented to the proposed purpose of the team's work, which the team members can modify as they see appropriate. The leader reads the team's proposed opportunity statement, which the team reexamines and usually rewrites. The current team composition (who work in the process of care) and process boundaries are also determined. Not all workers who perform the process are invited to attend, but at least one representative of each task of care should be involved. The process of establishing the team's opportunity statement, the process boundaries, and the team composition is iterative, often revisited periodically as the team moves through FOCUS-PDCA,* Health Corporation of America's (Nashville) framework for understanding systems and performing small scientific experiments on the system. The establishment of an opportunity statement, the best team composition, and the process boundaries may take several meetings.

At either the first or the second team meeting, the facilitator explains to the team a vision of direct patient care quality improvement, usually using the obstetrics team at West Paces Ferry Hospital as an example[8] because it is the longest running and most experienced direct patient care team and is a good conceptual model of the possibilities of quality improvement in clinical care. New team members learn the importance of making the process of care explicit, as well as examining the outcomes of care from the point of view of those who benefit from it. Through an explicit process of care—as seen by all persons who interact with the patient—and explicitly defined and measurable outputs of the care process, the team members are able to infer a causal link between their (collective) actions and the results of their actions. The example highlights the statistically valid way to connect each individual's actions in the clinical process with the results of care. With this understanding, the team can manage "upstream" from the results; that is, they can manage the process of care in a way that obtains the desired results.

---

*The nine steps to FOCUS-PDCA are Find a process to improve; Organize a team that knows the process; Clarify current knowledge of the process; Understand causes of process variation; Select the process improvement; Plan the improvement; Do data collection, data analysis, and improvement; Check data for process improvement and customer outcome; and Act to hold, gain and continue improvement.

Through FOCUS-PDCA, a team examines the process of care, which is defined as all thoughts, actions, and communications that lead to the result of care. A process focus is a new paradigm for most direct patient care team members. For example, the team examining cesarean sections (C-sections) makes the process of obstetric care explicit—how the patient gets into the hospital, how the patient gets to the floor, how the diagnostic workup proceeds, how care is delivered, and so on. By making the process explicit, developing a flowchart with all those involved in the process of care, and checking the flowchart against what really happens at their hospital, the team members have created the equivalent of a "catwalk" for their process. They can examine how the process actually works, and then improve it. Once the process of care for a certain body system is made explicit (flowchart), the team can examine the care a patient gets regardless of the type of pathophysiology. A patient may have cephalopelvic disproportion, failure to progress, placenta previa, or any number of other conditions that are indications for a C-section. The processes of performing pelvic examinations, ultrasound tests, pelvimetry, and other diagnostic tests are remarkably similar. Further, it takes all people who care for a patient present together in one room to describe the care processes (thoughts, actions, and communications) of a patient. FOCUS-PDCA is a framework to describe and address system failures.

After the obstetrics example is presented to the team, usually at the third meeting, the team begins to make the process of care explicit by developing a flowchart. Once the team members complete the flowchart (two to eight meetings), they verify it against the process as it actually happens by collecting process and output data. The team members design a data collection tool and a data collection form. They plot the collection of data on the process of care for about two weeks and then reexamine the flowchart for accuracy. The team revises the flowchart as often as necessary in order to reflect the reality of the process.

Using the obstetrics example, the team is introduced to the process focus of quality improvement in health care. The process focus of quality improvement is a great advantage for health care workers, especially physicians, because clinicians are fed up with feeling harangued and hassled by the current quality assurance structure that watchdogs the results of care and rewards behavior by punishing the individual practitioner. As all workers begin to understand the variation in the process of care—often by identifying places where the system fails—they can begin to improve the process of care. Teams identify the elements of care—called key quality characteristics (KQCs)—that are most important to the customers of care. The team also identifies in a statistically significant manner the parts of processes that have the most impact on KQCs. Using statistics, one can link a process to its results and thereby infer causality with a known alpha error. Teams can

111

then make changes in the process, leading to a change in results. The causal link allows scarce resources to be allocated more efficiently.

Making the link between variation in work processes and results provides ample opportunity to teach the team about systems thinking. Groups of providers are not accustomed to an explicit study of their process and need new skills and social supports to understand the system in which they work. Each team meeting becomes an adventure in helping team members start to understand their system, its interactions, and their interdependence. Each meeting is an opportunity to help team members envision a new working situation, a new order of affairs where processes work with predictable reliability. As the team progresses, the facilitator's job is to help the team discover new ways to work together, new ways to understand their system.

Once the team knows the system of care and its variations, they can select a process to improve, plan and make the improvement, continue to collect data on the process of care (key process variables) and the customers' views of the results of care (KQCs), check to see that the change in the process of care achieved the desired outcome, and plan to make further changes in the process of care (S-PDCA).

The team makes many journeys through S-PDCA, moving to increasingly complex issues in the delivery of care.

RESULTS

HCA West Paces Ferry Hospital has 17 direct patient care teams—"doctor teams," representing more than 60% of the total patient volume in the hospital.

Case Example 1: The HIV Team

Find an opportunity. A group of physicians in an Atlanta health maintenance organization (HMO) who are practicing at the hospital became aware of a growing number of patients diagnosed with human immunodeficiency virus (HIV) in their ambulatory and in-hospital practice. Moreover, these physicians felt a need to stay as up-to-date as possible on treatment modalities, as well as on treatment actions. This group's infectious disease consultant physician suggested that they form a quality improvement team, since he had participated on several teams with striking results.

Organize a team. A team meeting was organized with six physicians (one family practitioner, three internists, and two infectious disease specialists), a quality management nurse, and a facilitator. The team leader met with one of the HMO's consultant physicians before the meeting, but not the facilitator. During the course of meeting, the quality improvement process was explained, an example was given, and the team was asked to brainstorm ideas for the team's work. Once the team had clarified and consolidated the brainstormed list, they rank-ordered the list to determine the group's greatest educational needs (Figure 5). From this list, the team constructed an opportunity statement (Figure 6).

The team ended this 1 1/4-hour session by planning the next meeting agenda (two weeks from the date of the first meeting) and evaluating the meeting (Figure 6). Plans were made for the team leader and facilitator to spend time together before the second meeting to discuss its content. At the second team meeting, the team refined the opportunity statement (Figure 7).

Clarify the process of care. As the team started to describe the process of care, they found that they had developed no clear processes of care because they were uncertain of current best practices. The team decided to shift its focus from the quality improvement process to a more didactic focus in order to define appropriate care for patients with HIV-related disease. The team is now codifying current literature, and disseminating it to providers, as well as collecting current baseline information on the patient population. The team decided to resume the process description once all clinicians had a better understanding of the best current practices from the literature.

The HIV team demonstrated excellent use of CQI tools to solve problems. The team members used the tools to run their meetings efficiently, identify and rank order of their concerns, and describe goals and boundaries for their concerns. However, the HIV team did not engage in process improvement. Rather, the team chose to work on a problem the team had identified—they found the clinicians' understanding of HIV treatment to be lacking, leading to a haphazard and ill-defined process. The team's actions are typical of many teams when first exposed to the quality improvement process. They used a team meeting to rapidly and explicitly identify problems. A typical team reaction is to want to solve the problem without taking the time to describe, study, and measure the underlying process that produces the problem. In this case, when the facilitator pointed out this common error to the team, the factors that lead to a vague process of care were identified. The clinicians on this team, contrary to most other teams, were unclear as to the best care recommended in the rapidly changing literature for treatment of HIV-positive patients. One important lesson learned from this team is that in specialties in which information changes rapidly, process improvement through the entire FOCUS-PDCA cycle may not be the first "tool" of choice to improve care. Clinicians may improve care more effectively by first understanding the medical decision-making processes before designing, redesigning, and innovating a system of care to

HIV Team's Second Team Agenda and Meeting Evaluation

Objective: Begin to develop a process map of current process of care for HIV-positive patients in the group practice

Timekeeper: (unassigned until meeting time)

Leader: RM

Recorder: (unassigned until meeting time)

Facilitator: EM

  I. Revisit opportunity statement (5 min)

  II. What's the current process and knowledge base (15 min)

  III. Break out discrete processes (routine surveillance, prophylaxis, and antiviral use) (30 min)

  IV. Plan next agenda and evaluate meeting (5 min)

Individual assessments by team members of the meeting:
did well, could improve, a lot accomplished with the needs list, we could understand the CQI process better, finished opportunity statement, team's time management could be better, integrated our systems to accomplish more than one task, we wandered—could be more focused.

Figure 6.   At the first team meeting, the HIV team assessed the meeting and planned the next meeting agenda.

HIV Team's Second Opportunity Statement

There is an opportunity to study and create a cost-effective system to provide HIV care including routine surveillance, follow-up and prophylaxis of opportunistic infections and to provide experimental antiretroviral drugs in a managed care setting. The team's process starts with the HIV-positive diagnosis and ends with terminal care.

Figure 7.   At the second team meeting, the HIV team refined the opportunity statement.

Chest Pain Team's Opportunity Statement

An opportunity exists to study the causes of admission for chest pain (not the cause of chest pain).

Figure 8.   The chest pain team developed its opportunity statement at the first meeting.

114

best carry out the decisions of the clinician. By using FOC-PDCA, this team have improved care first by establishing a demonstrable process. After a process is established, often after running through several FOCUS-PDCA cycles, the team can move on to the U (understand process variation) phase and S (selecting a process to improve) phase, and then PDCA.

A second lesson learned is that all people involved in the care of a patient are needed to describe the current process of care, not simply a collection of clinicians as traditional quality assurance dictates. It is possible that this team failed to describe the process because it did not have all caregivers present at the team meetings. The team is now working on its literature review and provider education process. Once all providers are educated, team members hope to understand the sources of variation in the process of caring for patients with HIV-related conditions.

Case Example 2: The Chest Pain Team

Find an opportunity to improve. A group of physicians who belonged to the same HMO realized that they were not as efficient as they could be at admitting patients for chest pain. The team leader and the facilitator decided to use the FOCUS-PDCA method to understand the system of chest pain care and perform small experiments on the system of care to improve it (Figure 8).

Organize a team. The team leader and facilitator decided to invite several physicians representing each site of the HMO (three internal medicine specialists, one family practitioner, one cardiologist, one quality management nurse, and one physician facilitator). At this meeting, the FOCUS-PDCA method was explained using an example and the team developed its opportunity statement (Figure 8).

Clarify the process of care. The chest pain team worked through its understanding of the process as it actually happened, picked boundaries for the process they wanted to study, and developed a flowchart of the team members' best understanding of the system (Figure 9). After four meetings, the team's flowchart was completed; it took three iterations to get to the final version of the current process. Considerable study of the process was made between meetings.

Understand the variation in the process. In an effort to determine how the process of chest pain care varied over time, the team decided to collect data from a retrospective review of charts (Figure 10).

The chest pain team was shocked by the data they found. All physicians in the group were board-certified physicians, yet the data showed that only about 20% of all hospital admissions for chest pain were appropriate

Chest Pain Progress Flowchart

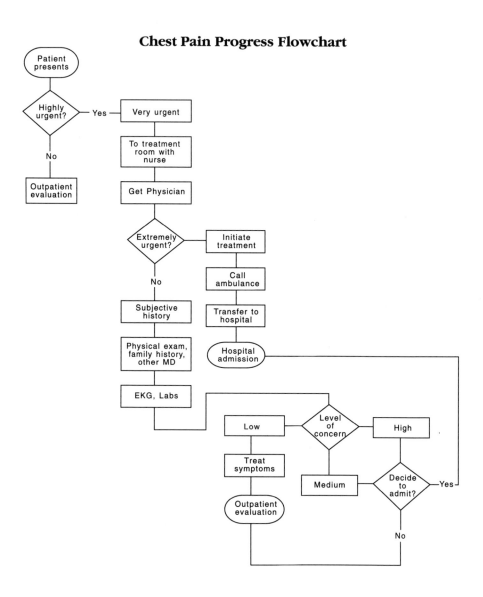

Figure 9. It took the chest pain team four meetings to complete a flowchart of their best understanding of the process.

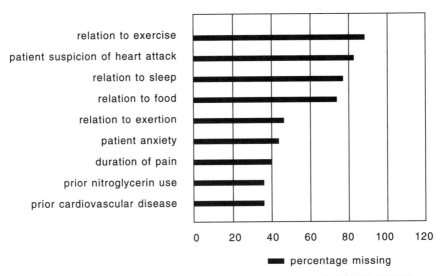

Figure 10.   Percentage of charts in which no data were recorded (1990, HCA West Paces Ferry Hospital). The chest pain team collected data from a retrospective review of charts to discover as much as possible about the process.

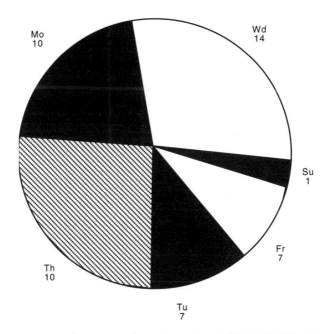

Figure 11.   Admissions of patients with cardiogenic pain (1989, HCA West Paces Ferry Hospital). No patients with cardiogenic pain were admitted on Saturday for the entire year.

117

admissions for cardiogenic pain. They also found that no patients were admitted on Saturday for the entire year (Figure 11). Likewise, the pattern of admission time was more consistent with system failures than with pathophysiologic state. The team members thought that they could learn from the process of weekend admissions and began to inquire about how the weekend process of admissions differed from the weekday chest pain admissions process. In studying the flowchart and result, the team came up with two potential causes for the process variation. The first was found in the process of information transfer between the outpatient physician and the inpatient admitting physician, often working in the emergency room. The team found that the information transfer process, particularly information about the patient's physiologic state, was at best unreliable—many assumptions were made about the referring and receiving emergency room physician's role in evaluating the patient. Second, as the team members studied the flowchart and the data, they became aware that the decision of whether to admit a patient often was greatly influenced by providers' trust of the process of outpatient follow-up as opposed to inpatient follow-up.

Select a process to improve. Team members felt that if they could trust the processes of outpatient follow-up, they might better admit patients and send patients home appropriately. The team selected two intervention points and made a process change (Figure 12).

Plan, do, check, and act on the selected interventions. The team Planned the intervention in the process, Did the intervention, Checked to see if progress had in fact been made in the process of care, and Acted to hold the gain (Shewhart/Deming PDCA cycle). At the end of the year, the team collected data sheets on the patients the hospital had admitted and studied the results (Figure 13). Through its efforts in CQI, this team not only increased the efficiency in its primary care processes without untoward effects, it also saved $147,054 in operating costs, and payers saved $331,951 (Table 2).

After studying its success, the team decided to reconfigure itself to encompass representatives from all those involved in the care of chest pain patient: the new chest pain team comprises two general internists, three cardiologists, one cardiac catheter laboratory technologist, one pharmacist, one emergency department physician, one utilization review/medical records specialist, one quality management nurse, and one facilitator (J.E.M. or L.S.).

Lessons learned. Many lessons have been learned from the chest pain team during its two-year journey toward continuously improving the care of chest pain patients at West Paces Ferry (Table 3). The team's experience shows that customers and suppliers can work together across institutions at several sites to improve care for patients. Further, unlike the HIV team, the domain of clinical knowledge for chest pain care is "what everybody

Chest Pain Team's Process Improvement

1. Design a chest pain data collection sheet to help providers clearly and concisely communicate their understanding of the patients' pathophysiology as well as make informed decisions about treatment.

2. Work with the cardiologist to develop a process to see patients reliably in the outpatient setting for workup.

3. Communicate the team's progress to all providers of chest pain care in the practice.

Figure 12. The chest pain team made a process change.

Patient Volume for Chest Pain Admissions (HCA West Paces Ferry Hospital)

	1989	1990
Total admits for chest pain	64	48
Final diagnosis AMI	6	12
Final diagnosis USA	7	7
Total AIHD	13	19
Percentage of chest pain admits w/AIHD	20%	40%
PruCare Membership	36,600	41,800

AIHD, acute ischemic heart disease; USA, unstable angina; AMI, acute myocardial infarction.

Figure 13. Even though patient volume and number of patients with AIHD increased, more patients were admitted appropriately, leading to fewer overall admissions; outcomes between the two years were equivocal.

knows." Therefore, the care is likely to break down not in the decision-making processes, but in the execution and coordination of the clinicians' thoughts. The execution and coordination of clinical decisions are described as a process of care, made explicit in a flowchart. It follows, then, that an all-physician team cannot adequately describe the process of care for a patient. The team had a difficult time developing a flowchart because

- the process is not uniform from site to site (nor from one incident of care to the next); and
- all persons in the process of care were not present to provide information about how the process worked.

119

Table 2.   Direct and Indirect Costs for Chest Pain Patients for Two Years (HCA West Paces Ferry Hospital).

	1989	1990
Direct costs	$293,424	$146,370
Indirect costs	662,357	330,406

Table 3.   Accelerators and Pitfalls to Success with Direct Patient Care Teams.

ACCELERATORS
- Understanding that patient care involves not only decisions about care, but also the actions and communications of every individual involved in the delivery of care
- Having teams examine the complete process of care as it actually happens
- Listening to our patients and other customers—a tremendous opportunity to learn about where we can make improvements in care
- Strong, directed facilitation as needed to keep the team on track
- Teaching team members team tools they need to use at the meetings
- Having one physician on the direct patient care team who has spent time working on other nonpatient care teams
- Diligent reading and facilitated learning about CQI by interested physicians
- Convenient meeting times (with food provided)
- Helping team leaders with team leadership skills between meetings
- Help with data

PITFALLS
- Starting "doctor teams" without significant organizational readiness
- Placing only doctors and nurses on teams without involving all people who work in the process of care
- Starting a team without significant cross-functional team experience
- Not keeping a storyboard of progresses made
- Not sharing lessons learned
- Too much help with the team's clerical work—team must own the data
- More than eight people on a team
- Involvement by many different people with competing interests

Without all the people who actually work in the process present, describing the complete process is, at best, difficult and slow. Without complete process knowledge, the team cannot know what the current process's strengths are nor where the current process fails and thereby might be improved. Nonetheless, when the team collected data retrospectively with an eye toward examining the process, opportunities for improvements were glaringly obvious. Interestingly, the team members never once identified problems in an individual physician's performance (and still don't know of performance problems in terms of individuals), quite unlike traditional quality assurance. The lesson here is that if one diligently studies the process—not the individual—systems improvements are made, and clinicians are given a method for continuously improving the care they deliver. Finally, as the team matured, it was found that members could not adequately describe the process of care, and they decided to add new members to the team to capture more process data. The team's interactive process of continuously improving care does not stop; the team simply moves on to other opportunities as it identifies them in its study of the care delivered. Success is always work in progress.

DISCUSSION and CONCLUSION

Facilitating direct patient care teams is an adventure in growth. It is often slow, often painful, often with setbacks, but always tremendously rewarding. The task of the facilitator is to move the ubiquitous tension present in health care today toward peaceful, productive, and creative resolution. The facilitator moves the team toward growth by taking the opportunity to create mental models—viable alternatives to the current structure of health care as the team encounters difficulties with the current system. Through active facilitation, clinicians begin to realize that thought processes are only a small part of care. Both clinicians and nonclinicians realize that their activities relate significantly to the care of the patient. They also realize that very little is known about how care is delivered. The team usually recognizes that the more common failure in health care is not a failure of the diagnostic process, but a failure of the complex series of actions that are required to deliver care (therapeutic treatment), which result from and relate to the diagnostic process. FOCUS-PDCA provides a way to address systems failures. As the team discovers its system and creates new solutions to age-old problems in a journey through FOCUS-PDCA, the facilitator creates a new wealth of skills and builds social supports for the team. Finally, the facilitator helps the team learn to depend on its own resources to improve the processes in which the team works daily. In doing so, the facilitator helps the team create its own future.

REFERENCES

1. Personal communication between author and PB Batalden. MD, Vice-President for Medical Care. HCA Resource Group, Nashville, TN, January, 1991.
2. McEachern JE: Understanding of quality management processes. In Melum M. Sinioris M (eds): *Pioneers in Health Care Quality.* Chicago: American Hospital Association, in press (1992).

3. McEachern JE. Halum A. Schiff L: The C-section experience. *J Occup Med* 33:372-373, 1991.
4. Neave HR: *The Deming Dimension*. Knoxville, TN: SPC Press, Inc. 1990.
5. McEachern JE. Neuhauser D: The continuous improvement of quality at the Hospital Corporation of America. *Health Matrix* 7:5-11, 1988.
6. Sholtes PM: *The Team Handbook*. Madison, WI: Joiner and Associates, 1988.

5

DATA MANAGEMENT for TOTAL QUALITY

A. F. Al-Assaf, MD, MPH

Total Quality (TQ) is an amalgam of many management philosophies presented with a unique list of principles that are primarily customer oriented. Customers may be internal or external. Internal customers are the organization's employees. External customers include all individuals and agencies an organization deals with in conducting its regular activities. Of course, the most important external customer in a healthcare organization is the patient. Physicians can be classified as either internal or external customers, depending on the type of organization. Customer satisfaction includes not only reacting to and addressing a complaint, but also methodically researching the origin of a problem, as well as its magnitude and impact. Therefore, TQ seeks an aggressive, proactive customer-oriented approach to the identification and solution of a problem.

Two approaches can be used to evaluate the service provided by an organization to its customers—the qualitative approach and the quantitative approach. The qualitative approach can be used to satisfy the internal evaluation process. This approach focuses primarily on the "do it right the first time" processes. The quantitative approach is best for evaluating external processes, those that determine the extent of customer satisfaction. This approach includes collecting and analyzing data on the nature and scope of the problems or potential problems facing the customers. Data on needs and expectations, as well as number of occurrences and level of customer dissatisfaction, should be collected and divided into categories for analysis.

This chapter will present two main issues in data management for TQ. The first is the concept of transforming data to information. The second is data collection, display, and analysis. In each of these areas, several tools and methods will be presented and illustrated.

TRANSFORMATION of DATA to INFORMATION

Data versus Information

The definition of data can be stated as all the raw numbers, figures, and individual responses collected from a sample or a population. Data are unprocessed facts and alone are meaningless and worthless. Information, on the other hand, is meaningful, interpreted, or processed data. Whenever one set of data is analyzed and used in specific relationship with another data set, the end product is information. For example, the number 18 is without a meaning by itself, but it becomes meaningful if it relates to the number of diagnosis coding errors per month in a hospital. Therefore, only information and not data can be used to answer a question or make a judgment on a hypothesis.

Processed data can be either discrete or continuous. Each is explained as follows:

- *Discrete Data:* Facts that are determined by responses such as yes or no, female or male, success or failure, etc. For example, the number of coding errors, the number of personnel in the information systems department, the number of discharges from a hospital per month, etc.
- *Continuous Data:* Facts that are variable in quantity and can be explained by answering questions such as how old, how tall, how much, etc. For example, the average length of stay in a hospital, the cost of nursing services for a patient, the response time to an emergency call, etc.

Data Reliability

According to Longo and Bohr (1991), the reliability of a measure is the extent to which it is reproducible. This means that if a measure is applied repeatedly (even by a different analyst), it will produce the same results over and over again. A tape measure is a reliable measure of the length of a sofa. Similarly, the number of medication errors is a reliable measure because the same measure can be used by another analyst at any other time to obtain the same result, given the same definition for medication error. The reliability of a measure is important to ensure the collection of accurate data. Accurate and reliable data are dependent on the level of training and expertise of the data collector and data processor. Incorrect or missing entries in a data set may render that set of data unreliable; thus, any judgment based on this data set may be inaccurate and not representative of the true facts.

Data Validity

To ensure the accuracy of the data collected, one must not depend only on the reliability of a measure. The validity of the measure is equally important. Validity considers whether one measured what one really meant to measure. In our earlier example, using the measuring tape to measure the length of the sofa is valid because the result indicates the desired information. Measuring medication errors in a hospital is valid if the result answers the question: did a number of medication errors occur. This same measure may not be valid if our intent is to measure the quality of services rendered. After all, to what extent does the occurrence or absence of medication errors indicate that an unexpected adverse condition did or did not occur? To access the accuracy of a measure one must know the predictive value of the measure. This can be further understood by explaining the concepts of sensitivity and specificity.

Sensitivity and Specificity

The accuracy of a measure or a test is determined by the calculation of its sensitivity and its specificity. Sensitivity is the proportion of times that the measure or the test is positive when the adverse condition or the disease is present. Specificity is the proportion of times that the measure or test is negative when the adverse condition or the disease is absent. This is to say that the accuracy of a test or a measure is dependent on the number of occurrences of false positives and false negatives. The number of false positives and/or false negatives should be very low for the task to be considered accurate. To illustrate these points, let's examine the following table designed to measure the accuracy of a test to detect the presence of a disease in a population.

Using the principles in Table 5-1, the measure in our earlier example (the number of medication errors) can be related to the quality of care as follows in Table 5-2. We can then conclude that the number of medication errors as a measure did predict 10 *true* adverse conditions out of a total of 17 adverse conditions detected, i.e., a predictive value of 59%.

From the above, it is obvious that for the data collected to be transformed to information, they must be defined in detail and their measures must be accurate. The accuracy of a measure is dependent on whether it is reproducible (reliable), whether it measures what we want it to measure (valid), and whether it predicts true occurrences of what we want it to measure (predictive value).

Table 5-1.   Measuring Test Validity.

Test	Disease		
	Present	Absent	Total
Positive	a	b	a + b
Negative	c	d	c + d
Total	**a + c**	**b + d**	**a + b + c + d**

a = the number of cases with disease that the test detected
b = the number of cases the test *falsely* detected as diseased
c = the number of cases with disease that the test missed
d = the number of cases the test *truly* labeled as not diseased
Sensitivity = a/(a + c)
Specificity = d/(b + d)
Predictive value = a/(a + b)

Table 5-2.   An Example of Relating a Measure to Quality of Care.

Medication Errors	Unexpected Adverse Condition		
	Yes	**No**	**Total**
Yes	10	7	17
No	2	81	83
Total	**12**	**88**	**100**

Sensitivity = 10/12 = 0.83
Specificity = 81/88 = 0.92
Predictive value = 10/17 = 0.59

DATA COLLECTION, DISPLAY, and ANALYSIS

One of the main principles of TQ is statistical thinking (Deming, 1986). Using statistical methods in data collection and analysis increases the credibility and accuracy of the information obtained. Statistics is a science based on quantitative measures of data and their elements. It is therefore not surprising to find that TQ emphasizes the use of statistics to interpret data accurately and produce meaningful information in order to understand, improve, and monitor processes in an organization.

This section will introduce several tools and techniques used in TQ in the quest for continuous process improvement. Leebov and Ersoz (1991) suggest several quantitative and qualitative tools for use in TQ. These tools can be divided into two categories based on their usual cited use:

Tools for Identifying, Collecting, and Displaying Data

- Surveys
- Brainstorming
- Brainwriting
- Logs
- Check Sheets
- Pie Charts
- Scatter Diagram
- Histograms

Tools for Improving and Monitoring Quality

- Nominal Group Technique
- Multiple Voting Technique
- Weighted Voting Technique
- Rank Ordering Technique
- Balance Sheets
- Trend and Run Charts
- Flowcharts
- Pareto Diagram
- Control Charts
- Cause-and-Effect Diagram
- Decision-making Matrices

Tools for Identifying, Collecting, and Displaying Data

It is imperative to understand that the process of collecting data is preceded by several steps. The objective of collecting data is to obtain adequate, comprehensive, accurate, and representative data elements. Thus, data collection processes should be preceded by the identification and listing of all the limitations and biases that the data might encounter during the collection process or the analysis phase. One must also consider the different internal and external sources of data. Caution should always be applied when collecting and interpreting data from different sources. Data collection sources may be heavily biased from one source to another. Also, the list of data sources should be exhaustive and every effort should be made to ensure that data are collected from all actual and potential sources. If, however, exploring all sources of data is not feasible due to certain barriers (for example, resources, logistics, etc.), then a statement to this fact should be provided with the report on data collection and analysis. Therefore, data collection barriers should be identified early and attempts should be made to overcome these barriers. Accurate and useful information depends heavily on the comprehensiveness, validity, and applicability of the data collected.

127

Surveys

One of the most widely used techniques to collect data is the survey. Using a survey to collect data from a target population is considered a simple and fairly accurate measure of the target population. There are, however, several questions that must be asked when conducting a survey to ensure adequate and true representation of the population under study. These questions may include: What is our objective(s)? Is there a need to select a sample of the population? Which method should be used in surveying the population? What questions should be asked?

Each of these four major issues concerning survey techniques will be explained next.

Objective(s)

Each survey must have an objective or a set of objectives that it is to achieve. The objective(s) has to be realistic, measurable, and applicable to the target population. For example, the objective of our survey could be to determine the percentage of patients discharged from our hospital in a specific year that have used our "hot line on patient education" during the three months following their discharge. Objectives are excellent measurement items and are useful in the evaluation of surveys before, during, and after data collection.

Sample

The population sample is defined according to the type and size of the target population. First, we must define and identify the target population. The next step is to determine if this population is accessible, if there is already existing data on it, and if the size is too large (if so, a smaller sample of the population should be selected), based on resources available and logistics. Calculating sample size is discussed below.

If we decide to survey the total target population, as in our earlier example (all the patients discharged from our hospital during a specific calendar year), then this type of sample is called a *census* sample. This is obviously the least biased sample. If, on the other hand, we decide to survey a smaller number of individuals in a population, then we would need to determine two major elements: sampling method and sample size.

Sampling Method

Sampling methods will select either a probability or a nonprobability sample of the population. A probability sample can be a simple random sample, a stratified random sample, or a systematic sample. A nonprobability sample can be a convenience sample, a purposive sample, or a quota sample. The following is a brief explanation of each of these sampling methods:

- *Simple random sampling* is a process in which the required sample size is selected at random from the total population under study by randomly generated number tables, random-number-generating computer programs, or a lottery. This type of sampling methodology produces a simple but unbiased sample.
- *Stratified random sampling* requires the determination of a sample based on one or a set of categories, usually demographics. In our earlier example, we could select a random sample from the population by specific age, income level, or other specific categories.
- *Systematic sampling* utilizes generating one random number and then selecting a constant interval. Thereafter, every case that falls at that interval will be selected. For example, if our random number was nine and the constant interval was six, we would then select the ninth patient discharged and then every sixth patient discharged thereafter, i.e., 15th, 21st, 27th, etc. Here, of course, we are assuming that those patients were not discharged using any systematic interval.

The other type of sampling method is nonprobability sampling. Three different sampling techniques that use this method are discussed below. For the following nonprobability sampling techniques, we must keep in mind that samples of these categories may not be representative of the target population. Therefore, inferences should be strictly related to the sample of the study, while projections on the total population from sample studies alone' should be accepted with the caution of potential nonrepresentation.

- *Convenience sampling* is performed to select readily available data. For example, we could select those patients discharged from the surgery unit during the month of March in a given year. This method is considered to be the weakest to withstand the test of sample representation of the population or bias.
- *Purposive sampling* is a technique used to select a sample for a specific purpose. For example, following a 30-day probationary period to re-accredit a hospital, the accrediting agency would only consider the activities of the hospital during the probationary period.
- *Quota sampling* is usually chosen to select a sample based on an arbitrary quota. For example, we select only 5% of the target population to be included in our sample.

Sample Size

Calculating the sample size is the second element of sampling. To determine sample size, one would require the availability of several preliminary data elements. One method of determining sample size uses the following equation:

$$N = (z/e)^2 p(1 - p)$$

where N is the sample size, z is the level of confidence determined by the z-score, e is the error rate, and p is the proportion of the target population in the total.

The following example might be helpful in understanding the above equation. Let's say that we want to survey private hospitals in the U.S. regarding TQ in their facilities. We find out the total number of U.S. hospitals (6815), of which (according to the current American Hospital Association Directory) only 4696 are private (nongovernment) hospitals. We also want to obtain a sample that is adequate, with a 90% confidence level and an error rate of not more than 5%. Using the above formula, we find that the z-score (from the standard z-score table) at the 90% confidence level is equal to 1.645. Also, we calculate p, the proportion of cases (private hospitals) in the total population (U.S. hospitals), which equals 0.6891 (4696/6815). Therefore, substituting for the symbols in the formula above, we find:

$$N = (1.645/0.050)^2 (0.689) (1 - 0.689) = 232$$

Survey Methodology

Once we have determined the sample size and selected a sampling technique, the individual members of the sample can be identified. To proceed, we must determine the method by which to survey the sample population. Selection of the method is dependent on the availability of resources (human and physical), time, accuracy, bias, and convenience.

There are at least three means of surveying a population: through the mail, by telephone, or through an interview. All require a predetermined and pretested questionnaire. Appendix A at the end of this chapter contains a sample questionnaire used in a recent study on TQ in Veterans Administration medical centers.

A mail survey will be able to reach a larger number of individuals with the least amount of expenditure and human resources. This method also provides honest (especially if the respondent's identity is anonymous) and the least biased answers. However, the major problem with this type of survey is the response rate, which, if low, renders the responses nonrepresentative of the total population. Of course, misinterpretation of the questions or not completing all of the questions may cause a problem in accurately analyzing the results. Mail surveys also require at least three to four weeks to complete and analyze.

A telephone survey is very accurate, but answers could be biased in response to leading questions. Because the human element is involved in collecting the data over the phone, specific training and coaching are required to record and extract data accurately from the respondents. This method has the advantage of receiving a potential 100% response rate and can be completed within a relatively short time period, especially if responses are collected electronically.

The face-to-face interview is the most accurate method, but again could be biased because the identity of the respondent, albeit protected, is not anonymous. Again, data collectors (interviewers) should be adequately trained in interviewing techniques and should be instructed to avoid leading questions in order to minimize the bias of responses. Interview surveys usually enjoy a much higher response rate than other types of surveys, but are considered the most expensive and most inconvenient type of survey due to scheduling problems and potential unavailability of respondents.

Implementation

It must be noted here that the integrity of the data collected through any of the above three types of survey methods depends on the content and the quality of the questionnaire. A questionnaire should be designed to provide information that can adequately answer the objective(s) of the survey. Each question included should be composed and designed relative to the sample population. Therefore, questions must be clear and simple to understand and should require a minimum of effort (and time) from the respondents to answer. It is suggested that closed-ended questions are easier to answer and certainly easier to analyze. For questions where the opinion of the respondents need to be captured and quantified, the questions may be designed in the form of a statement. Each statement is followed by a choice of several possible answers (on a numeric scale), based on the level of agreement or disagreement with that statement (see Appendix A for a sample of such a question). Once the questionnaire is designed and the questions are constructed, one must proceed to administer the questionnaire to a small number of individuals who share the characteristics of the sample population. This process is called pretesting, and it mimics the survey in terms of survey process and methodology. This process is important because it gives the analyst the ability to predict the behavior of the sample population. It also provides the analyst with feedback regarding the design, quality, and efficiency of the survey instrument to collect the desired data. Pretesting the questionnaire will provide the researcher the chance to modify the questions for clarity, making them simpler to understand and easier to answer. Data captured from the questionnaire are further analyzed using specific statistical techniques, e.g., descriptive statistics, correlations, difference tests, etc. The reader is encouraged to read more about these techniques in a statistics textbook.

Brainstorming

Although brainstorming is listed here under tools for identifying, collecting, and displaying data, it is a quick, simple, and very useful tool that is equally important in making quality improvement decisions. This technique is usually group oriented, whereby a group of individuals meet to generate an exhaustive list of ideas regarding an area or a topic at hand. It is a process that stimulates and encourages creative independent thinking. This is facilitated by one of the rules of brainstorming—any individual is allowed to list any idea he or she chooses without being criticized for it. The generated list can be used to either answer a question or trigger other questions in problem identification and solving. The purpose of brainstorming is to generate the information needed to proceed to other steps in the quality improvement process. This technique becomes especially useful when all members of the group participate and no boundaries of thought are adopted. The following is a description of the brainstorming technique:

- Members of a group are gathered to discuss an issue, e.g., the causes of long patient waiting time in the emergency department. After a few minutes of silence to think about the issue, a group facilitator is selected and is asked to record the list of all the ideas generated by the group on a board or a flip chart that can be seen easily by everyone in the group. Each member is then given a turn to voice any of his/her ideas on the issue. This is done by using either a freewheeling technique (anyone can call out an idea) or a round-robin technique. The facilitator lists these ideas with no discussion, judgment, or criticism. Brainstorming sessions should move quickly; therefore each member is given only a short time (15 seconds) to voice his or her ideas. Each idea is recorded in the words of the person who generated it. Group members can expand on ideas that were generated by others. Several rounds of soliciting ideas from the group members occur, until all members have exhausted all their ideas or until an agreed upon time limit is reached. Sessions usually last for about 15 minutes or less.
- The next phase is to examine the generated list, and discussion is encouraged to clarify each idea and its objective. All members can ask questions about any or all the ideas in order to reach a level of common understanding of the true meaning of each idea.

- Once these ideas are further clarified, then the entire list is evaluated, and those ideas that are similar are consolidated. In this step the list of ideas is revised and duplication is eliminated. Ideas can be sorted into related themes or subtopics. The final list is adopted by the group and is used for the purpose it was originally intended to serve.

Brainwriting

This technique is similar to brainstorming, where members of a group gather to generate a list of ideas on a topic. Unlike brainstorming, however, the ideas generated are evaluated and used aggressively by other members of the group to expand their own lists of ideas. In brainwriting, each group member is asked to write his/her list of ideas on a piece of paper. All the papers are then placed in the center of the table or the room for all the members to view and use to either add to or modify ideas on their own lists. Another method is where each member is given 20 to 30 minutes to generate ideas and record them on various flip charts that are then posted around the room. Each member is asked to read the ideas recorded by the others and then go back to their own sheets to list additional ideas that were stimulated by those of the others in the group. The advantage of brainwriting over brainstorming occurs in situations where a few members of the group dominate the idea-generating process. It also provides all members an equal opportunity to participate and eliminates ideas that are not well thought-out. Brainwriting can have the same uses as brainstorming in collecting and displaying data, as well as in quality improvement efforts.

Logs

This tool is both simple to construct and easy to use. It is used to keep track of a sequence of events or the period of time during which certain data occurred in order to chart trends or frequency analyses. Logs are constructed by identifying the data to be captured, as well as other associated elements. For example, one may want to keep a log of all the medical charts reviewed by date, by time, and by finding. Figure 5-1 is a sample of such a log sheet. It is important to keep in mind that logs should be designed to be simple and user-friendly. Logs are usually drawn as rows and columns with a summary of the statistics at the bottom. Recorders should be given a brief orientation session on using the logs. They should be encouraged to record only the raw data requested and discouraged from trying to identify or elicit a trend in the data.

Medical Record #	Reviewer	Date	Time	Finding(s)

Figure 5-1.   An example of a log.

Check Sheets

To answer the questions "What do you want to know?" and "What is the most reliable way to collect the data?," we must construct a check sheet. Check sheets can be prepared in the form of either a table or a diagram. When an observation or event occurs, the recorder makes a check mark or enters the appropriate data across from the item on the sheet. Figure 5-2 illustrates an event entered on a check sheet.

Check sheets are useful to collect data that answer questions regarding resource allocation, to analyze a current problem, or to identify potential problem areas.

Pie Charts

Pie charts are useful tools to provide an efficient and powerful presentation of data. The pie chart is a form of graphic representation of data elements that are part of a whole. Figure 5-3 shows an example of a pie chart displaying the percentages of ethnic minorities in a patient population. This tool is helpful in visualizing the differences between the parts compared to the whole. Pie charts can be used in place of bar graphs. However, several rules must be followed when constructing a pie chart:

- The segments of the pie chart must add up to 100% of the whole.
- The number of segments in a pie chart should not exceed more than six, so as to avoid a cluttered appearance.
- Each segment should indicate the percentage of the whole in order to facilitate comparisons.
- If one or more categories have a value of zero, then a pie chart should not be used.

134

Days	8–11	11–2p	2–5	5–8	8–11	11–2a	2–5	5–8	Total
Monday Tuesday Wednesday Thursday Friday Saturday Sunday									
Total									

Figure 5-2. An example of a check sheet for the number of emergency department patients per shift.

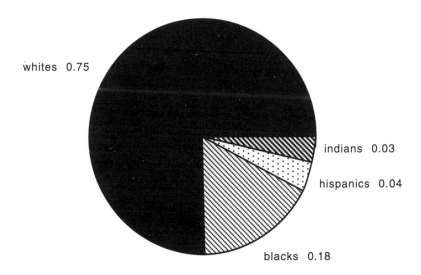

whites 0.75

indians 0.03

hispanics 0.04

blacks 0.18

Figure 5-3. An example of a pie chart, showing the percentage of patients by ethnicity.

Scatter Diagram

This technique is useful in displaying data obtained from two variables that may relate to (but not necessarily have an impact on) each other. The data collected from the two variables are plotted on a graph, with one variable on the *x*-axis and the other on the *y*-axis. If a pattern is detected, then a positive or a negative relationship may be concluded. This technique is considered the easiest way of recording correlation analysis without actually quantifying the strength or the significance of the relation between the variables. It is, however, simple to construct and is useful in showing data patterns and providing support data to construct a cause-and-effect diagram (described later in this chapter). Figure 5-4 shows an example of a scatter diagram between paired data. Although scatter diagrams are sometimes used to plot pairs of discrete data (e.g., number of charts), they are most useful when plotting continuous data (e.g., patient temperature).

Histograms

This tool is a modified bar graph, where the data on the *x*-axis are continuous data, and thus the bars are adjacent to one another. Histograms are used to present a pictorial view of the data elements and to show data patterns. They are constructed primarily to display data. Figure 5-5 is an example of a histogram. The *x*-axis shows when (during which time intervals) routine outpatient visits occurred, while the *y*-axis shows the number of routine patient visits completed during each time interval.

A histogram is constructed in steps. In the above example, we collect data by constructing a table of patient visits in the outpatient department, segmented by time interval. First, we arrange the total time into equal intervals. The next step is to construct a check sheet to record each patient visit that occurred within each time interval. A histogram can then be constructed using the above information by plotting the number of patient visits on the *y*-axis and the time intervals on the *x*-axis. Each time interval represents the width of a bar, while the number of patient visits will determine the height of the bar.

Tools for Improving and Monitoring Quality

Once the data have been collected and tools are constructed to display the data, analysis begins. Several tools can be used to aid in this process. Quality improvement tools are important in decision making and in evaluating the progress and the success or failure of a decision implemented to improve a process. There are several process improvement tools, most of which are presented on the following pages.

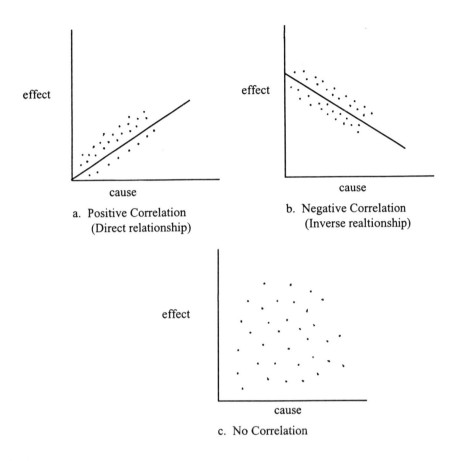

a. Positive Correlation
(Direct relationship)

b. Negative Correlation
(Inverse realtionship)

c. No Correlation

Figure 5-4.   An example of scatter diagrams.

Nominal Group Technique

This technique is a continuation of brainstorming and brainwriting. Once a list of ideas is generated, then the process of prioritizing or ranking of ideas begins. Ranking is accomplished by one of three popular methods (described below): multiple voting, weighted voting, or rank ordering. A second list is generated, with the ideas ranked accordingly, and is presented for implementation in process improvement. This technique is especially helpful in condensing the number of ideas into a shorter, more manageable list of "best" ideas.

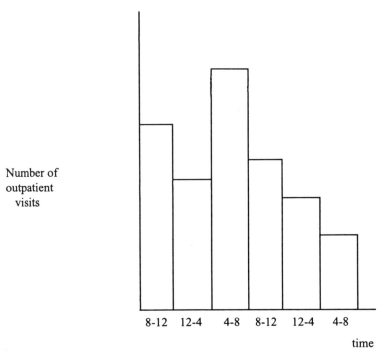

Number of
outpatient
visits

8-12   12-4   4-8   8-12   12-4   4-8

time

Figure 5-5. An example of a histogram: number of outpatient visits per day.

Multiple Voting Technique

As a complementary technique to brainstorming and brainwriting, multiple voting is another way to shorten, evaluate, critique, and rank a long list of ideas. Multiple voting is performed by the members of the group who generated the original list of ideas. The group arbitrarily chooses the number of votes each member may have. Each member then casts his/her vote on the set number of ideas. All those ideas voted on by group members are posted on a flip chart visible to all members. Discussions follow to determine which ideas received the most votes and whether these ideas are adequate to describe the group's choices. Further consideration of other ideas may be required if the group decides that more ideas are needed on the final list. The new and final list of ideas is then presented for implementation in the processes involved.

Weighted Voting Technique

This technique, similar to multiple voting, is useful in preparing a final list containing the best ideas. As with multiple voting, each member is allowed to cast his or her vote to determine whether the full list of ideas or a short list will be submitted. Each group member is allowed a set number of votes. (Usually the number of votes per group member is 1.5 times the number of ideas to be voted on). Members have the freedom to spread their votes across the ideas generated. A grid or a matrix is set up to record the voting pattern of the members and determine the total number of votes each idea receives. Figure 5-6 is an example of a weighted voting matrix.

Rank Ordering Technique

In conjunction with brainstorming and brainwriting, this technique is used to rank ideas for further consideration or implementation. Rank ordering requires working on a short list of ideas (ideally less than ten) generated by the group. Here each group member is asked to rank the shortened list of ideas (using any of the above techniques), starting with one as most important and ending with the least important idea. The recorder for the group posts the list of ideas on a flip chart and records in columns the ranking given by each member to each idea. After recording all the rankings for each idea, they are added together to obtain the total ranking score given to each idea by the group members. Because a score of one is given to the most important idea, the idea that receives the lowest score is the most important, and so on for the rest of the ideas. This is considered the most effective way of ranking, because it gives every member an opportunity to vote, and the final ranking order is clearly a collective effort of all involved.

Balance Sheets or Force-Field Diagrams

This technique is used to help a group of individuals select a shortened list of ideas, options, decisions, etc. All the ideas under consideration are listed on a two-column table. One column contains the positive aspects, advantages, strengths, or driving forces. The other column contains the opposite. Each idea is discussed and a listing is produced by the group members indicating the positives and negatives. After considering all the ideas on the list, the group weighs the positives against the negatives (i.e., the forces for it versus those against it) and then determines if some of the ideas should be eliminated. This technique is again very useful in selecting the best ideas for further consideration and implementation. It is therefore another important technique in the process of quality improvement.

Trend and Run Charts

A trend or run chart is a line graph used to visualize a pattern of behavior of certain data over time. It is therefore a pictorial indicator of the extent of fluctuation of performance of a data element over a period of time. Trend

	A	B	C	D
Jim	1	2	2	1
Jack	1	0	1	4
Allen	3	1	1	1
Diann	4	1	1	0
Jane	1	1	1	3
Totals	10	5	6	9

A: Mail Survey
B: Interview
C: Telephone
D: Combination of Two

Figure 5-6. An example of a weighted voting technique used by a 5-member team trying to reach consensus on which survey method to use to survey patients. Each member had six votes to distribute among four options.

charts are very useful in displaying and monitoring the behavior of data, as well as predicting future performance of the data.

Figure 5-7 is an example of a trend chart showing the number of patient complaints by month for one calendar year in a hospital. The figure shows a sharp increase in patient complaints during the last three months of the year. This information could allow the process improvement team to investigate the reasons for this sudden increase and determine whether this trend will continue over the next months. Used in this way, trend charts can play a major role in identifying the causes of problems, thus further improving the process of quality improvement.

Flowcharts

Flowcharts provide a graphic representation of a step-by-step sequence of processes and subprocesses, including events, reactions, and decisions. This tool provides a detailed list in the form of a sequenced diagram outlining all the actions and steps required for each process in an organization. It also provides a common language that can be used by teams when discussing the different elements of a process. For example, one could prepare a flowchart for any process in a hospital from patient registration

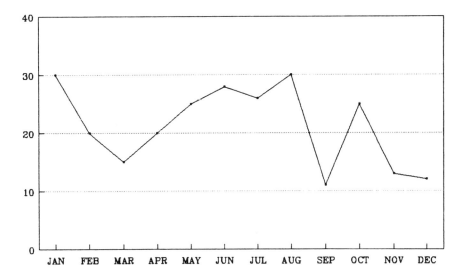

Figure 5-7.   An example of a trend chart: patient complaints by month.

to admission and discharge. Each step in the process is denoted by a symbol indicating the nature of the action or reaction. Figure 5-8 shows a flowchart for the process of a hospital outpatient visit by a patient. The symbols used in the flowchart make it easier for the examiner to identify the different types of actions or transactions that occur during the process.

Flowcharts can be one of several types: detailed (with loops of rework), top-down (only outlining the major steps in a process), or work-flow (based on the actual steps that are related to a specific work process). Team members should be collectively involved in flowcharting a process. They should start by defining the process under consideration. Next they should identify the beginning and the end of the process. The team should then start to list the steps of the process in the sequence in which they occur. Certain members of the team, or specific action teams, should be responsible for flowcharting the technical steps in the process. Once a flowchart of the process has been produced, the team should review it and then revise it (if necessary) to incorporate any missing steps or correct any errors. The final version of the flowchart is then transferred to a sheet of paper, using symbols to denote the steps of the process. It is now ready to be used by the organization. Figure 5-9 provides a list of the symbols commonly used in flowcharts.

A flowchart is an important tools for displaying a process and for understanding the steps in the process. It supports the principle that if you

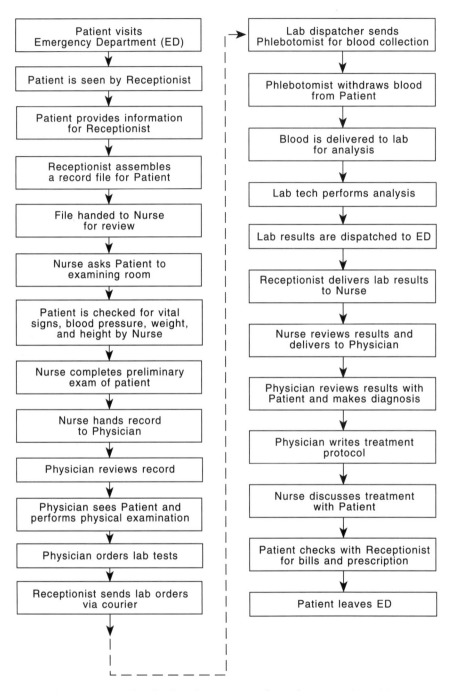

Figure 5-8. An example of a flowchart: process flow of an outpatient visit.

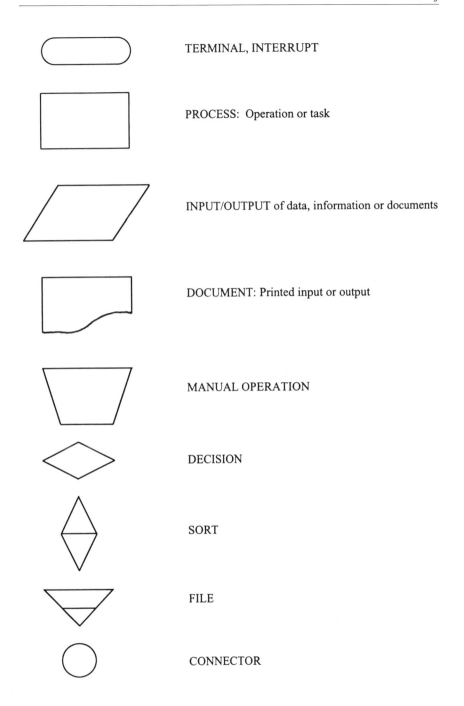

TERMINAL, INTERRUPT

PROCESS: Operation or task

INPUT/OUTPUT of data, information or documents

DOCUMENT: Printed input or output

MANUAL OPERATION

DECISION

SORT

FILE

CONNECTOR

Figure 5-9. An example of flowchart symbols.

143

understand a process and how it works, then you will be able to identify its requirements and any bottlenecks. Flowcharts are management tools that support the quality improvement efforts of an organization.

Pareto Diagram

According to Omachonu (1991), in 1897 Alfredo Pareto (an Italian economist) and in 1907 M. C. Lorenz (an American economist) developed the concept that only a small portion of the population hold most of the money. Quality expert J. Juran applied this principle to the problems of quality, dividing them into the vital few and the trivial many, i.e., most of the problems are linked to only a few causes. The procedure that classifies these problems is called Pareto Analysis.

The Pareto concept is also known as the 80–20 rule. In healthcare this can be applied by saying that 80% of documentation errors are caused by 20% of the staff. Another example is that 80% of the medication errors are caused by 20% of the nursing staff, and so on. One can further analyze data utilizing this principle with the aid of bar and line graphs. To do so, a few steps must be followed to display the data according to this principle:

1. Identify a quality problem to be studied (e.g., patient complaints about dietary services).
2. Select data collection method and conduct a data survey (e.g., mail survey).
3. Categorize the complaints cited by respondents according to type (e.g., temperature, taste, promptness of service, esthetics, etc.).
4. Calculate the frequency of complaints by category (e.g., temperature, 78 complaints; taste, 34; etc.
5. Plot the frequency of each category of complaint on a bar graph and arrange the categories in order of descending frequency, from left to right on the horizontal axis (x-axis). Two vertical axes must be designed. The left vertical axis (y-axis) is divided into equal intervals based the highest frequency (78 in our example), while the right vertical axis is divided into percentages from 0 to 100%.
6. Add the percentage values of the bars and calculate the cumulative total for each bar. Plot these totals on the same graph, but as a line graph, as shown on the left side of Figure 5-10. The right side of Figure 5-10 is the same problem replotted after improvements were implemented.

Pareto diagrams are important not only to display the causes of a quality problem, but also to provide the quality team a diagnostic and monitoring device that can be used to identify and monitor progress made after improvement measures are implemented. The importance of Pareto dia-

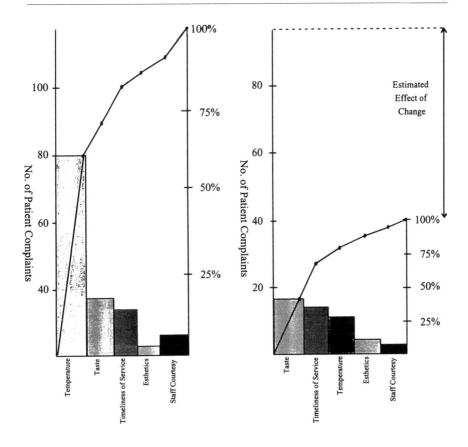

Figure 5-10.   Pareto diagrams for patient evaluation of Dietary Department, Carefree Hospital.

grams becomes evident when they are used to achieve an eventual flattening of the bars that represent frequency of problems in quality.

Control Charts

Control charts are tools designed to monitor a process over time and to study its trend and variation. They are constructed to display the stability of a process around an historical (acceptable) trend with a capability of measuring small changes in the process. A control chart provides an analysis of process behavior and indicates when certain factors had an impact on the process trend. It is a useful tool in process improvement efforts in that it identifies when a process became "out of control," i.e., outside the calculated control limits. It is therefore useful in identifying opportunities to improve a process. It is also used to determine whether process variation

145

from the norm (average) is due to special or common causes. Special causes tend to occur sporadically and acutely and therefore need to be addressed by the management team. Common causes, on the other hand, are long-term causes that are not able to destabilize a process but can slightly impact on process variation away from the norm. Common causes of process variation are the result of the interaction of several causes over time and need to be studied by appropriate quality improvement teams within an organization. Control charts are useful in controlling variation to keep it at an acceptable level.

Control charts are basically run charts with three additional horizontal lines. The average value is the line between the upper and lower control limits. A process is said to be in control if the trend lies within the upper and lower control limits around the average (Figure 5-11a). In this case, variation is due to common causes and therefore intervention by a quality team is necessary. However, if the trend falls outside these limits, then the process is considered to be out of control (Figure 5-11b). Here the causes of the process falling outside the control limits are considered to be special causes, and it is therefore management's responsibility to resolve them. There is, however, one additional element to this concept. The process is again considered to be out of control if at least three consecutive points on the process trend line fall below, or at least three consecutive points fall above, the average line, even though the process trend line is between the upper and lower control limits. Two successive points out of three must be at least two standard deviations from the mean. Special causes are also attributed to this type of trend (Figure 5-11c). A few other rules apply to the concept of process control and the reader should consult the list of references at the end of this chapter for further information. An important point that needs to be mentioned here is that control limits are not thresholds or standards. They are measures that describe the behavior or the nature of a process. Therefore, if a process is in control, it is not necessarily a good process; conversely, if a process is out of control, it is not necessarily a bad process.

To construct a control chart one needs to calculate the averages for a process or quality problem over time (for example, the number of medication errors per day per week over a five-month period). It is recommended that twenty data points be used to construct a control chart. An overall mean (average), X, is calculated, which represents the middle horizontal line on the chart. The standard deviation of the mean, S, is then calculated, using the following formula:

$$S = 1/(n-1)\{(x_1 - X)^2 + (x_2 - X)^2 + ... + (x_n - X)^2\}$$

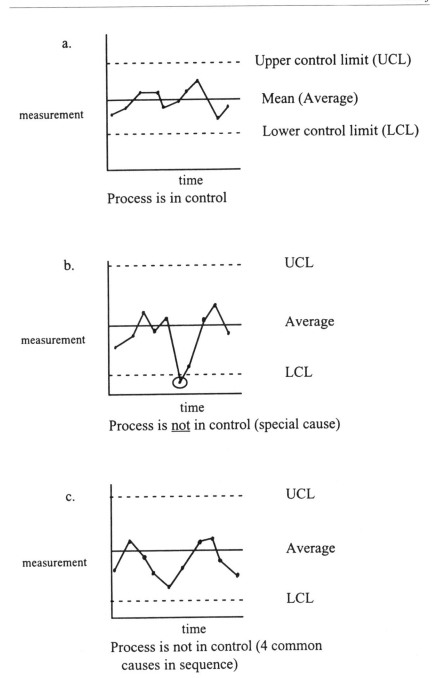

Figure 5-11. Examples of control charts.

where n is the number of observations, x_1 is the value of the first observation, x_n is the value of the nth observation, and X is the mean (average) $= (x_1 + x_2 + ... + x_n)/n$.

The upper control limit is calculated and is equal to 3 standard deviations above (plus) the mean, while the lower control limit is equal to 3 standard deviations below (minus) the mean. A line graph of the data points is plotted, with the number of weeks on the x-axis and the average number of errors per day per week on the y-axis. The graph is then examined to determine whether the trend of medication errors is in or out of control. The process is attended to accordingly, as discussed above.

It should be noted here that the control chart described is only one type, called an X bar–S bar chart. This type, however, is considered to be the most useful in analyzing healthcare data. Other less common types of control charts are available and their use and selection depends on the type of data to be analyzed. The references at the end of this chapter are selected to provide the interested reader with additional sources of information on control charts.

Cause-and-Effect Diagrams

Sometimes called the Fishbone diagram or the Ishikawa diagram, the cause-and-effect diagram is a tool useful in the identification of the causes and subcauses of a problem. A cause-and-effect diagram, as the name implies, displays the root causes of a problem situation in several related categories. Each category is further displayed in several subcategories, each of which either branches off into additional subcategories or displays a number of causes related to it. Fishbone diagrams utilize a few other quality improvement tools, such as brainstorming, surveys, etc. An example of such a diagram is shown in Figure 5-12.

Cause-and-effect diagrams are constructed by the quality improvement team in few steps. Once a problem is selected for study, its causes are listed. The list is refined to reflect realistic and trackable causes meriting further study. The list of the causes is then classified into categories (and subcategories), which are displayed on a diagram with arrows directed toward the main problem, as shown in Figure 5-12. Categories are either selected randomly by the team or are selected from a standardized list of possible causes of variation by category. A separate list of causes may be generated for each of the following categories: people, materials, machines, methods, and measurements.

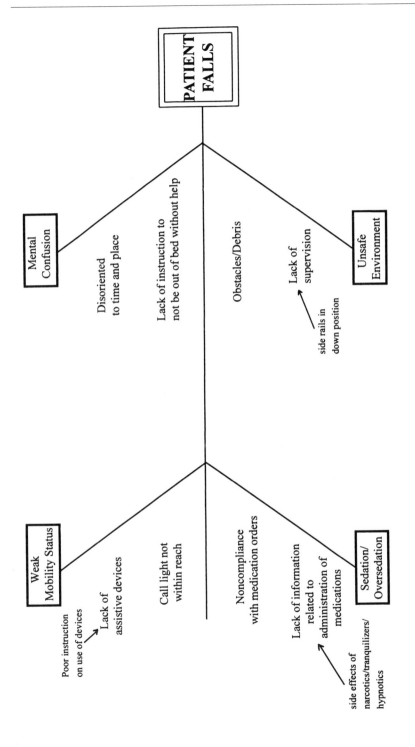

Figure 5-12.   An example of a cause-and-effect diagram for patient falls. (Figure supplied by Chris LeGrande.)

Decision-making Matrices

A matrix that can be used for decision-making is composed of a table of rows and columns. The rows display the list of possible decisions or solutions for improving a quality problem, while the columns represent the criteria for judging among these decisions. Criteria can be given different weights by the team to indicate the importance of one criterion over another. Examples of criteria are cost, politics, staff support, impact, administration, etc.

Decision matrices are very useful in making rational and democratic decisions to solve a problem or improve a process. Figure 5-13 shows an example of a decision-making matrix. The alternative decisions are listed in the left-hand column, and the evaluation or selection criteria are listed across the top row. Also note that each criterion is further weighted according to its importance and feasibility.

A decision-making matrix should be constructed by the quality improvement team in a few steps. After identifying and listing the causes of a problem (prioritized), the team will decide to study the most important solutions. Once possible solutions are selected, the team should then identify the selection or evaluation criteria for judging the solutions. This step is very important and a consensus should be reached on the list of criteria. A weight may be assigned to each criterion, denoting the importance of one over another (e.g., one may assign a weight of 3 multiplier units to cost, a weight of 2 multiplier units to impact, etc.). A scale for rating each decision is selected (e.g., 1 = low and 5 = high). Each team member is then asked to rate each decision from 1 to 5 based on the criterion. The score is placed in the cell below the criterion, as shown in Figure 5-13. However, if the criterion is weighted, then the rating is multiplied by the weight and entered in the cell. Each member adds the scores for each of his or her decisions (total of scores in each row). The totals for each decision from each member are added to arrive at a team total for each decision. Those decisions with the highest total scores are considered to be rated highly by the team and warrant further study and possible implementation.

Decision-making matrices are helpful in selecting an acceptable decision. They shift the burden of responsibility for decision-making to an interdisciplinary group of individuals and away from bureaucracies. They instill confidence and pride in team members, providing them a sense of responsibility and assuring them a role in the decision-making process of an organization.

Criteria/Weight

Alternative Solutions	Quality 3x 1=Low 10=High			Cost 3x 1=High 10=Low			Impact 2x 1=Low 10=High			Coordination 1x 1=Poor 10=Excellent			Total	Rank
	Rating	Weight 3	Subtotal	Rating	Weight 3	Subtotal	Rating	Weight 2	Subtotal	Rating	Weight 1	Subtotal		
Train Staff	10	3	30	6	3	18	10	2	20	10	1	10	78	1
Increase Staff Per Shift	5	3	15	1	3	3	5	2	10	6	1	6	34	3
Double Check Charts	3	3	9	10	3	30	8	2	16	1	1	1	56	2

Figure 5-13.   An example of a decision-making matrix: how to decrease medication errors.

CONCLUSION

This chapter presented an overview of the more common tools and techniques used by quality improvement teams to manipulate data and transform that data into meaningful information. The list of tools that can be used to meet this objective is even longer than what has been presented. I believe that these tools are the most widely used, but the reader is encouraged to seek more information on the subject. The objective of a quality improvement tool is to provide a method for managing data in order to support an organization's efforts to achieve improvement in the most rational and cost-effective method possible. According to Deming (1986), the use of statistical thinking will identify the causes of process variations and will lead to ways to reduce variation. Statistics in quality management tells us that the results of a process are not necessarily equal to the summation of all the factors composing it, but reflect the synergistic interaction of these factors with each other. Applying statistical principles to process improvement will eventually decrease waste, eliminate rework and duplication, and increase efficiency.

REFERENCES

Deming, W. E. (1986). *Out of the Crisis*, Cambridge. Mass.: Massachusetts Institute of Technology.

Finison, L. J., Finison, K. S., and Bliersbach, C. M. (1993). "The Use of Control Charts to Improve Healthcare Quality." *Journal for Healthcare Quality*, 15(1):9–23, 1993.

GOAL/QPC (1988). *Memory Jogger*, Methuen, Mass.: GOAL/QPC.

Hart, M. K. and Hart, R. F. (1989). *Quantitative Methods for Quality and Productivity Improvement*, Milwaukee: American Society for Quality Control.

Joiner Associates (1985). *The Team Handbook*, Madison, Wis.: Joiner Associates.

Leebov, W. and Ersoz, C. J. (1991). *The Health Care Manager's Guide to Continuous Quality Improvement*, Chicago: American Hospital Association.

Longo, D. R. and Bohr, D. (1991). *Quantitative Methods in Quality Management: A Guide for Practitioners,* Chicago: American Hospital Association.

Omachonu, V. K. (1991). *Total Quality and Productivity Management in Health Care Organizations,* Milwaukee: American Society for Quality Control.

Ozeki, K. and Asaka, T. (1990). *Handbook of Quality Tools*, Cambridge, Mass.: Productivity Press.

Plsek, P. E. (1992). "Introduction to Control Charts." *Quality Management in Health Care*, 1(1): 65–74.

APPENDIX A

SECTION ONE:

The following questions concern perceptions and attitudes about Quality Assurance (QA) and Total Quality Improvement (TQI). Please read each item below and circle the answer which best represents your views. Use the following scale to record your answers.

1. Strongly agree with   (SA)
2. Agree with   (A)
3. Neither agree nor disagree   (N)
4. Disagree with   (D)
5. Strongly disagree with   (SD)

	SA	A	N	D	SD
1. The QA program in my facility can identify all quality needs as they arise	1	2	3	4	5
2. The incorporation of TQI in my facility would increase the quality of care provided in the long run	1	2	3	4	5
3. If QA and TQI are separated (work out of different offices), employees will consider them as two separate quality programs	1	2	3	4	5
4. QA and TQI will compete to become the dominant quality care process in my VAMC * If agree or strongly agree, what can be done to minimize the competition: _____	1	2	3	4	5
5. There is a vital need to use outside consultants to aid the implementation of TQI in each VAMC	1	2	3	4	5
6. The TQI management process will continue to grow in the healthcare industry during the next decade	1	2	3	4	5
7. Excitement concerning TQI as the best way to provide quality in healthcare has been frustrating for QA professionals * If **agree** or **strongly agree**, please list why this is occurring: _____	1	2	3	4	5
8. QA professionals are continually reminded of QA as the "BAD" process of producing quality in healthcare	1	2	3	4	5
9. TQI philosophies currently functioning in the manufacturing industry will work in the healthcare industry	1	2	3	4	5

10. As a member of management, I am willing to provide as much time and energy as it takes to make the TQI process work   1   2   3   4   5

11. The management philosophies associated with the TQI process are aligned with my personal philosophies of management   1   2   3   4   5

12. **(QA personnel only)** As a quality assurance professional, I would like to be involved in the implementation of TQI in my VAMC   1   2   3   4   5

13. TQI is a temporary fad in the healthcare industry which will decline in popularity and use in the next 5 years   1   2   3   4   5

14. If QA and TQI are separated, there will be duplication of work produced by the two quality processes   1   2   3   4   5

15. TQI is a *quick* fix to the quality problems in the healthcare industry   1   2   3   4   5

16. QA and TQI will function more efficiently if headquartered in one centralized office   1   2   3   4   5

17. The TQI process should be implemented in all VA facilities using a standardized structure   1   2   3   4   5

18. TQI process teams should begin in nonclinical areas of the hospital   1   2   3   4   5

19. I would like to take a leading role in the implementation of TQI in my healthcare facility   1   2   3   4   5

20. TQI is a management tool which will help VA health care facilities increase the level of care given   1   2   3   4   5

21. TQI is a process which requires the leadership of the institution to constantly demonstrate commitment to quality   1   2   3   4   5

22. TQI should be included in the daily activities of management   1   2   3   4   5

23. Our management is ready to make a long-term commitment to TQI   1   2   3   4   5

24. The QA department in my facility should be responsible for TQI and its implementation   1   2   3   4   5

25. QA and TQI need to be integrated into one quality program.   1   2   3   4   5
    * If you **agree** or **strongly agree,** when should the two programs be integrated?
    [ ] During the 1st year   [ ] During the 3rd year   [ ] >4 years
    [ ] During the 2nd year   [ ] During the 4th year

26. TQI will decrease total healthcare costs   1   2   3   4   5

27. TQI will result in a reduction of FTEs   1   2   3   4   5

28. QA is complimentary to the TQI process   1   2   3   4   5

29. Management at my VAMC works well together as a team   1   2   3   4   5

SECTION TWO:

Please indicate your thoughts and perceptions concerning the following questions. This can be completed by simply indicating with a check mark, filling in of a comment(s), or circling of the number which most accurately reflects your perceptions towards the following question.

---

1. Please rank in order of importance the following areas of experience you see as important for a TQI Coordinator?
   _____ Clinical   _____ Financial   _____ Previous TQI
   _____ Quality Assurance _____ Administrative   experience
   _____ Human Resources   _____ Management   _____ Masters Degree
                                                   _____ Other

2. On a scale from 1–5 (five representing the highest level of enthusiasm), what is the level of enthusiasm for the following employees in your VAMC towards the implementation of TQI?
   _____ Upper Management   _____ Employees: Not in
   _____ Middle Management   Management Positions
   _____ Lower Management   _____ Union Representative

3. How far into the total quality improvement process is your facility?
   [ ] Not started   [ ] In place, pleased   [ ] Achieved significant
   [ ] At the beginning   with results   results
   [ ] In place, no results   [ ] In place, frustrated   [ ] Don't know/
                                                        no answer
   * If you have started the TQI process, how long has TQI process been underway?
            # of Years: _____   # of Months: _____

4. If TQI is implemented, or will be, in your facility, what is the expected amount of your administrative/management time required to steer the TQI process in the proper direction for success?
   [ ] Less than 10%   [ ] 31%–40%   [ ] 61% or greater
   [ ] 11%–20%   [ ] 41%–50%
   [ ] 20%–30%   [ ] 51%–60%

5. To date, what is the total number of days you have received in training on the philosophies and techniques associated with TQI from internal and/or external resources?
   [ ] 1 day or less   [ ] 6–7 days   [ ] 5–6 weeks
   [ ] 2–3 days   [ ] 1–2 weeks   [ ] 7–8 weeks
   [ ] 4–5 days   [ ] 3–4 weeks   [ ] Greater than 8 weeks

6. How would you rate your current level of knowledge regarding TQI philosophies and techniques:
   1 -------- 2 -------- 3 -------- 4 -------- 5 -------- 6 -------- 7 -------- 8 -------- 9 -------- 10
   poor   fair   moderate   good   excellent

155

7. From the start of TQI in your facility, what is the expected length of time you anticipate until results are seen?
   [ ] One–six months   [ ] Two–three years   [ ] Greater than six years
   [ ] Six–twelve months   [ ] Three–four years
   [ ] One–two years   [ ] Five–six years
8. What do you see/consider as barrier(s) to the implementation of the total quality improvement process into the Department of Veteran Affairs?

_____

9. Please list any additional information you believe is important concerning QA, TQI and/or any additional comments concerning this survey.

_____
_____

SECTION THREE:

Finally, we would like to know just a little about you so we can see how people of different backgrounds feel about the issues we have been examining.

AGE: [ ] Under 30   [ ] 36–40   [ ] 46–50   [ ] 56–60   [ ] Over 65
      [ ] 31–35   [ ] 41-45   [ ] 51–55   [ ] 61–65
SEX: [ ] Male   [ ] Female
Position Title   [ ] Director   [ ] QA Coordinator   [ ] Additional _____
Highest Level of   [ ] PhD   [ ] Associates Degree
Educational Attainment   [ ] Masters Degree   [ ] High School
             [ ] Bachelors Degree   [ ] Other
Please indicate the number of operational beds in your facility:
     [ ] 1–100   [ ] 251–400   [ ] 551–750   [ ] 1001–1250
     [ ] 101–250   [ ] 401–550   [ ] 751–1000   [ ] More than 1250
Please indicate the type of VA facility you are working in:
     [ ] Regional Office Center   [ ] Domiciliary
     [ ] Medical Center   [ ] Outpatient Clinic (independent)
Please indicate if your medical facility is affiliated with a university:
     [ ] Yes   [ ] No   [ ] Don't know
Please indicate the number of years you have been working in the following areas:
     _____ In a management position   _____ In present position
     _____ With the Department of Veteran Affairs   _____ Working in QA

**THANK YOU FOR TAKING THE TIME TO
COMPLETE THIS QUESTIONNAIRE!**

PART III

TOTAL QUALITY ENVIRONMENT

6

COST and HEALTHCARE QUALITY

A. F. Al-Assaf, MD, MPH

One of W. Edwards Deming's major points of quality management is not to award a contract on the basis of price alone. Both price and quality should be utilized as measures of efficiency and effectiveness. Quality has a major impact on the cost of healthcare services. Quality in healthcare means providing needed services to the customer and meeting his or her expectations with efficient utilization of resources. In the current healthcare environment, healthcare expenditures are increasing so dramatically that scarce resources are becoming even more scarce. Price competition has almost been eliminated and providers deliver healthcare services with little variation in price. Competition unrelated to price is being emphasized. The quality of services provided is a deciding factor in this competition.

Quality of service becomes a critical factor when providers can only survive by being fit and lean. Providers who survive this fierce competition will be those who deliver quality healthcare services in a cost-conscious environment. However, there is a limit to the amount of cost reduction that can be achieved without affecting the quality of care provided. Eliminating useful therapeutic methods or important diagnostic procedures may negatively affect quality. Therefore, delivering efficient care should not be at the expense of the appropriate and necessary services needed to provide quality.

An important principle of quality improvement is that if we study, analyze, and improve each process in an organization, then cost reduction will be a byproduct. Improving process control should initially focus on meeting the needs and expectations of the customer, not on cost reduction. Efficiency and cost reduction are achieved when rework, duplication, and waste are reduced and eventually eliminated. Quality is improved by instituting preventive management techniques whereby real or potential problems are identified and then solved or eliminated. Nonperformance increases our expenditure on fixing rather than improving.

The following recently published article addresses the relationship between cost and quality. In particular, it provides an analysis of the impact of improving quality on the efficiency and operating costs within a system. The authors have introduced the topic of cost and quality management very effectively. The reader is encouraged to seek additional references on this subject because it is a critical area for future discussion and research.

ACCOUNTING for the
COSTS of QUALITY

James D. Suver, FHFMA, DBA, CMA

Bruce R. Neumann, PhD

Keith E. Boles, PhD

Total Quality Management (TQM) rapidly is becoming the principal focus of senior managers in the healthcare field. TQM describes "a philosophy (and actions) of an organization that is dedicated to continuous quality improvement (CQI) throughout the organization. A hospital with total quality management, for example, will set specific quality goals, choose a number of high-priority quality improvement projects (QIPs), make quality improvement part of job descriptions throughout the organization and legitimize time spent on quality improvement, provide necessary resources (financial and otherwise), provide essential training for staff involved, and formally recognize quality improvement efforts."[1]

TQM logically may be considered an expansion of CQI, which is defined as application of "the management theory of quality to a healthcare setting. The management theory of quality is based upon principles of quality developed by W. Edwards Deming (who helped Japan improve its competitive position in the production of consumer goods, such as automobiles, after World War II) and Joseph M. Juran, a proponent of TQM in this country.

"While traditional 'quality control' theories seek out problems, assign 'fault,' and attempt to effect improvement by exhorting people to change their behavior, continuous quality improvement seeks to understand processes and revise them using data about the processes themselves. CQI sees 'problems' as opportunities for improvement. The CQI process involves a project-by-project approach to systematically improve quality, not just to maintain the status quo."[2]

Reproduced with permission from *Healthcare Financial Management,* 46(9):29–37, 1992; originally adapted from *Management Accounting for Healthcare Organizations,* 3rd edition, Chicago: HFMA and Pluribus Press, 1992.

One of the most important requirements of TQM is the total focus on the customer or client. With other management styles, organizational changes are evaluated from the perspective of the employee or the organization itself. In healthcare settings, the client usually is considered to be the focus of the process. However, many healthcare facilities are designed for the convenience of the provider. Excessive waiting times, lack of input, conflicting or missing records, piecemeal approaches to the delivery of services, and inadequate discharge planning often are functions of protection of professional domains and roles, lack of attention paid to designing comprehensive services, or perpetuation of a culture that fosters, among healthcare employees, the attitude: "It's just not my problem." TQM shifts the focus to the user of services, whether the user is the patient, another healthcare professional in the organization, or an external party.

Another essential feature of TQM is the concept of continuously seeing improvement in quality by eliminating all activities that do not add value to the process of providing quality. In a healthcare facility, non-value added activities include checking, filing, sorting, moving, copying, waiting, reworking, retesting, etc. Non-value activities are considered "waste" under TQM and are candidates for elimination.

COST of QUALITY

The standard theme of TQM is that poor quality is expensive and high quality does not have to be expensive. The challenge of TQM is to reorient employees so they think about the high cost of non-value added activities.

Improvements in quality can improve revenues or reduce costs, both of which improve the bottom line. As clients needs are better satisfied, revenues usually increase. For example, new services or revisions of existing services to better meet specific client needs often generate more revenue. Elimination of waste and non-value added activities, such as scheduling gaps or testing errors in ancillary departments, reduces costs. Similarly, producing any service without errors the first time lowers costs.

The American Society for Quality Control (ASQC) defines quality costs as: "a measure of costs specifically associated with the achievement or non-achievement of product or service quality—as defined by all product or service requirements established by the company and its contracts with customers. More specifically, quality costs are the total of the costs incurred through (a) investing in the prevention of non-conformance to requirements; (b) appraising a product or service for conformance to requirements; and (c) failure to meet requirements."[3]

A more concise definition of quality costs is: "all costs incurred to help the employee do the right job every time and the cost of determining if the output is acceptable, plus any cost incurred by the organization and the customer because the output does not meet specifications and/or customer expectations."[4]

For the management accountant, this concept must be expanded to identify the direct (visible) and indirect (hidden) costs of poor quality. In healthcare facilities, direct visible costs of poor quality include such obvious expenditures as the costs associated with unnecessary, inaccurate, or lost laboratory and x-ray tests; excessive overtime; errors in insurance billing; and the operation of the quality control department.

The indirect or hidden costs of quality in healthcare facilities include the economic consequences of such intangible factors as ineffective communication among physicians, nurses, and patients; lack of teamwork among physicians, nurses, technicians, and staff; and upset or frustrated staff members. Hidden costs also may include the financial effects of medication and prescription errors, and overdue receivables, inaccurate or missing insurance information.[5]

The costs of quality also can be separated into three major cost categories: prevention, appraisal, and failure.

Prevention Costs.   Prevention costs are incurred due to steps taken at the beginning of any process to protect against errors and defects and to incorporate quality into the service delivery process. Prevention costs are incurred before services are provided. They are prospective in nature and include costs associated with:

- Identification of clients' needs,
- Education and training of employees,
- Development of quality monitoring and reporting systems,
- Institution of quality administration, and
- Planning and design.

Although prevention costs result in additional cost outlays during the development of healthcare delivery systems, they then have a major impact on the quality of the services.

Appraisal Costs.   Appraisal costs represent the outlays associated with inspecting and evaluating the extent to which service delivery processes meet customers' requirements. Appraisal costs usually are incurred after a process has been completed, and they are retrospective in nature. Appraisal costs include:

- Quality audits, accreditation and state surveys, and licensure and certification reviews;
- Calibration and maintenance of equipment;

- Inspection and testing of purchased items;
- Documentation of services or processes; and
- Inspection or evaluation of services or process.

Any medical record, billing, or professional review organization (PRO) audit of patient services represents an appraisal cost. Flow charting and industrial engineering reviews of processes or services also constitute appraisal costs.

Failure Costs. Failure costs may be subdivided into the costs of internal failures and the costs of external failures. Internal failure costs are associated with correcting or replacing defective products or services before they reach the patient. Internal failures typically occur during the service delivery process and represent costs that could have been avoided. They include:

- Waste of any kind (e.g., use of unnecessary tests or supplies),
- Investigation of defective tests or other errors,
- Unnecessary repetition of activities,
- Idle time or any other wasted time, and
- Reinspection and correction.

Internal failure costs are difficult to identify. Most are buried in administrative overhead and in the labor costs of provider departments; most, such as the costs of labor associated with wasted time, are rarely identified separately in financial reports.

The costs of external failures are identified after defective services have been delivered to clients. They are generally discovered by the patient. The resulting cost of correcting the error or minimizing the negative feelings to prevent a loss of revenue in the future can be substantial. Typical external failure costs include those for:

- Responding to patient complaints,
- Insuring against liability or exposure to malpractice risk,
- Loss of client goodwill or referrals, and
- Lost revenue due to word-of-mouth complaints.

These last two categories may result in the most significant of any quality costs in terms of their long-term effects on the patent's perception of the quality of services provided and the provider's ability to sustain itself in a competitive market. Unfortunately, these lost opportunities represent costs that usually are not included in financial reports or in the estimated costs of quality noted above.

Prevention and appraisal costs are inversely related to failure costs; the more preventive or appraisal costs an institution bears, the fewer failure costs it will incur. However, in many organizations, the costs of failure far exceed the other costs of quality. One estimate puts the costs of external failure at 30 percent, the costs of internal failure at 45 percent, and the costs of prevention at 5 percent.[6]

It should be stressed that prevention costs reduce appraisal costs; the more steps taken to reduce the potential for failure (e.g., improving design, intensifying employee education) the less need there is for appraisal costs. At some level of appraisal costs, it is impossible to achieve further quality improvements without increasing prevention costs by enhancing design and other planning efforts.

Prevention and appraisal costs fall into the category of control costs. However, appraisal costs also fall into the non-value added category and should be eliminated whenever possible.[7]

TQM encourages institutions to expend more in prevention costs than appraisal costs to prevent failures. Prevention activities reduce or eliminate appraisal and failure costs and should reduce the total cost of quality. Ideally, the objective of any healthcare provider should be to reduce the total cost of quality by improving the processes of service delivery through expanded planning efforts.

The importance of determining the costs of quality should not be underestimated. For the management accountant, determining the best estimates of these costs and reporting them in a meaningful fashion is crucial to the successful implementation of TQM.

CALCULATING QUALITY COSTS

Several methods are available for calculating the costs of quality for a healthcare provider. For example, Exhibit 1 presents a cost of quality worksheet that tracks prevention appraisal, and failure costs.[8] Some of the data needed to complete this worksheet can be obtained from activity reports or graphs, some can be obtained from accounting records, and some must be estimated on the basis of observation, patient surveys, and intuition.

A key factor in the assessment of the costs of quality is determining the time spent in various activities. Because these time measurements may not be readily available, the development of a formal process for identifying the time involved in various activities will facilitate the TQM process and lead to quality improvements.[9] For example, process flow charts may be used to develop estimates of non-value added time or waste time.

Actual calculation of the costs of quality (see Exhibit 2) involves several operations. First, the specific activity associated with a type of quality cost, the time required to perform the activity, the frequency with which the activity is performed, and the members of the staff who perform the activity must be determined. Second, the total number of hours performing the

Department: _____ **Date:** _____

Internal failure costs

Description (1)	No. Hours per month (2)	$ Rate per hour (3)	$ Labor per month (4) (2) × (3)	$ Supply per month (5)	$ Other expenses per month (6)	$ Quality cost per month (7) (4) + (5) + (6)	$ Quality cost per year (8) (7) × 12
Total							

Exhibit failure costs

Description (1)	No. Hours per month (2)	$ Rate per hour (3)	$ Labor per month (4) (2) × (3)	$ Supply per month (5)	$ Other expenses per month (6)	$ Quality cost per month (7) (4) + (5) + (6)	$ Quality cost per year (8) (7) × 12
Total							

Prevention costs

Description (1)	No. Hours per month (2)	$ Rate per hour (3)	$ Labor per month (4) (2) × (3)	$ Supply per month (5)	$ Other expenses per month (6)	$ Quality cost per month (7) (4) + (5) + (6)	$ Quality cost per year (8) (7) × 12
Total							

Appraisal costs

Description (1)	No. Hours per month (2)	$ Rate per hour (3)	$ Labor per month (4) (2) × (3)	$ Supply per month (5)	$ Other expenses per month (6)	$ Quality cost per month (7) (4) + (5) + (6)	$ Quality cost per year (8) (7) × 12
Total							

Exhibit 1.   Cost of quality worksheet.
Source: Robin D. Daigh, "Financial Implications of a Quality Improvement Process," *Topics in Health Care Financing,* Vol. 17(3) 1991, p. 47–48.

Type	Description	Estimated volume	Annual volume	Position type	Minutes per occurrence	Annual hours	Average wage rate	Salary expense	Benefits (20 percent)	Estimated cost of quality
Prevention	Train technicians on equipment	8 hours per year × 20 technicians	160	Diagnostic imaging technician	—	160	$12.75	$2,040	$408	$2,448
Appraisal	Check registration for proper information	100 percent of 50,000 inpatient and outpatient visits	50,000	Diagnostic imaging technician	1	833	12.75	10,621	2,124	12,744
Internal failure	Locate master jacket not in file room	22.5 per day × 365 days	8,213	Diagnostic imaging file clerk	22.5	3,080	7.05	21,714	4,343	26,057
External failure	Retake film	4 percent of 70,000 exams	2,800	Film plus labor cost	—	—	10.00[a]	28,000	—	28,000

[a] Estimated cost of labor and materials for retaking an exam, per industry figures provided by imaging department director.

Exhibit 2. Sample cost of quality calculation.
Source: Anderson, Craig A. and Robin D. Daigh, "Quality Mind-set Overcomes Barriers to Success," *Healthcare Financial Management*, Feb. 1991, p. 31.

activity per year (annual hours) is multiplied by the employee's hourly wage to yield the total annual salary expended for the activity. Third, the annual salary expenditure is multiplied by a factor of 20 percent to incorporate employee benefits.[10]

Cost Drivers. TQM requires the identification of "cost drivers," or the specific activities that cause cost to be incurred. These activities are characterized by the complexity of the service that is performed and the environment in which it is provided. Complexity includes the type of equipment used, the number of setups required, the number of reworks performed, and the number of bad outputs produced. The environment includes the number of vendors, number of direct and indirect staff members, and the number of material moves and schedule changes.

In most cases, the number of transactions adds to the cost of providing a service. Many transactions involve non-value added activities such as movement from one area to another, waiting time caused by inefficient scheduling, copying and filing time, etc. Proper identification of cost drivers and other contribution to cost expansion increases the likelihood that nonvalue added activities will be eliminated.

STANDARD COST SYSTEMS

The introduction of standard cost systems in healthcare organizations has been facilitated by management's desire to know the cost of a specific product line or service. This has resulted in the identification of cost elements such as labor, material, and overhead. As the standard cost systems have become more complex, overhead has been segregated into two categories:

- Direct overhead that can be traced to specific products, and
- Indirect overhead that includes general and administrative expenses.

The direct and indirect overhead costs must be allocated to specific services or product lines in order to obtain the full cost of a service.

Since direct labor costs are routinely collected by service or product line in many systems, direct labor hours have been used as the allocation activity. However, direct labor hours are not the primary contributor to overhead costs; because overhead has been misapplied, the costing of services has been erroneous. For example, in a pharmacy, the number of prescriptions filled may be a more valid indicator of the activities that incur costs (i.e., cost drivers) than the labor hours of the pharmacy staff. In a like manner, the number of meals served may be an appropriate cost driver for cafeteria costs.

In selecting activity measures, many healthcare providers rely on macro measures such as diagnosis-related groups (DRGs), charges, visits, treatments, and tests. However, macro measures do not adequately reflect the intensity of services delivered. Micro measures such as relative value units, person minutes, and intensity of care or activity level, allow for more precise identification of cost drivers.

Activity-based costing systems for allocating overhead have merged labor and overhead into a category called conversion costs which are then allocated by cost drivers. An advantage of this approach is a reduction in the amount of information collected and a reduction in collection costs, both of which are goals of TQM.

VARIANCE ANALYSIS

The use of a standard costing system also has facilitated the use of variance analysis. Variance analysis is the determination of the difference between standard and actual costs and the fixing of responsibility for the difference by calculating spending, wage, and efficiency variances. Under TQM, the use of standards for performance measurement can result in dysfunctional behavior. For example, lower per-unit costs result from long production runs (batching all similar procedures to run at the same time) and reduces the cost of each procedure. However, long production runs result in increased patient waiting time, delays in delivering test results to physicians, and other non-value added activity costs.

Basing performance measurement on the achievement of a standard also may result in a relaxation of performance by managers and employees once the standard is reached. This is the antithesis of the TQM approach, which emphasizes the continuing pursuit of increasing quality. For example, strict reliance on nurse staffing patterns based on estimated acuity levels and standard hours can be dysfunctional in a CQI environment. When the standard hours are accepted as appropriate in terms of the quality and cost of care, the motivation to reduce them is lessened. TQM requires a continuous evaluation of standards and seeks ways of reducing non-value added activities included in standards.

REPORTING QUALITY COSTS

In many organizations, the costs of quality are not reported in financial statements because the information is not readily available in accounting systems. In particular, the hidden costs of lost customers show up only indirectly in reduced revenues and profit margins, and loss of market share. This weakness in financial reporting has made it difficult to sustain the interest of some top managers in the importance of continuing to reduce the cost of quality.

Quality costs typically are not collected and reported separately under most management accounting systems. Quality costs often are viewed as a percentage of underlying expenses, labor hours, or volume of services. Reports encompassing the entire organization often are based on percentages of revenue, while departmental reports are based on expenses, labor hours, or volume measures.

Another measure used in tracking quality costs is the percentage of per-unit costs. Since per-unit costs can be distorted by volume changes or by allocations of fixed costs, this measure may not be accurate enough to form a basis for decision-making.

Special studies and special reports are often needed to identify and track quality costs. These reports should be simple and straightforward. Their purpose is to help plan improvements in quality and evaluate the effectiveness of the changes. It should be stressed that quality cost reports should not erect barriers to improvement. One TQM guru, Philip Crosby, warned: "Don't get so involved with the technique of calculating the costs of quality that you forget what it should be used for: to call attention to the problems and identify those areas needing corrective action."[11]

To summarize, TQM stresses the identification and elimination of poor quality and its related costs. Implementation of TQM is having a significant impact on the accounting information reported for management decision-making in the area of quality costs.

TOTAL COST MANAGEMENT

Total cost management is a natural outgrowth of TQM. An effective cost management system should provide the necessary information that enables managers to make better decisions. Because TQM requires continuing improvement of the processes of providing services, historical financial data can be inappropriate for making many management decisions.

Total cost management incorporates the use of both financial and non-financial indicators to support decision-making. For example, total cost management integrates management and systems and links technology, human behavior, and information systems. It matches processes to cost information, captures strategic and financial measures, reflects the costs of a product's total life cycle for comparisons with competitors, focuses on profitability and cash flow rather than cost, and shifts orientation from variable to fixed costs.[12] It requires a proactive cost accounting system instead of the typical reactive approach.

As a result, total cost management can link an institution's operating position to its strategic goals; cover all business functions and relate the cost of business to the creation of value; adapt to changing technology; support customer demands; focus on important product cost elements from procurement through distribution; coordinate human resources, technology, cost, and planning elements of business; and serve as a catalyst for organizational improvement.[14]

One of the principal goals of the changes in accounting systems to meet TQM requirements is simplification. Financial managers must be integral members of the TQM process and take the initiative in facilitating change.

REFERENCES

1. Slee V. and D. D. A. Slee, *Health Care Terms*, 2d ed., Tringa Press, St. Paul, Minn., 1991.
2. Adapted from Slee, op. cit., p. 363.
3. Hagan, J. T., *Principles of Quality Costs,* American Society for Quality Control, Milwaukee, Wisc., 1986, p. 3.
4. Harrington J. H., *Poor-Quality Costs*, American Society for Quality Control, Milwaukee, Wisc., 1987, p. 5.
5. Milkavoick, M. E., "Creating a total quality health care environment," *Healthcare Management Review*, 16(2):9–20, 1991.
6. Harrington, J. H., op. cit., p. 121.
7. Adapted from Muthler, D. L. and J. B. Simpson, "Quality costs: Facilitating the quality initiative," *Journal of Cost Management for the Manufacturing Industry*, 1(1), 1987.
8. Daigh, R. D., "Financial implications of a quality improvement process," *Topics in Health Care Financing*, 17(3):47–48, 1991.
9. Anderson, C. A. and R. D. Daigh, "Quality mind-set overcomes barriers to success," *Healthcare Financial Management*, Feb., 1991, p. 31.
10. Ibid, p. 47–48.
11. Crosby, P. B., *Quality Is Free: The Art of Making Quality Certain*, Mentor, New York, N.Y., 1979, p. 181.
12. McIlhattan, R. D., "The path to total cost management," *Journal of Cost Management for the Manufacturing Industry*, 1(2):5, 1987.
13. Ibid.

7

The LAW, ETHICS, and TOTAL QUALITY

Carol Lee Hamilton, RN, JD, MPA

Laws impact Total Quality (TQ) in two fundamental ways. First, laws create much of the external structure of TQ—through national and state public laws along with their concomitant regulations. Second, attempts to manage the quality within healthcare organizations fail despite the presence of a TQ system. When this failure occurs, a number of aggrieved parties resort to the judicial system. Patients or others who are in search of remedying the substandard quality of care will typically bring action against both the physicians involved and the institution in which the care was rendered. Likewise, when institutions attempt to sever their relationships with physicians who have not met quality standards, these physicians will often appeal to the court system, seeking restoration of full clinical privileges.

The ROLE of LAWS and the LEGAL SYSTEM

This chapter explores the role of the judicial system in shaping healthcare quality. It presents a limited scope of legal opinions that have challenged the attempts of healthcare institutions or the public, through state licensing agencies, to regulate quality. Institutions typically place restrictions on the clinical privileges of physicians and other clinicians who have limited privileges. Licensing agencies may restrict or revoke the license of the physician or clinician. In these situations it is relatively common for the health professional to attempt to regain full privileges or licensure status through the court system.

Thus, the laws and the legal system play an integral role in molding, enforcing retrospectively, and revising quality management. Laws, regulations, and a myriad of lawsuits challenging efforts to ensure quality within the healthcare system provide an external framework for the policies and procedures operating in every healthcare institution.

The ROLE of ETHICS

What about ethics—is ethics relevant to a TQ system? Because laws and regulations, as well as healthcare organization policies and procedures, can never be complete, ethics becomes the supreme ringmaster. Ethics keeps the players within the circle of standards that represent quality. While standards are written according to various laws, the true commitment to achieving and maintaining the highest possible quality of care results from having an internal code of ethics. Every manager and every clinician must carry within themselves this codification of what decisions concerning quality are morally correct. The following discussion regarding the interplay between law and ethics will help to clarify the importance of ethics in conducting TQ in all healthcare organizations.

The significant impact that legislative and judicial bodies have had in shaping today's TQ systems cannot be overemphasized. Likewise, ethical standards along with a growing regard for greater individual ethical awareness have had an impact on the practice of quality healthcare. Yet no presentation of legal and ethical issues in TQ would be complete without exploring the role that laws and ethics *should* play in the realm of quality healthcare. While attempting to understand some of the major legislative thrusts into the quality of care movement, the student of TQ must question continuously the appropriateness of "legislating quality." Similarly, the student might ponder whether it is legislative and judicial interventions or, rather, a devotion to professional ethics that is most productive over the long term in achieving TQ goals.

The INTERPLAY between LAWS and ETHICS

Laws codify standards of acceptable conduct and often represent only a minimum standard of acceptability. For example, the deliberate killing of another individual is clearly illegal and will result in being charged with murder according to applicable state criminal codes. Murder is also indisputably immoral. In contrast, ethical standards usually represent models for behavior consistent with high levels of morality. For example, it is considered ethical to come to the aid of a motor vehicle accident victim and perhaps unethical not to render assistance. However, there is no law *requiring* that a private citizen assume the role of rescuer.

The term *ethics* carries at least two meanings that are pertinent to quality of healthcare. First, as a discipline, ethics is the field of study that centers on a systematic approach to understanding morality. Perhaps of greater importance to healthcare professionals is the definition of ethics as a set of moral values. Kurt Darr (1987) proposes that healthcare professionals view ethics as "a special charge and a responsibility to self and profession, the patient, the organization and its personnel, and ultimately, but in a less direct fashion, to society." Regarding the creation and implementation of TQ systems, then, ethics can be viewed as an ethical responsibility to deliver the highest possible quality of health services.

Therefore, when considering how laws and ethics impact quality of care in health organizations, one must be cautious in making assumptions about the value of laws and ethics. Together, they contribute to the framework in which TQ is practiced. Laws that govern quality do not necessarily reflect the standards for which health professionals strive. As such, these laws alone cannot ensure that the highest possible quality is established as a bench mark.

In short, not all actions and inactions that are considered legal are tantamount to ethical actions and inactions. Consequently, it is naive to conclude that the most ethical quality standards are automatically created merely because they pass legal muster. The health professional must insist upon TQ guidelines that are legal and ethical. Likewise, the implementation of these guidelines must always be consistent with each health professional's codes of ethics—the delineated code for that given health profession and the personal code derived from one's moral fabric. Implementation must reach above the legal foundations to arrive at an ethical summit of quality of care. That is, laws establish a procedural baseline for standards of quality, but only the individual set of moral values merged into the practice of TQ will result in achieving and maintaining the substantive standards of quality sought.

LEGISLATIVE IMPETUS

"Quality is…a central concern for much that is timely in healthcare politics and law" (Furrow et al., 1987). This is so because deviations from the quality standards of care too often lead to professional and institutional negligence lawsuits. Classical malpractice lawsuits, like any tort action, have required a deviation from a standard of care. Defining exactly what that standard of care should have been in each instance is a murky task, never subject to an exact definition. As TQ has advanced, proffering more sophisticated and exacting standards of care in various treatment situations, clearer standards have been developed. Thus, ascertaining the nature and extent of deviations from the standard of care becomes a less onerous task. Additionally, some experts argue that certain reform legislation, particularly earlier efforts, have had an adverse impact on the quality of care, e.g., Medicare cost saving measures that resulted in premature discharge of frail elderly patients from hospitals. This section examines selective legal problems stemming from key reform legislation enacted to improve the quality of healthcare services.

One of the most sweeping and controversial legislative enactments to emerge in the post-prospective payment system era of healthcare reform is the Health Care Quality Improvement Act of 1986 (HCQI).[5] (See also Chapter 1 for a discussion of this act.) Several legal cases have challenged this national legislation or have relied upon the mandates of the act to support a legal claim. A review of the major provision of the HCQI will be followed by a discussion of selective cases that have challenged the quality of healthcare as mandated by it.

Health Care Quality Improvement Act

Many of the recent developments in risk management can be attributed to enactment of the HCQI. This act became law on November 14, 1986, signed into law by President Reagan. Codified at 42 U.S.C.A. Section 1101 et seq., it "is intended to promote effective professional review, improve the quality of medical care, and restrict the ability of incompetent physicians to move from state to state to avoid licensure difficulties" (NAHQ, 1993).

Table 7-1 offers a summary of the most commonly discussed provisions of the act. Each provision should be analyzed critically. Among the questions to ask about each are: How effective are they in improving our healthcare delivery system? Are they fair to healthcare organizations and insurance companies, that is, not unduly burdensome and costly to carry out? Are they fair to patients and to healthcare professionals? In particular, do health professionals enjoy the extra challenges inherent in complying with these laws?*

As shown in Table 7-1, there are three central areas of regulation established by the act: promotion of peer review activities for physicians (including osteopaths) and dentists, establishment of the National Practitioner Data Bank, and creation of a duty on the part of hospitals to inquire. Each of these provisions interrelates intentionally to promote a cohesive quality management system. The goal is to ensure that high quality standards are met, but when deviations from the standards are found, measures are taken to protect the public from incompetent practice.

---

* Intrinsic job satisfaction may indeed be greater among employees who participate in large-scale TQ programs compared with those who do not. Responses of over 5000 employees found a significant level of intrinsic job satisfaction in the former group. *See* Counte, M. A., Glandon, F.L., and Oleske, D. M. (1992). "Total Quality Management in a Health Care Organization: How Are Employees Affected?" *Hospital and Health Services Administration*, 37(4):503–518.

Table 7-1. Capsule: Summary of the Health Care Quality Improvement Act.

A. Promotion of Peer Review

Limited immunity for peer review when actions:
- promote the quality of care
- follow reasonable efforts to obtain the facts
- provide adequate due process
- warrant themselves based on the actual facts

B. National Practitioner Data Bank (DHHS)

Mandatory reporting by state licensing boards and insurers of:
- actions taken against physicians
- awards and settlements given to patients

Insurers' reports must contain this information:
- physician identification
- amount of payment
- hospital affiliations
- description of the professional negligence (acts, omissions, injuries to patient, etc.)

Licensing boards must submit report to DHHS, including:
- revocation, suspension, or other licensure restrictions
- censures, reprimands, or probations for incompetence or misconduct

Healthcare entities must submit report to licensing boards, including:
- adverse decision regarding a physician's clinical privileges for more than 30 days
- acceptance of surrendered privileges pursuant to an investigation

C. Duty of Hospitals to Inquire about Physicians Seeking Clinical Privileges or Staff Membership

- hospitals must check Data Bank every two years
- HMOs and other entities may opt to inquire about reportable adverse actions taken against physician in their state according to the U.S. Department of Health and Human Services in its required monthly report

A typical fictitious scenario will demonstrate how the HCQI should monitor and report a deviation from the quality of care. The legislature, of course, does not establish the standards or the degree of latitude that each institution might garner as it conducts its peer review activities.

Quality Plus Health Center

The physician peer review committee at Quality Plus Health Center has found that Dr. Doe performed unnecessary cardiac surgery on Mrs. Moe. The committee determined that surgery was contraindicated due to Mrs.

Moe's age and unrelated pre-existing chronic illnesses. Consequently, in accordance with the hospital bylaws, and after complying with all due process requirements mandated in the HCQI, Dr. Doe's clinical privileges were suspended for one year. The hospital promptly reported its decision to the state licensing board, which in turn reported Dr. Doe's suspension, along with other similar actions, to the Data Bank.

Dr. Doe had no complaints or concerns regarding his practice at Quiet Plus Hospital in another city. However, a physician on staff at Quiet heard about Dr. Doe's suspension and reported it to Quiet's Peer Review Committee. No adverse action was taken, but Dr. Doe's surgeries have been under close scrutiny. Had Quiet not learned informally about the suspension, it would have learned of it when it conducted its required every other year inquiry to the Data Bank. A routine inquiry for Dr. Doe was due six months after his suspension occurred. Meanwhile, Dr. Doe, who had practiced at Quality Plus for 17 years, was irate about the action of the Peer Review Committee and brought suit against his former colleagues. However, the suit was dismissed because the judge ruled that the committee was immune from liability. The committee's actions met all the standards of the HCQI including having been taken "in the reasonable belief that the action will further quality healthcare."

Due process requirements include: (1) giving the practitioner notice of the proposed action, (2) providing an opportunity for a hearing and giving notice of the hearing (the practitioner may request a hearing within 30 days), (3) allowing representation by an attorney if desired, (4) providing the opportunity to call witnesses and to present relevant evidence, and (5) receiving a written record of the proceedings. Dr. Doe was granted a hearing in which these requirements were carefully followed. Thus, the committee, and each member, are immune from any civil action for monetary damages. There are exceptions to the granting of immunity, most notably those situations in which defamation, discrimination, or interference with business relationships can be proved. These are discussed in the section on judicial involvement in quality.

The Stark Laws

There are many other healthcare-related laws at the national level, which at least tangentially have as their purpose elevating the quality of healthcare delivery. An example of such is the so-called Stark laws, named after Congressmen Stark, who drafted the bill. This law prohibits a physician from initiating a referral to a healthcare entity providing clinical laboratory services for which Medicare would otherwise pay, if the physician has a financial relationship with that entity, that is, if the physician stands to gain monetarily from the referral. Of course, there are numerous exceptions. An example of an exception is a situation where the physician has an employment status with the entity or is under contract to provide administrative services to the entity. Arguably, this legislation is a form of quality management because it is designed to prevent unnecessary diagnostic procedures. Even though such procedures would likely be carried out with strict adherence to quality standards for clinical diagnostic procedures, quality is compromised whenever unnecessary services are rendered. Of course, one has to prove that said services are unnecessary.

The Consolidated Omnibus Budget Reconciliation Act

The Consolidated Omnibus Reconciliation Act of 1985 (COBRA) (42 U.S.C.A. S1395 et seq.) was enacted in response to documented concerns that patients suffered serious complications and even death because of the refusal of a facility to provide emergent care when it was clearly needed. Some facilities would refuse to render care after determining that the patient was unable to pay for the services. Ostensible agency, a common law principle, provides the legal backbone for prohibiting patient dumping. This principle, as it relates to healthcare facilities, posits that because the facility holds itself out to the public as providing these services in an environment of caring, it cannot draw patients into its doors and then completely abdicate its pronounced role as a helping agent of the patient. Arguably, the patient would not have sought care at that facility if they did not believe they would receive emergency care. The patient is then placed at even greater risk because of the delay in being routed elsewhere. Even more dangerous scenarios are those instances in which there are simply no alternate facilities in the area, for example, in sparsely populated regions.

The COBRA law is most notable for its so-called "anti-dumping" requirements. The central purpose of COBRA is to ensure that emergent care, examination, or screening is provided to patients regardless of their ability to pay for these services. The law generally applies to any hospital that receives Medicare reimbursement. Accordingly, any patient who enters a Medicare-affiliated facility is covered under COBRA. The facility must determine whether an emergency exists or, in the case of a pregnant woman, whether she is in active labor. The patient cannot be transferred to another facility until he or she is stabilized and appropriate services are available at a receiving facility (NAHQ, 1993).

JUDICIAL INVOLVEMENT in DETERMINING QUALITY

It is well beyond the scope of a text about TQ to provide an exhaustive discussion of case law. The student is referred to health law texts for in-depth discussions of the sampling of cases presented here. Much of the case law pertaining to healthcare quality can be characterized as challenges to one of the following:

1. The existing practices in institutions that have been developed to monitor the quality of care, particularly the physician peer review process. Also included here are Medicare Peer Review Organization decisions that deny physicians eligibility for Medicare reimbursement.
2. State licensing board regulations and procedures that have been established to protect the public. These cases often stem from hospital peer review actions which in turn lead to reporting to state licensing boards. The link is especially cogent since establishment of mandatory reporting to the Practitioner Data Bank.
3. Healthcare institutions for failing to comply with laws or with organizational policies and procedures for monitoring and reporting healthcare quality. These cases include those brought against healthcare institutions for failure to perform peer review properly or to take necessary measures to correct deficiencies in their healthcare services.

Physician Peer Review and Related Legal Challenges

In the past few decades the number of judicial opinions in the area of physician peer review has been disturbingly large. Lawsuits are often brought by disgruntled physicians who have been the target of adverse action regarding either (1) licensure by the state licensing board and/or (2) clinical privileges. In the former case, the physician has been found to have engaged in the egregiously substandard practice of medicine or, more likely, has been found to have a serious substance abuse problem that has interfered with his or her practice. Usually, the physician is placed under the supervision of other physicians or has particular limitations placed on his or her medical practice (e.g., another physician must prescribe narcotics for the physician with the restrictions). Suspensions of several months to one or two years are less common, and in severe circumstances the license is revoked.

Clinical privileges are often restricted as a result of findings made by physicians* conducting routine peer review. Such review is ordinarily a part of the continuous quality improvement program of an institution. However, if a physician is proscribed from admitting patients or must be under the

---

* A variety of clinical healthcare providers have brought challenges to clinical privileges, but these cases usually center on the hospital's bylaws which severely limit the scope of privileges for all providers in that group, e.g., psychologists, certified nurse midwives, etc. However, the vast majority of cases involving licensure *restrictions* resulting from quality concerns have physician plaintiffs.

supervision of a senior physician, the impact on that physician's practice is often devastating. Hence, physicians are motivated to challenge the restrictions. Antitrust is an effective legal theory on which to challenge removal from a medical staff or other clinical privilege restrictions. Thus, a peer review case relying on an antitrust ground is included.

The landmark *Patrick* decision was a significant force behind the enactment of the HCQI, having received a good deal of media attention. The act was passed before the 1988 Supreme Court ruling in *Patrick*. It brings to light the issue of the extent to which physician peer review committees fail to operate effectively in an environment of freedom and openness. The converse question is whether potential abuses of the committee's authority are adequately controlled by the immunity provisions and its exemptions. Refer to the earlier section outlining the HCQI after reading the summary of *Patrick v. Burget*, 108 S.Ct. 1658 (1988).

Dr. Patrick was a general and vascular surgeon who was an employee of the Astoria Clinic and a member of the medical staff of the only hospital in Astoria, Oregon. The partners of the clinic offered Patrick a partnership after Patrick had been employed for one year. Patrick declined and took up a private practice that provided competition for the clinic. The relationship between Patrick and the clinic physicians deteriorated. The clinic referred its patients to surgeons 50 miles away and did not refer any patients to Patrick. A clinic physician initiated a series of complaints to the hospital's executive committee that eventually reported the complaints to the state licensing board. Another physician at the clinic chaired the committee of the licensing board that investigated the allegations against Dr. Patrick. A reprimand was issued which was later retracted after Patrick sought judicial review of the board's actions. However, two years later, yet another clinic physician requested that the hospital review Patrick's clinical privileges. The committee voted to recommend termination of Patrick's privileges, and Patrick then resigned and brought suit. In the court trial, the jury verdict supported Patrick. Under the Sherman Act it awarded damages against several of the clinic physicians for antitrust violations. The jury verdict was reversed on appeal to the Court of Appeals for the Ninth Circuit. Although the appellate court found substantial evidence that the clinic physicians had acted in bad faith in the peer review process, it held that the physicians' conduct was immune from antitrust scrutiny. The court reasoned that Oregon's expressed policy in favor of peer review brought it under a state action exemption from antitrust liability. Finally, the U.S. Supreme Court reversed the appellate decision and held that there was no exemption from antitrust liability. The Court did discuss the policy argument that effective peer review, and hence the assurance of quality healthcare, might be hampered if physicians feel threatened by the possibility of antitrust liability. However, the Court basically concluded that it is the responsibility of

Congress to enact immunity from antitrust liability. Acknowledging the existence of the HCQI, the Court noted that it would not apply retroactively.

Case Law: Restrictions Placed on Licensure

A hospital has a duty to remove a physician from its medical staff roster for unprofessional conduct. The factual question in each of the following cases is the degree of misconduct, and there is no explicit answer. A case typifying what will ordinarily suffice as unprofessional misconduct serious enough to sustain a challenge by the physician is *Moore v. Carson-Tahoe Hospital* [88 Nev. 207, 495 P.2d 605 (1972), *cert. denied*, 409 U.S. 879 (1972)]. Moore was duly licensed to practice medicine in Nevada, was board certified, and was a specialist in OB-GYN. Pursuant to its medical staff bylaws, the hospital terminated his appointment for unprofessional conduct. However, the specific acts of misconduct that led to the termination were not specifically included in the bylaws or the hospital's rules and regulations. Dr. Moore had attempted to administer a spinal anesthetic, and among other questionable practices, he failed to use a sterile technique.

Dr. Moore sued based on a violation of his substantive due process rights, i.e., unprofessional conduct was too vague, having no specific meaning. (Dr. Moore did not claim a violation of his procedural due process rights which concern the steps or process that must be followed before an adverse decision, e.g., notice of a hearing and a properly conducted hearing on the allegations.) In a vindication of a public hospital's discretion to remove a physician from its staff, the Nevada Supreme Court held that the standard of "unprofessional conduct" was objective enough. The court stated that "The purpose of the community hospital is to provide patient care of the highest possible quality. To implement this duty...it is the responsibility of the institution to create a workable system whereby the medical staff of the hospital continually reviews and evaluates the quality of care being rendered..." (88 Nev. 207, 495 P.2d at 608).

On the other hand, a 1976 Supreme Court of South Dakota decision [*St. John's Hospital Medical Staff v. St. John Regional Medical Center, Inc.*, 90 S.D. 674, 245 N.W.2d 472 (1976)] clearly delimits a hospital's authority to revise the medical staff bylaws unilaterally. The board of directors of St. John's Regional Medical adopted new medical staff bylaws which were not approved by the medical staff. The hospital attempted to impose these new bylaws on its physicians, who then filed suit. The trial court held that the new bylaws were void because they were not adopted according to the procedures in the original bylaws (which required adoption by the medical staff). The trial court's judgment was affirmed by the state supreme court which stated that the hospital could not ignore the procedures set forth in the original bylaws.

Examined together the *Moore* and the *St. John's Hospital* cases demonstrate that there is a middle ground between a healthcare institution and the medical practitioner. The hospital must be able to protect its patients and itself from liability resulting from incompetent or unprofessional medical practice, while the medical staff must have some autonomy to police their own professional practice.

Another form of review and control of quality are the mandatory Medicare Physician Review Organizations (PROs) (discussed in Chapter 1). A recent case before an administrative law judge will exemplify how a physician challenges his or her exclusion from participation as a provider for Medicare. In *Inspector General v. Greece* (No. HIX-000000219, DHHS, Office of Hearings and Appeals, San Jose, Calf. 95113), the issue concerned a PRO exclusion of Dr. Greece from participation as a provider in Medicare for a period of two years. The PRO made this recommendation after concluding that Greece had not met the quality of care standards set out in Section 1156(a) of the Social Security Act (42 U.S.C. 1320c-5) which states, in part:

It shall be the obligation of the healthcare practitioner and any other person (including a hospital or other healthcare facility) who provides healthcare services for which payment may be made (by Medicare), to assure—that services—to beneficiaries (i.e., patients):

1. Will be provided economically and only when and to the extent medically necessary;
2. Will be of a quality which meets professionally recognized standards of healthcare; and
3. Will be supported by evidence of medical necessity and *quality* as may reasonably be required by a reviewing Peer Review Organization.

The physician did not cooperate with the PRO in providing evidence of medical necessity and quality as stipulated in Section 1156(a)(3) above. The opinion discussed at great length whether Dr. Greece's medical care should to be held to a local or a national standard, a long-standing debate in professional negligence law. The administrative law judge's decision was that Dr. Greece did not violate the quality of care standards imposed by Medicare, taking local circumstances into consideration.

This case demonstrates that administrative hearings serve to counterpoise the recommendations of a PRO to exclude a provider. Evidently, the basic requirements are broad; the reviewers must look to their local utilization and quality standards to make a determination of whether there have been violations. Even if a PRO is acting in good faith, application of the Medicare statutory requirements can be a tortuous exercise, involving at least as much adeptness in epistemology as in medical science. The "encyclopedia" of law involving licensure and licensure restrictions can be thought of as an external quality control process. A goal for TQ in healthcare organizations is to strengthen the linkages between their internal TQ and the functions of state licensing boards. The Data Bank has aided in tying these quality controls together, but additional steps must be taken to facilitate a flow of all appropriate information regarding quality concerns.

Case Law: Institutional Liability Involving Substandard Quality

Patients are often the plaintiffs in claims made against institutions for rendering healthcare of substandard quality. More often than not, one or more physicians are named parties in the lawsuit, but the hospital is also alleged to be liable under one of numerous theories that are not discussed here. These claims have met with mixed success, although there is an extensive body of case law in the area of institutional liability where the primary defendants are physicians who have allegedly engaged in professional negligence. However, the focus here is concerned with how pre-existing quality standards have been used as a tool to establish direct liability of a healthcare organization.

A leading example of such tinkering with quality management systems is the *Cospito* decision. Courts are reluctant to interfere to the extent called for to make a factual determination as to whether the quality fell below that expected by private or quasi-public (as opposed to public) bodies for accreditation such as the Joint Commission on Accreditation of Healthcare Organizations (JCAHO) (which until 1987 was known as the Joint Commission on Accreditation of Hospitals). The U.S. Court of Appeals decision in *Cospito v. Heckler* [742 F.2d 72 (3rd Cir. 1984)] explores a challenge to the quality of psychiatric care that relied upon the institution's loss of JCAHO accreditation. The relevant facts are as follows. Trenton Psychiatric Hospital is a state hospital in New Jersey that treats voluntarily and involuntarily committed patients for mental illness. The JCAHO found deficiencies in patient treatment, staffing, and other areas, which resulted in receiving only one year's accreditation. The following year the same deficiencies were found again, and one year after that the hospital's loss of accreditation became final.

Patients at the facility received Medicare, Medicaid, or Supplemental Social Security Income (SSSI). However, once the hospital was deaccredited, these benefits were discontinued. The patients alleged that the deprivation of their benefits was unconstitutional on various grounds including lack of procedural due process. The argument raised which is most germane to quality of care was that Medicare and Medicaid provisions improperly delegate the federal government's authority to JCAHO. The patients argued that because the JCAHO is a private organization, and because the delegation to the JCAHO is not accompanied by specific standards regarding decertification of psychiatric institutions, the delegation results in unconstitutional deprivation of their benefits.

However, the court held that the Medicare and Medicaid Acts provide enough explanation as to what institutions are eligible for participation in these funding programs, and therefore, no constitutional violations existed. This line of cases lends itself to policy scrutiny. It is arguable that the court in *Cospito* would have gone to even greater lengths than were necessary under these facts to preserve the relationship between Medicare and JCAHO. Courts will consider the policy implications of a contrary holding in deciding an important case. In this case, one major policy implication of deciding in the patients' favor would have been leaving Congress to the task of figuring how to link quality to the flow of federal dollars. Medicare would no longer be able to rely upon the expertise of the existing private organization (i.e., the JCAHO). Recalling that the JCAHO also accredits acute care facilities, should it have as much influence over who gets federal dollars?

An issue related to institutional liability is whether a medical staff as a body can be sued by a patient in an action against the treating physician. In *Corleto v. Shore Memorial Hospital* [138 N.J.Super. 302, 350, A.2d 534 (1975)] the plaintiff alleged that their decedent (a former patient) was subjected to professional negligence by the treating physician and that his negligence contributed to the decedent's death. The hospital administrator, the board of directors, and the medical staff were made parties as well, on the theory that they knew, or should have known, that the treating physician was not competent to do the type of surgery in question; however, these defendants allowed the physician to do so and to continue to treat the decedent.

The New Jersey court refused to give immunity to any of the defendants, over the argument that the public good would be promoted by not subjecting every administrator, director, or medical staff member to such lawsuits. The denial of immunity here should be distinguished from any immunity that might well have been granted had the medical staff attempted to review beforehand the treating physician's credentials and skill to perform the surgery. To what extent are medical staffs likely to do so?

Finally, consider that the scope of institutional liability expands beyond that of its medical staff. Consider the case of B*ernardi v. Community Hospital Association* [166 Colo. 280, 443 P.2d 708 (1968)], in which the quality of care given by a nurse formed the nexus of liability. The physician was named in the lawsuit, but because he was not present during the incident, the claim against him was dismissed by the court. The nurse injected her pediatric patient with a dosage of tetracycline, administered in the gluteal region. It was alleged that the nurse negligently injected the medication into the patient's sciatic nerve, causing permanent loss of normal use of her right foot. The court held that the hospital could be held liable for the alleged negligence of the nurse, reasoning that a hospital should be responsible for the care given by nurses it employs so long as that care is in the scope of their employment. Another sound rationale for integrating TQ throughout all personnel levels is the risk of liability from employee negligence that courts will unabashedly place upon the institution.

The Appropriate Role of the Courts

Few health law scholars will argue that there have not been abuses of the legal system as a forum for determining quality of care related issues. Such abuses have occurred on the part of healthcare professionals, institutions, and patients alike. Rather than serving to resolve substantive problems relating to quality (and there are doubts about the merits of the degree of involvement of the judiciary in such affairs) or to clarify the legislative intent about procedures relating to quality, courts have been asked to turn somersaults. Hospitals want the maximum possible protection from the risks of institutional liability that result from failure to monitor their clinicians closely. The clinicians, however, have often used, and sometimes abused, their right to seek redress for any action taken against their professional status by the state or by a healthcare organization. Many side entrances to the legal system have been used, such as finding flaws in the procedures that led to the adverse action or claiming defamation, tortious interference with business relationships or quite often, antitrust (i.e., the actions resulted from deliberate unlawful attempts to restrict competition, such as alleged in the *Patrick* case).

As part of gaining a better understanding of how the legal system is involved in regulating and judicially influencing quality, the student of TQ should reflect upon the proper scope of federal and state regulation and the court system at all levels. Have the cases presented here, or other cases with which you may be familiar, elevated the quality of care rendered to patients? Do some of the legal arguments seem strained, perhaps attempts to protect one's professional status in the wake of alleged misconduct? Likewise, is the vast array of regulations necessary, or are they cumbersome to the point that the patient may sometimes be the forgotten element? The complexity of these issues precludes the search for clear answers.

Nonetheless, this author questions the benefit of some of our regulations and believes that reform geared to simplification of the HCQI and other quality-related legislation would be a positive step in restoring meaning to substantive quality review. Second, the possibility should be explored of establishing a special board or commission to review the actions of hospitals in restricting the clinical privileges of physicians and other health professionals with clinical privileges. To avoid claims of antitrust or other ulterior motives, such panels should be composed of clinicians who do not practice in the service area and represent a balance of clinicians, health administrators, and citizens.

ETHICS and the ELEVATION of QUALITY

Standards of Ethics Affecting Quality

The American Hospital Association (AHA) Guidelines on Ethical Conduct and Relationships for Healthcare Institutions are but one example of direct attempts by healthcare professional organizations to impact quality positively through ethical standards. Guideline Six of the AHA guidelines is especially directed to the quality of care: Healthcare institutions should establish and maintain internal policies, practices, standards of performance, and systematic methods of evaluation that emphasize high quality, safety, and effectiveness of care.

Likewise, two of the principles found in the American Medical Association (AMA) Principles of Medical Ethics have bearing on the goal of delivering the highest possible quality of care: (I) A physician shall be dedicated to providing competent medical service with compassion and respect for human dignity, and (II) a physician shall deal honestly with patients and colleagues, and strive to expose those physicians deficient in character or competence, or who engage in fraud or deception. The latter AMA principle seems applicable to the hypothetical Dr. Doe case presented earlier, emphasizing the importance of ethical principles, as well as legal mandates, in elevating the quality of health services.

Finally, familiar to every healthcare professional are the various codes of ethics governing each clinical profession, for example, The American Nurses' Association's Code For Nurses. The healthcare clinician is under an obligation that is commensurate with licensure, to be thoroughly knowledgeable about and to practice according to the code of ethics governing his or her field.

Healthcare managers have also had available to them the Code of Ethics of the American College of Healthcare Executives (ACHE), adopted in 1973. The ACHE has an active Committee on Ethics that reviews the Code of Ethics and recommendations for revisions, and enforces the code when allegations of breaches are presented. The preamble states that the purpose of the code is to attempt to assure and facilitate accomplishment of the goals of health institutions and programs to further develop the integrity, skills, and impartiality of health administrators. Because most institutions today tout delivery of the highest possible quality of care as their preeminent goal, all healthcare professionals with administrative responsibility should become familiar with these ACHE ethical standards.

Individual Ethical Responsibility

Imagine for the moment that the sidewalks are swept clean. There are no laws dictating how or with whom or where we must conduct quality review programs. There are no professional codes of ethics that purport to govern the conduct of its professional membership. There is only the physician, the healthcare manager, the allied health professional, or other healthcare professionals who are charged with the responsibility of delivering the highest quality of care possible within the limits of the training, resources, and time that exist. Why imagine this uneasy state of affairs? Because, ultimately no amount of laws, regulations, policies, procedures— or ethical principles, guidelines, or codes—will directly control the quality of care received by any patient. Rather, the individual morality of the health professional and the level of responsibility that the professional is willing to assume will circumscribe the quality within that professional's realm.

The professional's responsibility incorporates three components: one's judgments about the correct response to a given situation, one's decisions based on those judgments, and the ultimate outcomes which are in turn dependent upon one's decisions. How an individual deals with each component is dependent upon having a theoretical framework or approach to handling ethical issues. "A well-developed ethical theory provides a framework for application of and adherence to fundamental principles that guide decision making and action" (Hiller, 1986). To be moral is not tantamount to being ethical; morals are purely internal judgments about what is right and wrong. It is ethics that provides the systematic approach to reasoning about how to apply one's morals in the decision-making process. In the context of TQ, this approach enables the health professional to make ethical decisions that positively affect quality. More bluntly, individual ethical responsibility means using one's set of morals in every professional and personal decision and course of action.

CONCLUSION

At the risk of oversimplification of the role of law and ethics, perhaps a fair conclusion is that both carry substantial weight in the TQ arena. The law carries a great deal of weight concerning what *should* be done about quality; ethics carries a great deal of weight regarding what *is* being done about quality. A Japanese proverb proclaims, "Wisdom and virtue are like the two wheels of a cart." Analogizing from this proverb, laws might be viewed as the wisdom, providing sound, rational guidelines based upon experience (history, precedent, etc.). Ethics might be analogous to virtue, having a character rooted in a strong sense of morality. Quality management, of course, is the cart itself. The system would be motionless without the wisdom of laws and the virtue of ethics, with no wheels to propel the TQ system along a continuum to infinitely higher levels of quality.

REFERENCES

Darr, K. (1987). *Ethics in Health Services Management*, New York: Praeger Publishers.

Furrow, B. R. et al. (1987). "Regulating the Quality of Health Care." in *Health Law Cases, Materials and Problems*, St. Paul, Minn.: West Publishing, pp. 1–67.

Harighurst, C. C. (1988). *Health Care Law and Policy: Readings, Notes and Questions*, Westbury, N.Y.: The Foundation Press.

Health Care Quality Improvement Act of 1986, 42 U.S.C.A. S 1101 et seq. (West 1987).

Hiller, M. D. (1986). "The Discipline of Ethics." in *Ethics and Health Administration: Ethical Decision Making in Health Management*, Arlington, Va.: Association of University Programs in Health Administration, pp. 7–35.

NAHQ (1993). "Risk Management." in *The NAHQ Guide to Quality Management*, Skokie, Ill.: NAHQ Press, pp. 324–39.

Rowland, H. and Rowland, B. (1990). "Legal Issues." in *Hospital Quality Assurance Manual*, 11:1–17.

8

TOTAL QUALITY and MANAGEMENT PHILOSOPHIES

Keith Curtis, MBA, PhD

No one is opposed to quality. How could anyone be, particularly in these times when the United States is being challenged not so much by foreign industrial might, but by higher quality foreign products—products that last longer, require fewer repairs, and are generally more acceptable to the consumer.

Discussion of quality occurs not only in terms of products, but in terms of service as well. The test of service may be how long the customer waits in line at the grocery store, how often the customer has to return before a problem is solved, or how long the customer is on hold. All are indicators of the quality of service.

Despite the emphasis on quality and the entire Total Quality (TQ) movement, there continues to be a disturbing resistance to TQ, particularly in the workplace. Perhaps some workers are too old to change, some do not work well in teams, or some perceive TQ as just another management gimmick to increase workload without adding resources.

The difference between successful and unsuccessful outcomes may just be a matter of how TQ is approached. Some might say that with the proper training, the TQ method has the potential to be successful in almost any industry—from automobile manufacturing to hospitals or from canned goods to computers. What seems to have been ignored by these entities is the idea that TQ is not just a technique or a tool that can be adapted to fit any situation. True, it is a managerial tool and a technique, but, like all tools, it should be used at an appropriate time and place. A screwdriver is not appropriate for every plumbing job, and TQ is not appropriate for every organizational arrangement. Each organization should be carefully diagnosed and analyzed before TQ is introduced.

TQ works well in organizations that meet certain cultural criteria. Its successful application requires that a certain belief system be in place before it is implemented. The belief system revolves around meeting customer needs. It must be steeped in the philosophy of using teams to solve system problems. The organizational philosophy must include the idea that process crosses organizational unit boundaries and that improvements in processes are made by people who have the best interests of the organization at heart. The organizational philosophy must embrace failure as an important part of the improvement process. "Tolerate failure—it is the price of success," is a common motto of a successful TQ application. The TQ philosophy must be based on an information system that is designed to collect statistical data, rather than monitor behavior or punish. The purpose is to reveal problems in the system that can be addressed by interdisciplinary teams.

Not all organizations carry an organizational culture that meets these philosophical and cultural demands.

ORGANIZATIONAL CULTURES

Culture is the way in which an organization forges a common sense of history, values, and purpose through the collective interpretation of its members (Moran and Volkwein, 1992). In other words, it is shared knowledge and understanding or the way members interpret their surroundings. In their excellent article, Moran and Volkwein point out that it is more than simply a psychological sharing, because it is more than just a collection of individual perceptions which are akin to the climate of an organization. Culture is a more stable and long-term sociological concept. The culture of an organization contains the essential elements of life within the organization. It is comprised of the historically constituted norms, ideologies, values, languages, myths, and even symbols that represent an organization. Culture involves a set of tangible or intangible standards that enable individuals to act in ways that are acceptable to other members of their organization. It is found in the shared perceptions that are shaped by the myths, ideologies, norms, and values of an organization. These perceptions may be expressed in the writings, thoughts, or language of an organization (Moran and Volkwein, 1992).

To some extent, culture governs the interaction among the members of an organization. Culture also helps people to interpret their experiences and guides their actions. Through its history, leadership, and social context, an organization creates its own cultural system of symbols and meanings that can be widely shared by its members. Culture can even be instrumental in eliciting commitment to the organization. Additionally, it can be learned by new members as the way to perceive, think, and feel about the organization. An interesting characteristic of culture is that it often is taken for granted and therefore drops from the awareness of those closest to it (Moran and Volkwein, 1992).

Culture becomes more obvious as cultural orientations are carried out in the philosophies of an organization. The *essence* of culture can be identified through observation. Shared behaviors provide the cultural essence of an organization. In sum, culture is not tangible, but rather it is an abstract frame of reference that can be identified or in some general way described through observing the behavior of the members of an organization (Moran and Volkwein, 1992).

Organizational cultures exist as empirically verifiable entities. One way to identify cultures, and determine whether or not TQ will work, is to examine types of organizations in terms of power orientation, that is, to determine how power is exercised in an organization. From the answer, distinctive cultures begin to emerge and clues begin to unfold to indicate the appropriateness of TQ in different organizational cultures.

The USE of POWER in ORGANIZATIONS

Organizations can be analyzed in a systematic way by focusing on how power is used to get things done. Some organizations are tightly integrated around a common goal or purpose. The goal or purpose of the organization is clearly understood and its value is widely shared by its members. This frame of reference can be identified as a unitary structure, where members of the organization are integrated around the task to be accomplished (Morgan, 1986). Power is used to focus energy and resources on a task. When there is little disagreement on the task, power is not used by people against each other or to improve position. When there is agreement, personal power is not a primary issue. Profit, patient care, and patriotism are example of values that may about unity of purpose. Successful businesses, sharply focused healthcare organizations, and the military are often characterized by unitary values.

The Unitary Organization

In his book *Images of Organization*, Morgan (1986) notes that unitary characteristics are most often found in organizations that have developed a cohesive culture based on respect for the goals of the organization. The interests of the individual and organization are generally synonymous. This unitary view emphasizes the sovereignty of the organization. Individuals subordinate themselves in the service of the organization. They realize and satisfy their own interests in the name of a higher purpose. Their focus is on achieving common objectives. The organization is united under the umbrella of common goals, and well-integrated teams strive to achieve them. Conflict is dealt with openly and objectively through appropriate managerial action, such as problem-solving teams or task forces. The system or its processes are believed to be the source of most organizational difficulties, rather than deviants, troublemakers, or persons working for their own self-interests.

In the unitary organization, power is used to focus on issues and to solve problems. Concepts such as goal setting, strategic planning, teamwork, and individual empowerment are highly held values and are also extremely effective managerial tools.

An important point in describing a unitary type of organization is that it not only must have a clear purpose or goal, but members of the organization must also subscribe to that goal and be willing to sacrifice for it. In other words, organizational commitment above personal gain is a common characteristic of the unitary organization. Much is made of the phrases "tightly focused" and "a clear vision" in unitary organizations.

Unitary organizations are only one of several organizational types. Clearly, there are degrees of commitment even in the most tightly focused organization. At other points on the organizational spectrum, however, other characteristics more adequately describe an organization. This is particularly true in those organizations where power is used not so much for the common good, but rather as a tool to resolve conflicts or enhance personal gain. These organizations, which are usually characterized by their diverse interests, are more aptly described as being pluralistic. Organizations primarily made up of professionals or white-collar workers, and particularly where autonomy is highly valued, often tend to fit the pluralist model (Morgan, 1986). Many types of organizations may be included in this model, such as universities, hospitals, and governments.

The Pluralistic Organization

Pluralistic organizations are typified by loose networks of people with divergent interests. They gather in an organization for many reasons, including earning a living, developing a career, advancing in a profession, or pursing a desired personal goal or objective. They resemble coalitions of interest groups bound together because their cooperation in relation to specific issues, events, or decisions advances their specific values. However, conflicts arise whenever interests collide (Morgan, 1986).

Conflict will always be present in an organization. However, the way it is managed is revealing. Conflict may be explicitly and directly confronted, as in a unitary organizational setting, or it may be covertly addressed, as in a political setting. Most modern organizations are characterized by various types and degrees of politics because they are both competitive and collaborative at the same time. People often must collaborate in pursuit of a common task, yet they are often pitted against each other in competition for limited resources, status, and advancement. Conflict is regarded as an inherent and ineradicable characteristic. In many respects it is even regarded in a positive light, as healthy and productive.

Power is the medium through which conflicts of interests are ultimately resolved. Power involves the ability to make another person do something that he or she would not otherwise do. One gains power in an organization through what is called *organizational politics.*

The pluralist organization places emphasis on the diversity of individual and group interests. The organization is regarded as a loose coalition that has a modest interest in the formal goals of the organization. The organization is viewed as a collection of various professions or special interest groups, each vying for position within the organization. Depending on the issue or circumstance, power must be more or less equally shared in order to maintain a semblance of balance. The hallmark of the pluralistic organization is acceptance of this inevitability of the use of organizational politics to accomplish one's purpose (Morgan, 1986).

Management is thus forced to focus on balancing and coordinating the interests of the members of an organization so that they can work together within the constraints set by the formal goals of the organization, which really reflect the interests of all parties concerned. The main goal is to manage conflict in ways that will benefit the overall organization. Compromise, collaboration, and accommodation are characteristic managerial approaches used in pluralistic organizations.

Both the unitary and pluralistic organizations portrayed above are more modern forms of organizations. However, there is a long history of success emanating from the more traditional organizations. These organizations are more highly structured and much more mechanistic than either of the above. They are often characterized as bureaucratic, authoritarian, or even autocratic. They have existed for centuries and continue to be effective today, especially in organizations that are characterized by a relatively stable environment.

The Structured Organization

The structured organization formalizes the use of power. Authority and superior–subordinate relationships are clearly defined and are distinctive characteristics. People work on a contractual basis, where "a fair day's work for a fair day's pay" is a common value. Organizational hierarchy and chain of command define communication channels. Job descriptions and pay rates define roles. Rules and regulations govern behavior.

The first and most obvious source of power is formal authority. It is a form of legitimized power that is respected and acknowledged by those with whom one interacts. Authority is also a form of social approval. Monarchs and bureaucrats win their rights to power through procedural means. A factory supervisor is given a right to influence policy because formal position on an organizational chart defines the spheres of delegated authority. Authority is seen as flowing from the top down, i.e., delegated by one's supervisor (Morgan, 1986).

There was a time when the people at the bottom of an organization were oppressed. However, during the industrial revolution, people joined unions, many of which still exist today. Workers gained benefits and rights through formally negotiated union–management contracts. One of the primary roles of the union is to protect the interests of its members. Contracts are negotiated, employee rights are specified, and benefits are bestowed.

Organizations in which there are sharp distinctions between different classes of employees, such as the division between blue- and white-collar workers, or where there has been a history of conflict between management and labor tend to reflect the characteristics of this structured industrial model. Although this view may seem somewhat narrow and old fashioned, it is more pervasive and influential than we are led to believe in the modern management literature.

The structured organization places emphasis on the oppositional nature of contradictory class interests. The organization is viewed as a battleground where rival forces (e.g., management and unions) work to achieve largely incompatible ends. Conflict is regarded as inevitable and as part of a wider class conflict that will eventually change the entire structure of the organization. As in the pluralistic organization, the use of power is a key feature of a structured organization. Rather than being used in organizational politics, power is exercised through more formal negotiations. Negotiation is a means to distribute power. Power is more closely aligned to a form of social control, economic control, and the legal system than is commonly found in a pluralistic organization.

TQ and CORPORATE CULTURE: FINDING a FIT

It is clear from the preceding discussion that TQ works best in organizations that have developed a unitary culture. In a goal-oriented organization, the focus is on problem solving, issue identification, formation of teams, open communication, collaboration, participation, and even empowerment, all of which are crucial to the success of a TQ program. TQ works best in organizations in which there is a clear sense of purpose that is shared by all members. One culture centers on a clearly defined, well-understood, and mutually agreed upon purpose and task. This organization is characterized as unitary because individual and organizational goals are generally synonymous. The individual gains personal satisfaction by contributing to what he or she perceives to be a larger purpose—deriving a personal identity by supporting that particular purpose.

Cultural Differences

The Japanese have found that TQ methodology fits very nicely into their culture. In Japan group consultation sessions are held to make important decisions, and there is a strong loyalty to both the peer group and to the organization. These values are much stronger than are commonly found in organizations in the United States (Hofstede, 1993).

As might be expected, many organizations in the United States and elsewhere are based on strong cultural values of democracy and individual rights. Diversity is one of the strengths of organizations that are built on democratic principles. Traditionally, organizations in the United States have been known for their inventiveness and creativity. New ideas are generated from the creative tension that exists around the highly held value that competition is good. The reactions of different people to these competitive tensions vary from situation to situation and produce a great variety of behaviors. Many people manage to achieve considerable degrees of overlap between competing personal and organizational aims and aspirations, shaping their general task or mission so as to allow themselves to achieve both personal and organizational aims at the same time. Thus, we can begin to understand how people relate to their work through their own personal concerns. We can detect the motivating factors that underpin the varied styles of careerism, gamesmanship, task commitment, turf protection, and free wheeling that are a part of the politics of organizational life.

The Right and Wrong Cultural Fit

The cultures of many organizations in the United States do not easily lend themselves to cultural requirements of TQ. Self-interest and politics are more akin to a pluralistic organization, where people with divergent interests create tension and conflict. Conflict arises whenever divergent interests collide. Most modern organizations promote various kinds of politicking precisely because they recognize the importance of divergent interests and the role of conflict.

As noted previously, power is the medium through which conflicts of interest are ultimately resolved in a pluralistic organization. Power influences how and when who gets what. TQ does not fit well in organizations where different groups bargain and compete for a share in the balance of power and use their influence to realize personal or group aspirations.

197

If TQ is a difficult technique to apply successfully in a pluralistic organization, it is even more difficult to employ in a highly structured organization. It is here where the organization itself is viewed as a battle-ground where rival forces strive to achieve largely incompatible ends. The automobile industry is a perfect example, where the long-standing culture is based on the industrial model of union–management conflict. In the United States, the automobile industry is struggling to transform its highly structured organizational model in order to more effectively compete with the Japanese and others. The concepts of TQ have not come easily to the automobile industry or the unions.

What is occurring in the automobile industry is a valiant attempt at cultural transformation. However, transforming culture is not at all like transforming short-term quarterly returns on investment.

Effective versus Ineffective Organizations

Look at the characteristics of the most effective organization you have known. It probably had a clear goal or purpose, was finely focused on the task to be done, balanced power throughout the organization, and had a minimum of conflict; what conflict was present was probably handled objectively, with focus on the issue, not personalities. In other words, the organization was in perfect equilibrium.

Now look at the least effective organization you have known. The environment was probably constantly changing. The old ways no longer worked, but those in charge were successful in using them; therefore, they resisted the change present in the environment. The eager young members wanted to adapt and do new things; as a result, power struggles developed. There was conflict between the more powerful and the less powerful, power centers developed, and people became self-serving and political. Even the CEO was self-centered, and organizational goals were used to enhance his or her self-image. If there were clear goals, they were inter-preted differently by the various specialties or functional areas. The orga-nization became more like a political system, with varying interest groups vying for power and influence. Decisions were made by voting in commit-tee meetings. In short, it was an organization in chaos, with everyone protecting himself or herself.

Studies have shown that there is a relationship between politics and performance. Top management teams of effective firms avoid politics, whereas the management teams of poor performers tend to use politics (Pfeffer, 1992). This is because politics consumes time and dissipated executive energy, restructures the flow of information, and results in distorted perceptions about the opinions of others. Politics and authoritarian management are almost perfectly correlated. Conflict can be bitter, focused on personalities, and unproductive rather than illuminating. To the extent that power struggles result in destructive conflict, organizations suffer (Pfeffer, 1992).

Cultural transformation, if it is to be successful at all, is a gradual process. Every journey begin with a first step, and there are things that managers can do to transform their organization, assuming that transformation is the right thing to do.

TRANSFORMING ORGANIZATIONS to a TQ PHILOSOPHY and CULTURE

Constant effort must be made to manage conflicts constructively and to unite the organization around a common vision and a common set of external threats. Trade-offs invariably must be made. The process of transforming an organization requires the ability to compromise.

The first step, then, in managing transformation and the accompanying power dynamics is to reduce political activity wherever possible. One of the critical tasks in managing power dynamics and attempting to reduce them is to figure out where the organization currently is and determine where it should be headed strategically.

In a truly political organization, where there will never be agreement and group interests will always be diverse, no attempt should be made to achieve a cultural transformation toward TQ. Here, TQ is not appropriate, nor will it ever be an effective management tool in a highly politicized organization. At best, it is an effective marketing technique that the politician can use to demonstrate that he or she is truly contemporary and up to date with the latest management fad.

However, to the extent that an organization can agree on core values (such as purpose, goals, and objectives), political activity can be reduced. The critical issue is whether the organization, in the absence of political activity, will be able to respond more positively and effectively to its environment or whether political activity is an integral part of the process of organizational change. If it will respond more effectively, then let the cultural transformation toward TQ begin!

Managing Cultural Transformation

Change is difficult because people really do not want to change. Change can be painful, and employees may resist embarking on a major new journey unless they perceive that the change will be an improvement over the current course. People hang on to old habits and old behaviors long past

199

their usefulness. Change always takes longer than planned. People learn slowly and forget easily. People expect too much. People want everything now (Belasco, 1990).

Transformational Leadership

Transformational leadership focuses on organizational vision and the task to be done, eliciting help from the people who will facilitate task accomplishment (Marszalek-Gaucher and Coffey, 1990). This differs from transactional leadership, where work is accepted as is, and people view their relationship with the organization from a contractual perspective.

The transformational leader must work with the people in the organization to develop a vision for the future, create an environment for change, and convince others to join in making the vision a reality. The leader can not do it alone, no matter what his or her position in the organization. If the personality, philosophy, or style of the leader is such that he or she cannot share power, the transformation process should stop. TQ will never work if imposed from the top down. There must be acceptance. However, if the motivation and incentive to improve quality exist, the leader should proceed with the transition.

The British provide an excellent example of how to adjust to change. They mark the passing of the old, while quickly making the transition to the new. "The king is dead, long live the king." This ritual marks the passage of the old ruler (the king is dead), while empowering the new (long live the king) (Belasco, 1990).

If you want organizational change, you must develop a bold plan, actively sponsor the changes, and support them tenaciously over a period of time. Donald Rice, Secretary of the Air Force, in response to deep budgetary cutbacks in the Department of Defense, stated, "We are not paring down the Air Force, we are building a new smaller Air Force from the ground up." He then moved quickly and resolutely to restructure the entire Air Force, based on a completely new, more effective organizational design.

Begin with Vision

Revisit and revitalize the purpose and vision of the organization. Start with a simple purpose, and use a rifle, not a shotgun. Vision is the focus— start with a compelling vision for the future as a guide to change; this is the key to long-term success. It is the vision that drives all action—focus on the results you want dearly to attain. A vision clearly identifies for all concerned (employees, customers, and suppliers) exactly what the organization stands for and precisely why they should support it. Vision tightly directs attention to the critical factors that produce long-term results and thereby success.

The new vision plants a stake in the ground. It guides decisions. It inspires action—and it is needed at all levels of the organization.

Focus on the New

A new vision is embodied in the purpose, philosophy, goals, and mission statements of the organization. Once established, you must live it and communicate it compulsively. Put it on the wall and talk about it in meetings. And live it—continually—every day. Be obsessed with it or it will become history (Belasco, 1990). Print it in employee handbooks, emblazon it on notebooks, and include it in memos. You may even go so far as to create saying, mottoes, or catchwords, such as "Quality is job 1;" "absolutely, positively, overnight;" "We deliver, we deliver;" "We love to fly and it shows." Words are important; they communicate purpose and empower action.

Vision Is Not Enough

Creating sayings to support a vision is not enough—the present drowns out the future. As John Gardner noted, most people do not listen. The noisy clatter of the present drowns out the tentative sounds of things to come (Gardner, 1990). Vision is an emotional appeal, but talk is cheap—lots of managers and organizations are long on talk. The walls of most organizations are littered with the graffiti of too many visions. Most organizations today are filled with rhetoric. An old Chinese proverb goes, "Lots of noise at the top of the stairs, but no one coming down."

It Takes Resources

Show me your budget and I'll show you your real priorities. It takes resources. Regardless of the intentions expressed in the strategic plan, where you place your key people and money is the direction in which your organization will move. Invest your resources in your strategic plan to create your new tomorrow.

Other Requirements for Change

Downsize, refocus, and improve productivity. Recruit, orient, train, develop, appraise, pay, and promote people based on the vision. Create a sense of urgency. Above all, use objectives to change and renew the organization and its people. Objectives are set at the process level—where the work gets done! Vision is important, but preoccupation with vision can result in neglecting the details that must be accomplished if that vision is to be realized.

Results versus Process

Being truly results-oriented means being aware that every outcome is preceded by a process. A process orientation not only sharpens our judgment, it makes us feel better about ourselves. TQ is based on the idea of continuously improving the thousand small details that make a process and a system effective.

Change must combine results and process. To change or not to change? That's the wrong question. The real question, however, is "How to change?" Results are the ultimate measure. Yet how we achieve those results is also important. We fail as managers if we simply tell someone "I want results," but do not share with them what we know about how to do it or, worse, help them achieve the results. You don't score many points looking at the scoreboard. The game is won or lost on the field. The scoreboard only records the results. Understand how to score touchdowns, not how to record them (Belasco, 1990). The game is the process by which you manage. The profit-and-loss statement is the scoreboard. Management is about results, but if you become obsessed with only the results, you forget about the "how" to do it. When you don't know "how," you cannot consistently produce the "what." The "what" is most important, for it represents your vision, but the "how" is the way to attain the "what." Once you know the "what," then you can concentrate on the "how." Thus, process is important as well. First its the grand vision, then its the little things.

MANAGING the PROCESS through CHANGE

The "big picture" is the result of thousands of exquisite strokes of a brush. Vision and process should be tightly intertwined. Each detail of every process should be examined continually and the question posed, "Are we doing the right thing in relation to the purpose of the organization?" By constantly revising objectives that need to be changed, an organization will undergo continuous process renewal and improvement.

How To Do It—Empowerment

Empowerment is the ability to take unencumbered action. It is providing people with the necessary skills and training, and then presenting the objectives to them and allowing them to figure out the best way to accomplish the tasks. Empower employees with the vision, and give those who live it special status. TQ requires a relentless pursuit of improvement—a system of collaboration that is facilitated by good communication.

Still, isolated attempts at empowerment (TQ, quality circles, participative management) are useless in the absence of the proper culture. What is the proper culture? TQ requires a secure environment that encourages risk, failure, and a focus on lessons learned.

Is the proper culture enough for people to accept the TQ concept? It is not likely. People do not feel the urgency to change unless they consider themselves to be a part of the vision. They are encouraged to accept the vision when they have a stake in the outcome. This incentive can be achieved by forming teams to solve problems that inhibit personal performance. Empowered teams can be a powerful force.

Business, the British management journal writes: "We are moving from the set piece trench warfare of Flanders in 1914–1918 toward the quick response jungle war of Vietnam. Seventy years ago great armies moved on detailed instructions of supreme commanders and their general staffs. Today we need the flexibility of response seen in a well-led fighting patrol, harnessed within the vision that ensures a victorious campaign." Flexible bands of disciplined people focused tightly on a vision is the key to success in the jungles of the marketplace—and government.

Integrating Multiple Teams

Teams can insulate themselves and be destructive to the organization. Therefore, they must be helped to achieve their goals, and they must help other teams to accomplish their goals. This can be done by establishing what James Belasco calls "Customer–Supplier contracts." Every team in the organization has a *customer*—every team produces outputs used by another team in the organization. Every team has *suppliers*—every team receives inputs from others in the organization. It is an interdependent system, and the web of customer–supplier contracts binds all the components together to produce an effective organization. The deliverables should be agreed upon, in writing if necessary, and they should be measurable (time, money etc.).

Empowering People

Change driven from the top of the organization—without significant across-the-board participation—is a recipe for failure. People are motivated to achieve what they can see, touch, and measure; they are goal oriented. Relate the goals and objectives to the strategic plan, to individual personal goals, and to the contribution each participant can make (i.e., you as an individual make a difference). The point is to implement the vision as a mid-level function. People must be committed to it because of an innate desire to limit change. People need to be reminded *every day* that they are empowered to make changes. Yet that is not even enough. People must be renewed by participation in their own goals and objectives, with a sense of high expectations. Participation empowers vision. Relate the vision as the path to personal success.

Renew People

Selective movement of people in and out of the organization promotes renewal. Effective organizations intentionally recruit even the maverick. They challenge what is. Training and development are key. Reassignment is one of the most promising strategies to developing talent. One goal (and a desired result) of any good organization must be the development of its people. Reorganization is another way to renew people. It changes the constellation of key players and keeps people refreshed.

Measure It or Forget It

What gets measured gets produced. The use of key *management indicators* is important. Whereas implementation is a mid-level function, measurement is a top management function.

Rewards are a key component of any measurement system. What gets rewarded gets produced again. Be careful with using money as a reward. Reward those who use the vision. Create heroes and tell stories about those who exemplify the vision in action. Reward individuals and teams. Celebrate and share the spoils.

TQ Integrated with Information

Information management is a key component of TQ. The data used to support management indicators must come from a sound information management system. The manager should look for trouble spots because, "Bad news is good news." To identify the early warnings of trouble, be alert to new information and to subtle deviations in the typical routine. Data collection is part of the continuous improvement process. Give me the bad news—then I can fix the problem. Use that information to improve the process. This will result in improved quality, which will thereby improve results.

The Keys to Change and Renewal

The leader of an organization may do well by considering the following key changes:

1. Work hard—change begins with you. Ask yourself, "What am I doing that either empowers people to change or prevents them from changing?" It won't be easy; you have years of programming that tell you the manager is the leader and is there to fix problems and provide answers to questions.
2. You must change from being a dictator to being a facilitator, or a coach. Today you have smart people working for you; could it be that they know more than you? The vision is the focus of all your activities.
3. Communicate the purpose, philosophy, mission, and goals (e.g., the vision).
4. Create a sense of urgency. Urgency is the energy to change today—it is the fuel for your rocket!
5. Measure the results of quality, customer service, employee growth and development, communication, ethics, on-time delivery, etc.

CONCLUSION

The following are key questions to be asked in determining whether you have empowered others to live your organization's vision: What goals and action plans do I have for executing the vision in my area? How can I help? What information channels can we establish through which we can discuss the vision and how to attain it? How can I stay informed without undercutting others? How can we force ourselves to recognize heroes? How can we ensure that the team stays focused on the vision? How do we deal with those who cannot change? Don't move too quickly—many will take a "wait and see" attitude. They want to see if your actions speak louder than your words. Others may need training.

REFERENCES

Belasco, J. A. (1990). *Teaching the Elephant to Dance*, New York: Crown Publishers.

Gardner, J. W. (1990). *On Leadership*, New York: The Free Press.

Hofstede, G. (1993). "Cultural Constraints in Management Theories." *Academy of Management Executive*, 7(1).

Marszalek-Gaucher, E. and Coffey, R. J. (1990). *Transforming Healthcare Organizations*, San Francisco: Jossey-Bass.

Moran, E. T. and Volkwein, F. (1992). "The Cultural Approach to the Formation of Organizational Climate." *Human Relations*, 45(1).

Morgan, G. (1986). *Images of Organization*, Newbury Park, Calif.: Sage Publications.

Pfeffer, J. (1992). *Managing With Power*, Boston: Harvard Business School Press.

PART IV

STRATEGIC DIRECTIONS

9

INTEGRATION of TOTAL QUALITY and QUALITY ASSURANCE

Bryan S. Tindill, MSHA

Douglas W. Stewart, DO

Even though the processes of quality assurance (QA) and total quality (TQ) differ, the ultimate goal of both is the improvement of patient care. This chapter contrasts the differences between TQ and QA. The functional connections between traditional QA and modern industrial quality management science (IQMS) are emphasized. These connections serve as a framework for the integration of QA activities into the organizationwide, continuous quality improvement process of TQ.

To avoid problems with semantics, terms used in this chapter are defined as follows: QA refers to a traditional evaluation of performance that relies on inspection to detect conformance to standards. TQ is a comprehensive management philosophy that focuses on continuous improvement by applying scientific methods to gain knowledge and control over variation in work processes. It is applicable to both manufacturing and service industries. Constant efforts to satisfy the requirements of internal and external customers drive the TQ system. The terms organizationwide quality improvement (OQI), total quality management (TQM), total quality improvement (TQI), continuous quality improvement (CQI), and IQMS are often used synonymously with TQ.

The history of quality assessment in healthcare dates back to the work of Florence Nightingale and her use of applied epidemiology to investigate hypotheses regarding problems with hospital care during the Crimean War. Later, during the Depression, however, interest in the study and its application to healthcare systems and outcome management waned. The practice of QA grew in the 1950s. During this time the Joint Commission was created to accredit hospitals. (Today it is known as the Joint Commission on the Accreditation of Healthcare Organizations, or JCAHO.) The original focus of this approach was inspection to ensure that hospitals met minimum standards of care and requirements for organizational structure. In the 1960s and 1970s the government emerged as an important purchaser of healthcare services. QA grew along with the expansion of federal and state healthcare regulations, seemingly in direct proportion to increasing government expenditures for healthcare.

The 1980s witnessed the evolution of IQMS in the United States. This new philosophy relied on building quality into production processes rather than inspecting and eliminating poor quality after the fact. Yet the health service industry was slow to adopt the continuous improvement, TQ paradigm. Healthcare organizations continued to focus on meeting internal and external requirements set by accrediting agencies and third-party payers, strengthening their QA departments and committees. Thus, during a time when other industries were beginning to implement TQI processes organizationwide, health service organizations simply tended to revitalize their QA activities. It would take a crisis in the 1990s before healthcare organizations would begin integrating TQ with QA activities and analyzing processes to improve standards of care and overall outcomes.

In the 1990s there was a strong impetus for manufacturing and other service industries to study and apply continuous improvement, or TQ. The incentive was threefold: increasing pressure of competition from Japanese industries, the rediscovery of several American scientists who had helped post World War II Japan rebuild its industrial base, and the beginning of a concomitant move toward customer-driven service. While some healthcare organizations have enjoyed great success in their transformation to OQI, many other hospitals, clinics, and departments are reluctant or unwilling to abandon their investment and experience with traditional QA programs.

QUALITY ASSURANCE ACTIVITIES in HEALTHCARE

Throughout the medical community there is little dispute that healthcare should be of high quality and reasonable value. As both healthcare costs and cost containment efforts increase, providers and patients are questioning whether they are receiving the greatest benefit for their dollars spent and whether the level of healthcare provided is being compromised. The primary response to this question has been a strong emphasis on traditional QA programs (Harris, 1990). QA professionals gather and analyze data in order to identify exceptionally bad examples of care. Harris (1990) indicates that this process of inspection is based on the long and honorable tradition that rose out of attempts to reduce surgical mortality and morbidity.

Involving professional staff in programs to inspect healthcare and its many elements is a main component of QA. Such programs take various forms: committee review structures, external review of cases and incidents, and criterion-based reviews of care by both internal and external reviewers.

QA activities are important in healthcare organizations for several reasons. One of the most prominent features of QA activities is to guarantee that organizations meet predefined healthcare standards. Healthcare organizations use these standards to measure activities involved in the delivery of care. In addition, QA standards are intended to help these organizations meet changing healthcare demands. For the most part, healthcare organizations have practiced QA as a limited set of activities. The scope of methods employed to ensure quality in healthcare mirrored requirements of the Joint Commission (JCAHO). In the late 1970s, JCAHO finally established formal and explicit QA standards.

QA approaches have undergone constant change since becoming formalized as QA standards. QA standards of the last ten to fifteen years have relied primarily on diagnosis-focused and procedure-focused audit approaches. Recently, however, QA programs have included the ongoing systematic monitoring and evaluation of critical aspects of care. TQ, on the other hand, focuses on improving the processes through which organizations deliver healthcare, as well as the overall outcomes. Berwick (1989) illustrates difficulties that have arisen due to structure-oriented QA approaches, explaining that most hospital-based QA efforts have attempted to detect "bad apples"—those providers who are unscrupulous, irresponsible, and/or incompetent. Even though these providers represent a very small minority, healthcare organizations have applied a large proportion of QA resources in efforts to identify them and institute some form of regulatory-based sanctions. Williams (1991) suggests that healthcare organizations should have applied these resources to improvement activities for the majority of providers; the cost of not doing so is staggering.

Current JCAHO initiatives stress the identification of opportunities to improve patient care, demonstration of appropriate action taken, and follow-up on the effectiveness of action taken (Green, 1991). JCAHO's "Ten-Step Process for Monitoring and Evaluation" embodies the essence of the current approach to healthcare QA (Batalden, 1991). Followers of JCAHO initiatives have noted an increased emphasis on TQ and diminishing references to QA. While JCAHO has expressed and demonstrated its commitment to TQ in healthcare, it continues to promote the ten-step process as one of several valid methodologies for improving quality.

TOTAL QUALITY

If quality has always been an implicit goal in healthcare, why have hospitals throughout the country recently started talking about quality as if it were a new idea? As Berger and Sudman (1991) explain, the talk is about taking quality to yet another level—extending the standard of quality that people expect in clinical care into every aspect of the service and management system in a hospital. The concept is called total quality (TQ) or organizationwide quality improvement (OQI). However, even though the principles and philosophy of TQ are logical and straightforward, their application in the healthcare industry is difficult. TQ requires extensive education, unavoidable interdependency with others, experimentation, willingness to be vulnerable, and above all, leadership (Berwick et al., 1992).

The conceptual approach of TQ differs from that of QA. TQ calls for continuous and relentless improvement in the total process that provides care, not simply in the improved actions of individual professionals. Thus, it bases improvements on both outcome and process (Kaluzny and McLaughlin, 1990). The philosophy of TQ also differs from QA because it recognizes that defects in quality are rarely the result of a lack of will or intention by the healthcare worker. Thus, organizations that practice TQ identify root causes of defects within the system. The systematic analysis of TQ often reveals that these causes of quality defects are due to poor job design, equipment failure, lack of leadership, or unclear purpose (Berwick, 1989). Some estimate that these system failures cause 85% of the errors that occur. Another substantial point of difference between QA and TQ is that TQ is a top-down management philosophy that implies an organizationwide commitment to the quality improvement process. Harrington (1987) explains this management commitment, "The employee is the hub of the process, but management is the axle that makes it turn."

If it is to succeed, management, as well as employees representing all levels of the organization, need to master and utilize the skills associated with the TQ process. TQ is a long-term, ongoing process that requires hard work and a step-by-step approach. It should not be viewed as a program or management fad, but as a set of philosophies and structured methods to guide the continual improvement of all aspects of business. TQ stresses improvement through more efficient and effective design and redesign of processes. A central focus of TQ is to control normal process variation, eliminate defects, and remove special causes of variation. In contrast to the reactive approach of QA, TQ is proactive in nature. Organizations use TQ to build in product and service quality when designing new processes or redesigning old ones. Thereafter, they use TQ to improve those processes continually. Compared to QA, TQ also demands a comprehensive change in the culture of the organization. TQ empowers employees at lower levels of the hierarchy to make decisions. Existing attitudes and management styles come under close scrutiny. TQ often involves a wide range of job functions at different organizational levels in combined efforts to study a process, identify the most important area for improvement, and develop solutions. When initially implementing TQ, organizations usually select a few specific areas in which to begin. In the long run, however, successful implementation requires comprehensive participation. All systems and processes become subject to evaluation and change. Thus, unlike QA, applying TQ locally defeats its purpose.

Often, we credit the Japanese with being the innovators of quality leadership and planning. However, during the 1950s, two American quality gurus, W. Edwards Deming and Joseph M. Juran, taught the Japanese statistical methods for quality control and introduced them to a new management philosophy which is now called TQ. The healthcare industry is just beginning to acknowledge the value of this TQ philosophy, as evidenced by the increase in quality-related material in healthcare literature beginning in the late 1980s.

TRANSITION to TOTAL QUALITY: MANUFACTURING and HEALTH SERVICE SECTORS

During the past several years, hospitals have been under many of the same pressures that U.S. manufacturers faced in the 1960s and 1970s: heightened competitive pressures, purchaser concerns about quality, escalating costs, and increased accountability to the public (Andrews, 1991). In this environment, more and more hospitals began to embrace TQ in the hope that it would improve quality and efficiency. Some organizations have failed, as in other industries, while others have enjoyed great success (Newbold, 1990). Each hospital has a unique and diverse environment that presents its own set of barriers that it must overcome before TQ can flourish.

Traditional QA approaches are being challenged, while numerous public and private sector initiatives are being developed to test new models in the quest for the ideal quality management system. Factors both internal and external to the healthcare industry are driving the evolution of healthcare QA. Initiatives for change in QA methods have arisen in response to scrutiny from prospective payment, cost containment movements, increased competition, and increased consumer and purchaser involvement (Batalden, 1991). In numerous medical facilities around the country, employees do not view the QA program in a positive manner. Many question whether healthcare organizations have used QA effectively as a constructive activity. Berwick et al. (1992) implicate review and assurance activities in drawing "the U.S.

213

into a costly cycle of surveillance, contention, and stagnation." These assertions and the apparent inability of QA to play a significant role in the resolution of cost and quality problems have led some healthcare organizations to adopt a new management philosophy—TQ.

Hospitals have begun to examine their definition of quality and to determine how physicians, payers, and patients define quality. It is suggested that while QA programs focus on clinical aspects of healthcare, many experts believe that consumers place equal emphasis on the quality of care given and an array of amenities. Medical care quality is a complex and abstract concept that eludes precise explanation. No universal definition currently exists for quality of care, which makes its measurement problematic (Beloff, 1991).

At this point, much of TQ remains unproven with regard to healthcare (O'Leary, 1991). We do know that manufacturing organizations have achieved astonishing results when TQ tools and methods have been used to measure and improve their processes. The question in healthcare is why results have not yet been seen. Newbold (1990) suggests that implementing TQ requires a minimum of three to six years before an organization can expect to achieve any notable results. Further, he finds that any commitment to a shorter period is likely to be ineffective, and the organization should withhold assessment of improvements until that length of time has elapsed. Hospitals are only just getting started, and too little knowledge is available in the industry to facilitate the discovery of useful data elements (Keil, 1991). An additional obstacle to TQ implementation in hospitals involves the traditional hierarchical culture, with roles and boundaries for physicians, nurses, administrators, and other support staff. This structure will not be easily dismantled or rebuilt. A recent study of Veterans Administration medical facilities (VAMCs) by Reeves and Bednar (1993) revealed that managers at all levels "identified their direct supervisors as having the potential to present significant barriers to TQ implementation." The study also noted that executive turnover was another formidable obstacle to the adoption of the new and innovative management philosophy. When the senior manager who championed the new paradigm subsequently leaves, the driving force for the management revolution disappears.

There are major differences between service industries and manufacturing industries which warrant a careful analysis of the quality attributes and requirements for quality improvement. According to Bliersbach (1991), in contrast to the manufacturing sector, the service industry has the following characteristics:

1. Services are dominated by subjective elements, not precise physical elements.

2. No inventory control can be established over services. Services cannot be stored, because they are extremely perishable.
3. Most service organizations must contend with a strong client or patient presence in providing their service.
4. The process of providing services requires a complex, highly efficient delivery system that is time sensitive.
5. It is difficult to create concrete, objective measures to evaluate the service delivery process.

Finally, the transformation from assessment of technical care (the science of medicine) to interpersonal care (the art of medicine) requires some additional discussion, which is beyond the score of this chapter. However, it is worthwhile to note that an increased appreciation of the significance of the patient's perception of care has led to the emergence of a customer-driven focus in healthcare and interest in the measurement of patient satisfaction (Donabedian, 1988; Aharony and Strasser, 1993).

COMPARISON of QA and TQ

Whether fairly portrayed or not, many have come to view QA as an activity to fix blame. In contrast, TQ searches for root causes of problems in processes within the healthcare system, rather than among the ranks of its employees. Although many hospitals have updated and improved their QA programs, most have focused these enterprises on departments or individuals, rather than on integrating them into the entire organization. They often build their QA programs around external accreditation agency requirements, and therefore the resulting programs are usually narrow in scope. Even though some hospitals have incorporated QA into their management philosophy, there is little emphasis on error-free work, management by prevention, and the sense of ownership or involvement in quality issues by employees or managers. In many healthcare organizations the QA department is tucked away and generally does not influence systems between accreditation surveys.

QA programs currently in use generally have three major foci: (1) assessing or measuring performance, (2) determining whether performance conforms to standards, and (3) improving performance when standards are not met (Laffel and Blumenthal, 1989). Once the healthcare organization meets the standards, however, the QA program often comes to a standstill until it notes another problem of nonconformance. On the other hand, the TQ process actively seeks opportunities for improvement and takes action to eliminate costly variations, thereby improving quality. Unlike QA programs, TQ is a continuous process that never stops.

Laffel and Blumenthal (1989) noted several limitations to the current approach to quality. First, QA often does not extend beyond meeting standards, thereby making the system static and reactive. Second, the QA coordinator and/or QA department is the main driver of QA. In contrast, focused and combined efforts of all departments and employees drive TQ. Where the TQ philosophy permeates the culture of an organization, all employees share responsibility for achieving excellence in quality. The organization empowers employees to assume this responsibility, providing training in a common set of TQ tools and techniques that enables healthcare workers to control, manage, and improve their work processes. Thus, in a TQ environment, employees can carry on their work without the all too common sense of frustration, waste, and helplessness (Berwick et al., 1992). Finally, QA has traditionally focused on the performance of the physician and other clinicians and has underestimated the contributions of nonphysicians and organizational processes. TQ, on the other hand, evaluates the contributions of nonclinical departments as well, so that they too can play an important role in the effort to improve healthcare service.

QA-driven changes usually involve specific structure or process elements. The assumption behind these changes is that QA will improve outcomes, but QA does not emphasize or validate the relationship between structure, process, and outcomes. In contrast, TQ-driven improvements focus on specific outcomes and then deductively identify those processes that, if changed, might result in measurable improvement. Compared to TQ, QA tends to be narrow in scope—focused on variables that are easily measured. TQ is more comprehensive—first defining the process and required outcomes, then seeking objective evidence to indicate that an opportunity for improvement exists, identifying the most important area in which to conduct improvement experiments, and finally verifying that the process outcomes have improved. QA outcome measures reflect an essential inspection process. They are designed to indicate poor outcomes. In this capacity, they will continue to be important as part of a broader TQ system for QCI. However, these measures have limited value because they do not provide insight into the causes of defects. TQ provides a system that can work in conjunction with traditional QA outcome measures to focus on identifying and eliminating root causes of defects within the processes involved in producing those outcomes (Laffel and Blumenthal, 1989). A further distinction can be made between QA and TQ regarding the more subjective, personal influence of TQ on participants in the healthcare system. Williamson (1991) points out that TQ more often involves internal rewards, such as professional gratification derived from personal growth or improved patient health.

As presented by Andrews (1991), six key elements distinguish TQ from traditional QA programs:

1. A focus on process, not people
2. Defining quality as meeting the needs of the customer
3. Improving quality to reduce costs
4. Building quality into the process
5. Using a scientific approach to problem solving
6. Approaching quality as a management strategy

Both the differences and similarities between QA and TQ are meaningful. In simple terms, healthcare organizations can integrate TQ with QA by using the positive aspects of QA as a foundation for developing a comprehensive systems approach to healthcare quality issues. Just as QA has been the common thread through current JCAHO standards, TQ progressively will become the central theme of the new standards framework that is evolving as a major component of the agenda for change in healthcare.

INTEGRATION of QA and TQ

While many healthcare organizations across the United States are implementing TQ, currently a number of them are not integrating their QA functions with the TQ process. Without proper integration, QA and TQ efforts parallel each other, duplications occur, and organizations send mixed messages regarding the degree of support for the role of QA (Green, 1991). Some leaders of healthcare organizations have reacted as though they face an either/or decision about QA and TQ. This is not so. Common ground exists between QA and TQ, and each offers complementary strengths. Together, QA and TQ can serve as a solid foundation for an optimal TQ healthcare system. Thus, the integration of QA and TQ presents the healthcare industry with an opportunity to build upon the best of these approaches in order to reach the goal of continual improvement in quality. (For a discussion of Dr. Berwick's views, see "Quality: How Do QI and QA Differ? An Expert Illustrates the Answer." *Hospital Management Review*, 9:2, 1990.) Table 9-1 lists the strengths of current QA programs that provide a foundation to bolster the success of quality improvement in a healthcare system.

The successful implementation of a TQ system offers resolution to many current barriers obstructing effective quality management for the healthcare organization. Clearly, quality in healthcare has multiple dimensions that dictate the need for an IQMS. These dimensions include clinical quality, patient and customer service, appropriateness of care, cost effectiveness and efficiency, reduction of clinical risk, and patient and employee safety (Green, 1991). Thus, by providing a coherent philosophy and methodology

Table 9-1.   Strengths of Quality Assurance.

- Experience in the development of indicators to evaluate healthcare structure, process, and outcome
- Identification of high priority areas
- Expansion of professionals knowledgeable about theory and methods of quality assessment
- Development of quality information systems
- Identification of a professional who is knowledgeable about information systems and data management

---

(Source: American Medical Records Association, 1991)

that can ensure continuous quality improvement, TQ offers a solution to long-standing and current obstacles to effective healthcare quality management. Table 9-2 lists the strengths of quality improvement.

While there is no recipe for successfully implementing TQ in a healthcare organization, the following observations indicate winning management strategies for organizational transformation:

1. The organization acknowledges that customers are the most important part of the healthcare system. They are both a beneficiary and a part of the TQ process. Customer requirements, or needs, determine both the desired outcome of the process and how it should work.
2. Management makes a long-term commitment to integrate the continuous improvement process of TQ into the management structure (through such elements as strategy, planning, and leadership—modeling desired actions and attitudes, etc.).
3. Reward systems reinforce new behaviors required in the TQ system. The organization appropriately recognizes both managers and employees for their successes and contributions.
4. All organization members focus on opportunities for improvement, convinced that these represent opportunities for future success.
5. Everyone contributes to the continuous improvement effort because they know that preventing problems is better than reacting to them.
6. Management empowers and supports all members of the organization so they can fully participate in the TQ system, within teams and as individuals. They place great value on both personal and mutual, team-based development, recognizing that human capital is the most important asset of the organization.

Table 9-2.   Strengths of Total Quality.

- Continuous commitment to quality by the leadership of the organization
- Strong reliance on the organizational structure for improvement of process
- Elevation of the support function for managing quality by appointment of a senior officer for quality, reporting directly to the chief executive officer of the organization
- Integration of quality focus into total management of the organization
- Reliance on scientific management techniques and tools for evaluating and improving quality of services
- Employee ownership of quality, with delegation of authority to evaluate, plan improvements, and take corrective action within the scope of the individual's responsibilities
- Focus on systems for service delivery and on performance of the average producer versus a focus on identification and correction of outlier performance

(Source: American Medical Records Association, 1991)

7. Everyone recognizes that problems are usually the result of system failures, rather than human failures. Instead, they analyze and resolve problems in the context of an overall process. Thus, the focus is on improving the process, not blaming the people within it.

SUMMARY AND CONCLUSION

As the level of information and interest in TQ in healthcare increases, so does the level of confusion among healthcare managers, physicians, and administrators regarding the distinctions between TQ and the traditional QA role. There is understandable hesitancy on the part of many healthcare providers to discontinue or modify established QA programs. They are more familiar with QA, and external accrediting bodies require QA. However, there is much value in utilizing common elements of both processes in order to obtain a TQ culture. Creating a TQ culture throughout an organization is a long, slow process. It requires significant time to realize the benefits of quality improvement, time to learn how to best apply quality principles, and time to allow the process to become institutionalized within the organization. The application of TQ to healthcare provides management with a means to expand critical evaluation to include all the systems that clearly contribute to the effectiveness of providers and organizations (Tyler, 1991).

219

REFERENCES

Aharony, I. and Strasser, S. (1993) "Patient Satisfaction: What We Know About and What We Still Need to Explore." *Medical Care Review,* 50:49–79.

Andrews, S. L. (1991). "QA vs. QI: The Changing Role of Quality in Health Care." *Journal of Quality Assurance,* 38:14–15.

Batalden P. B. (1991). "Organizationwide Quality Improvement in Healthcare." *Topics in Health Records Management,* pp. 1–12.

Beloff, J. (1991). "What Is Quality and How Is It Measured?" *Physician Executive,* (17)3:20–24.

Berger, S. and Sudman, S. (1991) "Making Total Quality Management Work." *Healthcare Executive,* March/April:22–25.

Berwick, D. M. (1989). "Continuous Improvement as an Ideal in Health Care." *New England Journal of Medicine,* 320:53–56.

Berwick, D. M, Enthoven, A., and Bunker, J. P. (1992). "Quality Management in the NHS: The Doctor's Role." *British Medical Journal,* 304:235–239, 304–308.

Bliersbach, C. (1991). "Quality Improvement: One-Third of the Quality Equation." *Journal of Quality Assurance,* September/October:58–61.

Donabedian, A. (1988). "The Quality of Care: How Can It Be Assessed?" *Journal of the American Medical Association,* 260:1743–1748.

Green, D. (1991). "Quality Improvement versus Quality Assurance?" *Topics in Health Records Management,* 11:58–70.

Harrington, H. J. (1987). *The Improvement Process,* New York: McGraw-Hill.

Harris, J. S. (1990). "The Bridge for Quality Assurance to Quality Improvement," *Journal of Occupational Medicine,* 17:1175–1176.

Kaluzny, A. D. and McLaughlin, C. P. (1990). "Total Quality Management in Health: Making it Work." *Health Care Management Review,* 15(3):7–14.

Keil, O. (1991). "From Quality Assurance to Quality Improvement: A Guide to the Joint Commission's Change in Emphasis." *Biomedical Instrumentation and Technology,* July/ August:278–281.

Laffel, G. and Blumenthal, D. (1989). "The Case for Using Industrial Quality Management Science in Health Care Organizations." *Journal of the American Medical Association,* 262(20):2869–2873.

Newbold, P. (1990). "Quality Improvement: Lessons From Experience." *Decisions in Imaging Economics,* pp. 14–17.

O'Leary, D. S. (1991). "CQI—A Step Beyond QA." *Quality Review Bulletin,* January: 4–5.

Reeves, C. A. and Bednar, D. A. (1993). "What Prevents TQM Implementation in Health Care Organizations?" *Quality Progress,* April:41–44.

Tyler, R. D. (1991). "From QA to TQM." *Physician Executive,* May/June:25–28.

Williamson, R. G. (1991). "A CEO's Perspective of TQM." *Frontiers of Health Service Management,* Summer:51–54.

10

OUTCOME MANAGEMENT and TQ

A. F. Al-Assaf, MD, MPH

Healthcare researchers and practitioners have used several methods in their attempt to measure and monitor the quality of healthcare. As early as the mid-1800s, Florence Nightingale (1859) endeavored to measure quality of care by examining outcomes. The most common indicators she studied measured mortality rates and specific morbidity rates.

Relying on outcome measures, however, was not the only way in which quality was measured. Flexner's famous report in 1910 on medical education and training relied on *structure* measures. Until recently, the Joint Commission on Accreditation of Healthcare Organizations (JCAHO) has relied on structure measures in drafting their annual hospital standards for accreditation manual. Peer Review Organizations (PROs), on the other hand, relied on *process* indicators in evaluating the quality of care provided to Medicare patients. Currently, however, a new movement called *outcome management* is evolving to include a number of areas that impact the quality of patient care. It focuses on using outcome measures to *manage* quality. The trend toward outcome management is driven by economics and, to a lesser extent, by the curiosity of providers and researchers.

This chapter introduces the topic of outcome management and attempts to link it with continuous quality improvement (CQI) and total quality (TQ). It presents the history and evolution of how the healthcare industry has used outcome indicators for measurement. Other areas related to outcome management are highlighted, with an emphasis on special studies and key players who are driving the movement. The chapter concludes with a discussion of the limitations and challenges facing outcome management and a special look into the future to consider what outcome management can provide for those in the healthcare industry.

BACKGROUND of QUALITY OUTCOME

In 1854 Florence Nightingale introduced outcome indicators to measure mortality rates and monitor the quality of patient care. During the Crimean War, she collected statistics on wounded soldiers who eventually died, as well as those who recovered. She correlated these outcomes with the intensity and quality of nursing care they received. She discovered that adequate nursing care was instrumental in reducing soldier mortality rates from 32% to 2% (Nightingale, 1859). Later, with her studies on hospital deaths stratified by disease category, Nightingale was effective in correlating this outcome indicator with sanitation and unsafe environments. Her arguments, supported by her studies on outcome measures, won national support to improve the quality of patient care and the hospital environment.

Other British researchers, in particular an epidemiologist named W. Farr, called for local physicians to publish the mortality statistics they collected (Daley, 1991). Farr was attempting to correlate patient mortality with overall community health. This was also another effort to link mortality data as an outcome indicator to the quality of care delivered to patients by physicians. In 1908, Dr. Emory W. Groves of Britain also conducted several studies on outcome measures. He collected data on patient mortality as an outcome indicator, as well as surgical procedures. Based on his findings, he argued that a standard classification of disease categories should be established for comparison of care. He also suggested that there should be guidelines for patient follow-ups after surgeries to ensure adequate care and to reduce adverse outcomes.

In 1914, a Massachusetts General Hospital surgeon named Dr. Ernest A. Codman pointed out that hospitals should look at the result of patient care as an indicator of the quality of care rendered while a patient is in the hospital. He argued that studying the end result will suggest where problems occurred and identify ways to prevent them from recurring. He also suggested that a measurable indicator, such as hospital mortality, is one way to evaluate the care. He stated that there are two types of hospital-related deaths: unavoidable and intentional. The latter is highly dependent on the care provided by the clinician and the services rendered by other hospital personnel. Although some outcome measures continued to be used in Europe and the United States, the trend began to favor structure measures and, later, process measures. Outcome measurement, however, did not fade completely. Researchers and practitioners continued to collected data on outcome indicators and used them in their attempts to understand and monitor the quality of care. Outcome indicators, however, saw a new revival when Professor Avedis Donabedian (1966) published his paper on evaluating quality of medical care. Dr. Donabedian referred to three approaches to quality measurement and monitoring: structure, process, and outcome.

He noted that all three are equally important in measuring the quality of care provided by a healthcare organization. He also emphasized that these three approaches are complementary and should be used collectively to monitor quality of care.

Several studies followed which emphasized outcome measures in monitoring and evaluating quality of patient care. In the late 1960s the National Halothane Study was funded to investigate the correlation between the use of the anesthetic halothane and hepatic necrosis in postsurgical patients. The study involved 34 university teaching hospitals and focused on variations in mortality rates. After adjusting for case mix and other variables, the study concluded that variation in mortality was attributable to the effectiveness of care (Moses and Mosteller, 1968; Bunker et al., 1969). Roemer and Friedman (1971) published another study relating outcome to variables in patient care. This study examined the quality of the organizational structure of a medical staff and concluded that it was inversely related to hospital mortality rates. Similar studies by Shortell and LoGerfo (1981) and Flood et al. (1982) supported the same correlation.

Several researchers found that the volume of surgical operations performed in any one hospital correlated inversely with the mortality rate from those hospital procedures (Luft et al., 1979; Flood et al., 1984a). Reviewing abstracts from the Commission on Professional and Hospital Activities for selected surgical operations, Luft et al. (1979) found that mortality rates were lower in those hospitals with higher volumes of certain surgical procedures. Other studies by Flood et al. (1984b) looked at similar variables and drew similar conclusions. As more surgical procedures were performed in a hospital, the mortality rates resulting from these procedures were lowered. These data suggested a negative correlation. As more procedures are performed, hospital staffs gain the experience that enables them to deliver better quality of care, resulting in fewer deaths.

The call to use outcome, process, and structure indicators in quality evaluation gained considerable attention among researchers. However, the healthcare delivery system lacked the driving force, or incentive, to apply them in practice—to subscribe to Dr. Donabedian's ideas. During the 1950s through the 1970s, JCAHO (then called the Joint Commission on Accreditation of Hospitals, JCAH) emphasized structure standards in its monitoring activities. Because accreditation is important to hospitals, their incentive has been to focus on meeting JCAHO structure standards and use them as indicators of quality service. This trend continued until the 1970s, when Professional Standards Review Organizations (PSROs) were established. They emphasized process in the evaluation of medical care delivered to Medicare patients. This emphasis was again adopted by the successors of PSROs, the PROs, which were established in the early 1980s. (For further information on PSROs and PROs, refer to Chapter 1.)

223

Some outcome measures have always been used to collect and analyze data on outcomes. However, they were limited to primarily internal use and academic investigations. Data were shared with outside agencies only on a selective and sporadic basis. This trend continued until 1986, when the Health Care Financing Administration (HCFA), operating under the protection of the Freedom of Information Act, published its first report on hospital mortality data. The results were captured in a March 16, 1986 *New York Times* article entitled, "U.S. Releasing Lists of Hospitals with Abnormal Mortality Rates." This report presented the mortality rates of the nation's hospitals based on information collected from Medicare reimbursement data. This crude analysis of mortality rates by hospitals attracted major attention nationwide, particularly from the hospitals named and JCAHO. With all its limitations, the report stirred a new movement toward outcome measurement and in 1987 prompted JCAHO (almost concurrently with HFCA) to publish its Agenda for Change (O'Leary, 1987). JCAHO's new outcome-focused direction was probably an attempt to recapture the hospital accreditation market, especially because the HCFA had become more interested in outcome measures. JCAHO launched a major publicity campaign for its initiative, which sought both clinical and organizational outcome measures. JCAHO capitalized on this new trend toward outcome-focused research, engaging several U.S. hospitals (selected as a representative sample) to collect data on predefined outcome indicators. The objective was to design a national norm of outcome indicators for inpatient services to evaluate quality of care delivered. This project is still in process.

Following these two events, several other organizations became interested in outcome research. As part of the Omnibus Budget Reconciliation Act (OBRA) of 1986, the U.S. Congress called for the Institute of Medicine (IOM) to review the quality of the Medicare program. As expected, the IOM report emphasized outcome and discussed several advantages in doing so. The most prominent point made was that outcome measures are systematic and closely related to process quality (IOM, 1989). Therefore, attempts to improve processes should have a positive impact on outcome and vice versa. The IOM report also called for expansion of outcome research and the inclusion of clinical practice guideline development. This report prompted Congress to pass the OBRA of 1989. This act included new initiatives for research in outcomes of care. In 1990, the Secretary of the Department of Health and Human Services, Dr. Louis Sullivan, created the Agency for Health Care Policy and Research (AHCPR). This became the eighth Public Health Service agency in place of the National Center for Health Service Research. The mandate of the AHCPR was to encourage research in the areas of quality, cost effectiveness, and outcome research (Nash and Markson, 1991).

AHCPR has become active in the area of outcome research and, in particular, clinical practice guidelines. In coordination with other agencies such as HCFA and the National Institutes of Health (NIH), AHCPR has supported several institutions and research organizations in developing Patient Outcome Research Teams (PORTs). Funding for such teams has been very generous ($5 million per grant). Their objectives are to evaluate disease conditions from a multidisciplinary standpoint and to develop appropriate and acceptable universal practice guidelines for the prevention, treatment, and management of these disease conditions. This initiative views clinical evaluation from a multidisciplinary perspective, which should allow a team to manage patient outcomes from the standpoint of prevention, treatment, policy formulation, and epidemiological analyses. This new emphasis should prove effective in managing outcomes from such different perspectives as clinical, economical, political, social, etc.

WHAT IS OUTCOME and
WHAT IS OUTCOME MANAGEMENT?

An outcome is the end result of a process. In healthcare, outcome research is usually patient oriented. The end result of a process, protocol, or procedure delivered by a structured system of health professionals must be customer oriented. Here, of course, the main customer is the patient. Therefore, to be useful to a healthcare organization, outcomes must be targeted at improving the medical status of the patient (Lohr, 1987). It is for this reason that outcome research is important in developing paradigms of clinical processes and patterns that are most efficient in achieving the objective of improving a patient's medical status. Examples of outcomes include patient satisfaction, patient mortality, unscheduled return to the operating room, readmission within 72 hours of discharge for the same medical condition, etc. These are obvious direct care outcomes, but what about behavioral, physiological, and psychosocial outcomes? Other outcomes receiving attention include rehabilitation potential, functional status, and quality of life (Jennings, 1991). Although outcomes are the end result, they must be analyzed as part of the total picture, i.e., patients and their environment. This is the only way that outcomes can have meaning and use in improving the quality of healthcare. Outcome management is the process of collecting, analyzing, evaluating, and disseminating the results of medical processes or procedures to improve the results of healthcare. The guidelines and protocols for these procedures are agreed upon by appropriate and widely accepted bodies. This process should be achieved through a collaborative effort by all players in the healthcare system—patients, purchasers, providers, payers, and regulators. This can only be accomplished through

225

total integration of the system, both vertically and horizontally (Geehr, 1992). Ellwood (1988) introduced four benefits of outcome management:

- Outcome management will provide physicians with widely accepted guidelines and standards to assist in the process of delivering medical care.
- Over routine and periodic time intervals, outcome management will provide the skills and tools necessary to measure the status and well being of a patient, both clinically and functionally.
- Information on clinical and outcome data would be available in large databases.
- This information would be disseminated widely, customized as appropriate for decision makers, and updated and modified to reflect changes in technologies, philosophies, and expectations.

According to Geehr (1992), outcome management can be achieved by focusing on the following four areas:

1. *Outcome Specification Process* (i.e., Which outcomes? What to measure?). Outcomes may be negative (e.g., mortality, morbidity, cost, complaints, etc.) or positive (e.g., satisfaction, quality of life, effectiveness, appropriateness, etc.). Outcomes of medical processes are collected and analyzed; they may be customized from the standpoing of a purchaser (buy-right strategies), a patient (participation in clinical decision making), or a provider (guidelines for appropriate, effective, and efficient care).

2. *Outcome Measurement Instruments.* The objective is not only to collect valid, appropriate, and comprehensive data regarding an outcome, but also to collect these data in an efficient, standardized, and error-free manner. Therefore, it behooves healthcare professionals to automate this process and to agree on a tool or collection of tools to achieve this objective. One example of such a tool is the Health Status Questionnaire or Short Form 36 (SF-36) developed by the Medical Outcome Study conducted by the Rand Corporation (Nash and Markson, 1991). This tool provides a measure of functional status, including social, physical, and mental health status (Ellwood et al., 1991). Another example is the work provided by Quality Quest (within InterStudy) to develop tools for severity-of-illness measures. These tools are collectively referred to as TyPE (Technology of Patient Experience). Other institutions supported by AHCPR's PORT grants are also developing standardized tools to collect data for managing outcomes. These efforts are being maximized by the development of optical scanners that can capture these data in a computer, making the process of data input and analysis more efficient and less cumbersome.

3. *Management Information Systems.* The main objective is to establish an automated system of data collection, input, analysis, and retrieval in an integrated manner. The system should support large database query and allow multiple users to share information simultaneously. The proposed management information system should be supported by a decision support system that enhances clinical and management decision-making processes through the intelligent (expert systems and neural network) integration of several databases and logic (fuzzy logic and artificial intelligence) pathways. Although the technology is currently available to simulate clinical cases and develop critical pathways, future technological advances should refine this function even further. A provider may be able to electronically test different clinical management modalities in simulated case scenarios and then choose the best possible outcome.

4. *Continuous Improvement.* Most continuous quality improvement (CQI) paradigms are process oriented and are either prospective problem prevention paradigms or (more commonly) retrospective problem-solving paradigms, or a combination of both. Outcome management, therefore, proves useful in determining the best outcome for a given process. Managing outcomes will have an impact on how processes are structured, conducted, and improved and provide the feedback necessary to develop appropriate, effective, and efficient guidelines. Outcome management is highly dependent on CQI in achieving such an objective in a manner that is equally acceptable to the key players in the healthcare system.

MEASUREMENT of OUTCOMES

The basic principles of measurement rely on well-defined standards, measurement objectives, and a tool to perform the measurement. The main objective of a measurement, of course, is to determine the *relative value* of an item, product, or process. Healthcare organizations have an added incentive to determine the value of their product and service because the quality of life is at stake. These organizations are under pressure from third parties to provide the highest quality product (and service) for the most reasonable (or lowest) cost.

There are three approaches in measuring quality: structure, process, and outcome (Donabedian, 1966). Healthcare organizations have been trained (at least those accredited by the JCAHO) to develop *indicators* that measure performance. These organizations were most often engaged in efforts to collect data from these indicators; their efforts were mainly focused on structure and, to a lesser extent, process indicators. Outcome indicators

227

have not been explored adequately by the healthcare field. Therefore, a new interest is surfacing to develop outcome indicators and then measure quality of performance based on these indicators. What are those measures and how can we use them more efficiently?

An article published in the *QRC Advisor* (1992) explains that outcome measurement aids in comparing past experiences. Experiences between similar groups within an organization seem to be valuable in benchmarking (comparing experiences among organizations in an effort to learn from the successes to improve performance). This same article further explains two reasons why healthcare organizations find it difficult to focus on outcome. One is that an outcome must be considered globally, that is, it involves *all* the results of patient episodes and nothing less. However, one should recognize that results are reached through a series of processes performed by a system structured to carry them out. Therefore, outcome is dependent on structure and process, especially when an adverse result occurs. All the elements that caused or resulted in such an outcome should be examined, and ways to improve them should be considered and implemented. Another reason (or myth) cited for difficulty of focusing on outcome is that healthcare organizations consider outcome to be either physician focused or, on the opposite extreme, dependent on too many individuals. Of course, both statements are debatable. Although physicians are vital to patient outcomes, they are not the only contributors. Other healthcare professionals contribute to producing an outcome. Certain outcomes, however, occur without (or with limited) physician participation (e.g., patient comfort and diet during a recent hospital stay, difficulty with visitor parking facilities, satisfaction ratings, etc). Further, an outcome is traceable to its original source, and the processes leading to it can be identified, studied, and improved. The focus should *not* be on individuals, but rather on processes (usually a manageable number), which can be improved. Therefore outcome is not dependent on *too many* individuals.

Developing an Outcome Indicator

Asking the right question is sometimes the most important step in developing an outcome indicator. First, the difference between structure, process, and outcome measures must be understood. We must then understand whether we are asking a question that actually measures an outcome.

Let us examine an indicator commonly used in academe: The student has received and understood the learning objectives of the course. This indicator is meant to measure an outcome (the student learning from the course), but does it? If the student received and understood the learning objectives of the course, does it also mean that the student learned? The indicator should be rephrased to state that the learning objectives for the course were achieved. Similarly, in healthcare, an outcome indicator commonly used is that the patient received and understood his or her dietary instructions or medication regimen. If the objective here is to measure an outcome, then the only one being measured is the outcome of the process of giving instruction. This is not an outcome that will improve the patient's health and decrease the possibility of the condition recurring. A more valuable outcome indicator would be measured by periodic checks on the patient (by phone or in person) with regard to following and adhering to instructions given for diet or medication. In this way, at least one meaningful and useful outcome to a patient encounter will be measured.

Clearly, outcome measurements are useful to the extent that they have been developed accurately and thoughtfully. The objective must be defined and the appropriate questions asked when developing an outcome measure. To assess measurement, one main question should be the focus: What does it really measure? Does it measure volume, process, resources, and input, or does it measure outcome? To qualify as an outcome measure, the answer to these questions must consistently be *outcome*. It is also important to keep in mind that we need to know *who* will be using it, *when* will it be carried out, and *how* the data will be collected. Of course, the ultimate test of any system of measurement is its validity, reliability, and usefulness (as described in Chapter 5).

Managing Outcomes

Outcome indicators should be directed at the effectiveness of care, the appropriateness of care, or the efficiency of care (Rowland and Rowland, 1992). Outcome measures should be *total* measures. They must be able to measure the end result of a process delivered by a structured system, including the human and physical resources involved. The outcome measure is used to achieve a greater objective—to improve the health status of the main healthcare customer, the patient. Therefore, the desired outcome of a patient encounter should be an improved health status of that patient, relative to his or her health status before the encounter. The degree of this desired improvement is dependent on patient expectations and perceptions and the efforts of the healthcare team to meet them. This is the difference between measuring the outcome of a process and *managing* total patient outcome. This process of outcome management looks at the patient episode as a process in continuum. Outcome management views outcomes in terms of the total process, measuring the extent to which a system accomplished its objective of improving patient care, all the way from health promotion and patient education to clinical intervention, follow-up, and rehabilitation.

QUESTIONS about OUTCOME MEASUREMENTS

Meltzer (1992) raised several questions regarding the usefulness of outcome measurements and the comprehensiveness of the process of outcome management. His article mentions five issues that should be studied when considering outcome management.

1. Accounting for the structural elements that impact an outcome (e.g., the skills and knowledge of the individual provider). The methods of providing care vary, and therefore so should the outcomes of their services.
2. Responsibility and authority for identifying, developing, measuring, and using these outcomes. Individual expectations of desired outcomes may be substandard based on the expectations of another individual. Also, desired outcomes from the perspective of the patient surely differ from those of providers, administrators, or payers.
3. A designed outcome may measure different things for different patients. All patients are not alike. It is possible to deliver a successful process and structure resulting in a desired outcome to one patient, but it may not produce the same desirable outcome for another.
4. Outcome measures are dependent on the quality of the statistical analyses. According to Rowland and Rowland (1992), outcome-based monitoring should be considered from both an epidemiological and a statistical viewpoint. The significance of difference between an observed and an expected outcome must be taken into account, as well as the probability that the expected outcome may recur for a given process or structure.
5. Where should we stop and who will make that decision? What will be the impact of that decision on the *total* outcome of healthcare? These decisions are difficult to make when other factors must be considered (e.g., cost, rationale, ethics, law, norms, etc). Will a decision by a payer to stop performing a diagnostic test that has a 30% success rate be justified from the patient's perspective? What about a test with a success rate of 35% or even 5%? Would rationing healthcare impact outcome management efforts to improve the quality of total patient care?

Returning to the original discussion, outcome measurements involve past experiences, current experiences with process and structure, as well as internal peer review comparisons and benchmarking. Collecting all these data and organizing a good process to measure and manage these outcomes is a formidable task. It is almost inconceivable that the intelligent use of collected data to generate useful and meaningful information can be accomplished without the use of computers. Information systems are invaluable in achieving continuous improvement. Automating medical records should be pursued vigorously to make them accessible on-line. Patient information should be available and easily traced to compare individual and group outcomes within the same facility and historically. Furthermore, technology can provide physicians and clinical decision makers with the ability to trend these outcomes and compare them with results from similar institutions, with the ultimate goal of improving quality of care.

Another issue in outcome management is its impact on the patient. The potential impact of computers was previously discussed, in order for "doctors to see their patients in some larger epidemiological context" (Ellwood, 1992). With the emphasis on outcome management, it will be important to obtain feedback (and lots of it) from patients about their medical care. This includes the efficiency of the treatment, the impact of the diagnosis on the prognosis, the patient's ability to function normally, etc.— all directly from the perspective of the patient. Again, according to Ellwood (1992), the aspect of quality of life is being considered in most major outcome management research activities. The challenge, however, is in determining how to measure quality of life. If such a tool were identified, the information obtained regarding quality of life surely would be more valuable in providing efficient medical care to patients than the current system based on deductibles and co-insurance.

Obviously, outcome management is still evolving, and many of the questions raised are still unanswered. Outcome management, however, has great potential. Its future depends heavily on new techniques for gathering and managing data. It will also reflect other factors that influence methods of delivering care. In the end, it will enable us to critically analyze new strategies for providing high-quality, cost-efficient healthcare to patients.

RESEARCH on OUTCOME and ITS MANAGEMENT

Outcome management is appealing to several groups, private and government based. For researchers, it is a new area, with the potential for breakthroughs and original data to be gathered. It is also an area that has received an abundance of funding, especially from the federal government. Availability of funding is a strong motivator for researchers to pursue the study of outcomes and outcome management. Let us look at some of the major studies and research activities in this area.

As mentioned earlier, in 1986 OBRA called for a review of quality of care received by Medicare patients. It mandated the IOM to perform a comprehensive review. The IOM concluded that research should be expanded on outcome of care. The IOM report prompted Congress to pass the 1989 OBRA. This act expanded these research opportunities. In 1990 the AHCPR was established under the Public Health Service of the Department of Health and Human Services. Its major emphasis is on outcome research, and it began funding support activities for a number of PORTs. According to a program note published by AHCPR in 1990, "PORT projects are designed to identify and analyze the outcomes and costs of alternative practice patterns for a specific condition, determine the best strategy for treatment or clinical management, and develop and test methods for reducing inappropriate variations in practice." PORT grants provide funding to study such conditions as back pain, cataracts, diabetes, hypertension, depression, hip fracture, myocardial infarction, prostatism, glaucoma, asthma, rheumatoid arthritis, chronic obstructive pulmonary disorders, substance abuse, and peripheral vascular disease, to present a partial list. An interdisciplinary team is assembled for each of these PORTs and is mandated to prepare a prospective clinical outcome evaluation of that specific condition. The purpose is to design specific clinical guidelines for the management of such conditions based on the collective and organized efforts of experts.

Another area related to outcome management research is measurement of severity of illness. The purpose of these studies is to develop and use severity of illness measures to adjust for case mix differences among patients. According to Nash and Markson (1991), several instruments have been developed and are being continuously tested. These measurement tools include Disease Staging, Computerized Severity Index (CSI), Acute Physiology and Chronic Health Evaluation (APACHE II), MedisGroups, and Patient Management Categories (PMCs).

Of the above systems, Disease Staging, CSI, and PMCs are diagnosis specific (i.e., they tend to differentiate severity of illness in patients with the same primary diagnosis). Thus, patients with acute cholycystitis are not compared to those with acute glomerulonephritis. The other systems (MedisGroup and APACHE II) are diagnosis independent. They tend to depend on clinical investigations and ancillary tests, without regard to the underlying diagnosis. They also rely on information extracted from the medical chart by trained abstractors (Lezzoni and Moskowitz, 1988) and in the MedisGroup are further compared with a national database of users (Thomas and Longo, 1990). Users of MedisGroup now exceed 500 hospitals in both the United States and Canada (Linder, 1992). By measuring changes in severity of illness, these systems are being used to evaluate patient outcomes and to assess the quality of care provided by different institutions. For further information on these systems, the reader is advised to review works by Hornbrook (1982), Cretin and Worthman (1986), Lezzoni and Moskowitz (1988), Geehr (1989), Lezzoni (1989), Ellwood et al. (1991), Linder (1991), and Markson et al. (1991) among others.

According to the Hospital Research and Educational Trust (HRET) of the American Hospital Association (Longo et al., 1990), several organizations currently collect and analyze data on patient and hospital outcomes. One widely monitored organization is the Delaware Valley Hospital Council in Philadelphia. The Pennsylvania Health Care Cost Containment Council (HC4), a state agency, was created in 1986 to identify ways to contain healthcare costs. HC4 continuously collects severity of illness data (adjusted for morbidity, mortality, and charges) on 57 diagnosis-related groups from every hospital in Pennsylvania with 100 beds or more. They subsequently publish a quarterly report ranking the performances of these hospitals based on this information (Nash and Markson, 1991). Based on these reports, an outcome-based project called *Buy Right* rewards the most quality-oriented, highly efficient provider with more patients (Nash and Goldfield, 1989).

Another project is developing a system for rating hospitals, similar to a Wall Street single bond-like rating, based on outcome information. The Wharton School's Hospital Corporate Rating Project is supported by the Hartford Foundation in New York City to undertake this task. Release of the work is expected in the near future.

Of course, when considering outcome research, the JCAHO's Agenda for Change (O'Leary, 1987) also comes to mind. According to O'Leary (1991), the president of JACHO, the quality of care provided, although heavily dependent on the clinical team of professionals, is equally dependent on "effective governance, management, and support services" in any healthcare organization. JCAHO's efforts to utilize outcomes, both clinical and organizational, have slowed down due to the fact that JCAHO has moved much faster than most hospitals are able to conform.

In the government, the HCFA entered into a project involving a select number of PROs. HCFA established the Health Care Quality Improvement Initiative (HCQII). This project is a collaborative effort between the two entities to collect outcome data and to examine patterns of care through the Medicare reimbursement patient database. According to Jenks and Wilensky (1992), HCQII has four important driving forces: variation research, peer review studies, new quality improvement models, and development of practice guidelines. The major objective behind such a project is to establish a centralized Uniform Clinical Data Set (UCDS) to capture information on some 1800 elements from a 10% sample of inpatient discharges. The goal is for all PROs to use the UCDS database to compare the practice patterns of individual providers with national patterns.

OUTCOMES MANAGEMENT and TOTAL QUALITY

Clearly, the main objective of using outcome measures is to improve the quality of care delivered by a healthcare organization to a patient. The idea is not only to study and improve individual outcome indicators, but to also

233

view outcomes from the standpoint of the total system. A specific outcome is dependent on all the structures and processes involved in its development. To achieve improvement, all factors, barriers, and strengths of the *system* should be reviewed, evaluated, and improved. Outcome measures are important tools to direct attention to the reasons why certain outcomes occur. They should direct our efforts to finding ways to address these challenges efficiently to achieve the desired outcome. This is the difference between *measuring* and *managing* outcomes. Managing outcomes is what TQ is all about—managing the total system to improve the quality of care rendered to the patient.

According to Bohr and Bader (1991), the Deming Cycle of Plan-Do-Check-Act (PDCA) is congruent with the processes of developing clinical guidelines (an aspect of outcome research). Appropriate care criteria are developed (plan), implemented (do), monitored (check), and tested and retested (check); those that prove to be successful are used and those that do not work are discarded (act).

Epstein (1991) presented the same argument. The principles of the two philosophies are very similar. In outcome management, criteria that are successful in improving the outcome of care are developed and monitored; Variations from these criteria are minimized and further eliminated, through continuous assessment. All of these activities are related to TQ and CQI. The fundamental principle of TQ is to eliminate variation, and this is what outcome management attempts to do: recognize *good* outcomes, study them, and eliminate variations in the process that may lead to undesired outcomes.

Geehr (1992) agrees with this. He also suggests that QI of structures and processes depends on feedback from outcome measurements. He goes on to suggest that this can be done prospectively, with the use of practice guidelines and expert systems, and retrospectively, through assessment of trends and outcomes of clinical practice patterns.

CONCLUSIONS

The field of outcome management is still undergoing refinement. As mentioned earlier in the chapter, outcome is in the eyes of the beholder. One must keep in mind the magnitude of the impact outcomes have on the key players in the healthcare system. Patients may find certain outcomes desirable, but those same outcomes might be considered undesirable from the standpoint of a provider or regulator. It is safe to say, however, that outcome-based assessment of the quality of care is gaining broader acceptance, and health professionals are becoming more aware of it. Health professionals must work collectively to assess their performance and develop appropriate criteria for care in an effort to achieve a desirable outcome. An outcome should be based on feedback from patients, providers, and third parties and take into consideration the process of continuous improvement of the system of care.

It is inevitable that future trends will include a stronger emphasis on patient and system data. Healthcare decisions will most definitely be data driven. According to Geehr (1992), the future of outcome management will involve physician privileging and credentialing, critical pathways (Coffey et al., 1992), practice guidelines, and peer review processes, among other elements. However, with vast amounts of data available (as in automation of medical records, on-line national databases on clinical practice patterns, and expert systems in clinical decision making), the use of computer technology will increase rapidly. Healthcare professionals will be forced to use these technologies to compare their outcomes with those of their peers.

REFERENCES

Agency for Health Care Policy and Research Program Note (1990).

Bohr, D. and Bader, B. (1991). "Medical Practice Guidelines: What They Are and How They're Used." *The Quality Letter,* 3(1):1.

Bunker, J. P. and Forrest, W. H., Jr., Mosteller, F., and Vandam, L. D. (1969). The National Halothane Study: A Study of the Possible Association Between Halothane Anesthesia and Postoperative Hepatic Necrosis, Bethesda, Md.: National Institutes of Health.

Codman, E. (1914). "The Product of a Hospital." *Surgical Gynecology and Obstetrics,* 18:491–494.

Coffey, R. J., Richard, J. S., et al. (1992). "An Introduction to Critical Paths." *Quality Management in Health Care,* 1(1):45–54.

Cretin S. and Worthman, L. (1986). *Alternative Systems in Case Mix Classification in Health Care Financing,* Santa Monica, Calif.: Rand Corporation.

Daley, J. (1991). "Mortality and Other Outcome Data." in *Quantitative Methods in Quality Management: A Guide for Practitioners,* Longo and Bohr (Eds.), Chicago: American Hospital Association.

Donabedian, A. (1966). "Evaluating the Quality of Medical Care." *Milbank Memorial Fund Quarterly,* 44:194–196.

Donabedian, A. (1988). "The Quality of Care." *Journal of the American Medical Association,* 260(12):1743–1748.

Ellwood, P. M. (1988). "Outcomes Management: A Technology of Experience." *The New England Journal of Medicine,* 318(23):1549–1556.

Ellwood, P. (1992). "Outcomes Management: The Impetus and Impact." *Health Systems Review,* 25(1):24–26.

Ellwood, P. M. et al. (1991). *The Future: Clinical Outcomes Management in Health Care Quality Management for the 21st Century,* J. Couch (Ed.), Tampa, Fla.: American College of Physician Executives Press.

Epstein, A. (1990). "The Outcomes Movement—Will It Get Us Where We Want To Go?" *New England Journal of Medicine,* 323:266–270.

Flood, A. B., Scott, W. R., Ewy, W., et al. (1982). "Effectiveness in Professional Organizations on the Quality of Care in Hospitals." *Health Services Research,* 17(4):341–366.

Flood, A. B., Scott, W. R., and Ewy, W. (1984a). "Does Practice Make Perfect? Part I." *Medical Care*, 22(2):98–114.

Flood, A. B., Scott, W. R., and Ewy, W. (1984b). "Does Practice Make Perfect? Part II." *Medical Care*, 22(2):115–125.

Geehr, E. C. (1989). *Selecting a Proprietary Severity of Illness System*, Tampa, Fla.: American College of Physician Executives Press.

Geehr, E. C. (1992). "The Search for What Works." *Healthcare Forum Journal*, 35(4):28–33.

Groves, E.W. (1908). "A Plea for Uniform Registration of Operation Results." *British Journal of Medicine*, 2:1008–1009.

Health Care Financing Administration (1987). Medicare Mortality Information: 1986, Vols. I–VII, Washington D.C.: Department of Health and Human Services.

Hornbrook, M. (1982). "Hospital Case Mix: Its Definition, Measurement and Use. Part II: Review of Alternative Measures." *Medical Care Review*, 39(2):73–123.

IOM (1989). Institute of Medicine Report.

Jenks, S. F. and Wilensky, G. R. (1992). "The Health Care Quality Improvement Initiative: A New Approach to Quality Assurance in Medicare." *Journal of the American Medical Association*, 268(7):900–918.

Jennings, B. M. (1991). "Patient Outcomes Research: Seizing the Opportunity." *Advances in Nursing Science*, 14(2):59–72.

Lezzoni, L. (1989). "Measuring Severity of Illness and Case Mix." in *Providing Quality of Care: The Challenge to Physicians*, N. Goldfield and D. Nash (Eds.), Philadelphia: American College of Physicians.

Lezzoni, L. I. and Moskowitz, M. A. (1988) "A Clinical Assessment of MedisGroups." *Journal of the American Medical Association*, 260(1):3159–3163.

Linder, J. (1991). "Outcomes Measurement: Compliance Tool or Strategic Initiative." *Health Care Management Review*, 16(4):21–31.

Linder, J. (1992). "Outcomes Measurement in Hospitals: Can the System Change the Organization?" *Hospital and Health Services Administration*, 37(2):143–166.

Lohr, K. N. (1987). "Outcome Measurement: Concepts and Questions." *Inquiry*, 25(1):37–50.

Longo, D., Bohr, D., et al. (1990). *Inventory of External Data Demands Placed on Hospitals*, Chicago: Hospital Research and Educational Trust.

Luft, H. S. and Hunt, S. S. (1986). "Evaluating Individual Hospital Quality Through Outcome Statistics." *Journal of the American Medical Association*, 255(20):2780–2784.

Luft, H. S., Bunker, J. P. and Enthoven, A.C. (1979). "Should Operations be Regionalized: The Empirical Relation Between Surgical Volume and Mortality." *New England Journal of Medicine*, 301(6):1364–1369.

Markson, L. Nash, D., et al. (1991). "Clinical Outcomes Management and Disease Staging." *Evaluation and the Health Professions*, 14(2):201–227.

Meltzer, R. (1992). "The Hazards of Outcome Measures." *Administrative Radiology*,11(1):51–52.

Moses, L. E. and Mosteller, F. (1968). "Institutional Differences in Postoperative Death Rates: Commentary on Some of the Findings of the National Halothane Study." *Journal of the American Medical Association*, 203(7):150–152.

Nash, D. and Goldfield, N. (1989). "Information Needs of Purchasers." in *Providing Quality Care: The Challenge to Physicians*, N. Goldfiole and D. Nash (Eds.), Philadelphia: American College of Physicians.

Nash, D. B. and Markson, L. E. (1991). "Emerging Trends in Outcomes Management." *Frontiers of Health Services Management*, 8(2):3–52.

Nightingale, F. (1859). *Notes on Hospitals*, West Strand, London: John W. Parker and Sons.

O'Leary, D. S. (1987). *The Joint Commission Agenda for Change*, Chicago: Joint Commission on Accreditation of Healthcare Organizations.

O'Leary, D. (1991). "CQI—A Step Beyond QA." *Quality Review Bulletin*, 17:4–5.

QRC Advisor (1992). "Teaching Ways to Measure Outcome." *QRC Advisor*, 8(9):3–6.

Roemer, M. R. and Friedman, J. W. (1971). *Doctors in Hospitals: Medical Staff Organization and Hospital Performance*, Baltimore: John Hopkins.

Rowland, R. and Rowland, B. (1992). "Outcome-Based Measurement of Quality." *Managing and Measuring Health Care Quality*, Aspen.

Shortell, S. M. and LoGerfo, J. P. (1981). "Hospital Medical Staff Organization and Quality of Care: Results for Myocardial Infarction and Appendectomy." *Medical Care*, 19(1):104–154.

Thomas, J. W. and Longo, D. L. (1990). "Application of Severity Measurement Systems for Hospital Quality Management." *Hospital and Health Services Administration*, 35(2):221–243.

11

RESEARCH and TOTAL QUALITY

June A. Schmele, RN, PhD

The rapid evolution of the science of healthcare quality, the advent of Total Quality (TQ) in the late 1980s and early 1990s, and the changes being made to the structures and systems through which care is delivered offer a present and future research challenge of unprecedented magnitude. A multitude of researchable questions call for investigation and enhancement of the knowledge base in the science of quality. The evolving paradigm of TQ in healthcare organizations calls for research-based practice in order to substantiate knowledge, test new patient care and organizational interventions, enhance practice, and thereby improve patient care.

QUALITY MANAGEMENT TERMINOLOGY

Over time, numerous definitions and uses have been developed for the word *quality*. Thus, in this and any other discussion about quality, a common understanding of terms is required. Although some still use the traditional term *quality assurance,* most experts have abandoned its use. For the purposes of this chapter, we will use the following terms to describe quality:

- Quality Management—an umbrella term for *all* systematic processes directed toward the improvement of care.
- Quality Assurance and Improvement (QA&I)—the traditional system generally for accreditation purposes that was formerly called Quality Assurance (QA).
- Total Quality (TQ)—the top-down consumer-driven organizational commitment to improve quality throughout the organization. It is also called Total Quality Management (TQM).
- Continuous Quality Improvement (CQI)—the ongoing improvement of quality of systems and work processes through the use of teams.

© St. Lucie Press CCC 0-9634030-4-4 9/93/$100/$.50

BACKGROUND and DEFINITIONS

Historically, there has been a fair amount of confusion about the relationship between traditional QA&I and research. Some saw a strong relationship, while others saw little or none. This lack of clarity results because the scientific process is inherent in both research and QA&I. Sometimes it is not difficult to differentiate between the two concepts. We will be careful to define the commonalties and differences between them, examining each concept closely. The basic differences between QA&I and TQ can be described as stated by Church Chason (1993):

> Quality Assessment and Improvement (QA&I) is essentially a checking mechanism driven by accrediting bodies external to the healthcare organization. Commonly we use it after the fact, to determine whether or not we met certain elements considered important in delivering overt or covert standards of care. The process of assessment requires us to gather and analyze data pertinent to these standards of care. These data become outcome indicators that tell us when we need to improve our healthcare delivery system. However, the usefulness of these data is limited because we have not used them to direct ourselves to the specific area we need to improve, upstream, in one of the many healthcare delivery processes. Traditional QA&I has had a limited impact on improving our healthcare system. Until now, the leaders and managers of healthcare organizations have not had adequate incentives to pursue the improvement opportunities it indicates. Accordingly, the improvements driven by quality assessment data rarely have scientific validity because we do not base them on a systematic investigation of the facts. Instead, in an effort to meet accreditation standards, we generally use our best guess, or gut feel, to identify the cause of the problem. Without the benefit of scientific analysis, we usually identify and solve a symptom rather than a root cause. Because we failed to attack the root cause of the problem, in time we find that the same problem recurs. For example, too often we simply lay blame for the problem with one of the providers in the healthcare delivery system. Yet, the true actionable root cause may be a lack of training, procedural consistency, or simple communication and awareness. Here, reprimanding or eliminating a provider simply solves a symptom, and the root cause is bound to occur again.
>
> Total Quality (TQ), on the other hand, provides a strong management incentive to pursue continuous process improvement, as well as a scientifically valid methodology for accomplishing it. Total Quality offers the healthcare organization a proven method for maintaining its Mission—enabling it to survive today's tough times through improving the processes of its healthcare delivery system. Similarly, TQ offers the healthcare organization a plan for attaining its Vision—high quality, affordable, and accessible patient care. In contrast to QA&I, TQ is essentially an organization wide continuous improvement process driven internally and proactively by an executive commitment to meet or exceed the reasonable needs of customers who are both

internal and external to the organization. Through education and training in a common set of statistical tools and teamwork techniques, all members of the organization come to share this commitment and are empowered to improve the work processes in which they have responsibility and control.

Burns and Grove (1993) define the research process as "diligent, systematic inquiry or investigation to validate and refine existing knowledge and generate new knowledge." We employ the research process to answer questions or test hypotheses about certain phenomena. The process requires us to gather, manage, and manipulate data carefully—often using statistical analysis. The purpose of research is to increase our knowledge about the phenomenon under investigation.

Research and TQ have two basic elements in common: both identify the phenomenon of interest and gather data. We find differences between these two processes in the way they manipulate, interpret, and manage data and the purpose of their investigation. TQ relies heavily on the use of statistical tools and techniques to drive improvement. Thus, thanks to the growth of the quality field overall, we are developing a much more sophisticated process for gathering and handling data, as well as requiring more valid and reliable instrumentation. In addition, with these latter changes we may be able to use data gathered in quality studies for secondary analysis to explore other researchable questions. Burns and Grove (1993) define research questions as "concise, interrogative statements developed to direct a study that focuses on description of variables, examination of relationships among variables, and determination of differences between two or more groups." If we apply this definition to TQ as a phenomenon of interest, we uncover a multitude of research questions. For example, in a TQ project we might gather data on the consumers' satisfaction with care and service. In a secondary analysis we could research other related questions such as the relationship between middle management's commitment to the concept of TQ and the consumers' satisfaction with care and services.

RESEARCH-BASED PRACTICE

If we consider TQ to be a phenomenon of interest, TQ and its key elements become the objects of research. Clearly, from both a practical and an academic viewpoint, we have major opportunities to gain knowledge in these areas. In the practical arena, we could focus on how to apply TQ effectively in a healthcare service setting. Here, research can provide healthcare organizations with vital information about TQ implementation that lets them build upon the experiences of others and generalize from research findings. To this end, researchers should consider building a TQ knowledge base, incorporating the findings of others and replicating studies. Further, research dealing with the TQ concept as a whole, or its component variables, is becoming increasingly important to counter the suggestion that TQ is merely a "buzzword."

New research is needed to deal with this new phenomenon. The rapidity of change and the introduction of new paradigms necessitate research in order to bring about knowledge-based practice. Deploying evaluation research to study TQ methodologies will increase our knowledge in this area. This kind of research should help healthcare organizations expedite the TQ implementation process. Accordingly, this chapter discusses research on the general object of quality, with specific emphasis on TQ.

To begin, we must isolate the critical elements, or variables, of TQ so we can consider them as researchable phenomena. TQ is *a consumer-driven, top-down leadership philosophy*. It requires both *organizational commitment* and *total employee involvement*. TQ also provides a process for *continuous quality improvement* through the use of *teams* and statistical *tools*. Having identified the critical elements, or variables, of TQ, we can develop researchable questions that relate one or more of these elements to other variables such as demographics or structure, process, or outcome measures. The unit of analysis may consist of organizations, units, teams, and/or individuals.

SOCIAL SCIENCE RESEARCH

Social science research offers comprehensive methodologies that allow us to address quality issues at various social levels. Social science research is the application of scientific research procedures to solve problems of a social nature. It is a social inquiry directed toward the domains of behavior, often within the scope of organizational problems or questions. According to Miller (1991), social science research may have three different foci: *basic, applied,* and *evaluation.* All three branches of social science research call for the inclusion of a guiding theory. Miller has developed a schema, which compares the differing research orientations—basic, applied, and evaluation—according to four criteria: the nature of the problem, the goal of the research, the guiding theory, and the appropriate techniques (Miller, 1991).

Basic research (sometimes called pure research) is intended to advance knowledge rather than suggest immediate application. The underlying value of basic research is that its quest for knowledge leads to a better understanding of the phenomenon and further development of relationships and predictions (Miller, 1991). An example of basic research on the subject of TQ might be such a research question as: "What is the relationship of Theory X and Theory Y leadership to the critical elements of TQ?"

According to Miller (1991), "applied research has been transformed as policy research, action research, and useful research." In contrast to basic research, the goal of applied research is twofold: to advance knowledge and to identify an immediate solution to a specific problem. An example of an applied research question might be, "Is there a correlation between improving the ventilatory care process and the occurrence of ventilator pneumonia in patients, and if so, what is it?"

Evaluation research, on the other hand, could provide healthcare organizations with a step-by-step methodology for assessing the appropriateness of various TQ models and the effectiveness of TQ implementations. Rossi and Freeman (1989) define evaluation research as "the systematic application of social research procedures for assessing the conceptualization, design, implementation, and utility of social intervention programs." These authors developed their ideas in the field of evaluation research over a period of 30 years. They suggest a number of questions that healthcare organizations might ask to assess the effectiveness of TQ models and implementations (Rossi and Freeman, 1989):

- What is the nature and scope of the problem requiring new, expanded, or modified social programs? Where is it located, and whom does it affect?
- What feasible interventions are likely to ameliorate the problem significantly?
- What are the appropriate target populations for a particular intervention?
- Is the intervention reaching its target population?
- Is the intervention being implemented in the ways envisioned?
- Is the intervention effective?
- How much does it cost?
- What are its costs relative to its effectiveness and benefits?

Evaluation research is a major field of study in itself. Those who would like to pursue this topic in detail should reference the *Program Evaluation Kit*, a resource which consists of a series of nine publications offering a step-by-step evaluation approach (Herman et al., 1987).

GUIDELINES and DATABASES

When uniform guidelines and data sets are developed at the institutional, regional, and national levels, researchers will have a mechanism to explore common variables and build on previous research. Various disciplines in healthcare are developing uniform patient databases (sometimes referred to as minimum data sets). Eventually we will be able to use these databases for both quality management and research purposes. The data they capture are associated closely with the key elements of care we have identified and often use as the basis of quality measures.

One such example is the Joint Commission's current clinical indicator project. The Joint Commission has developed standard quality indicators for major components of care in anesthesia, obstetrics, cardiovascular, oncology, trauma, medication usage, and infection control (Joint Commission, 1992). These indicators have implications for Joint Commission accreditation as well as for the development of national uniform data sets. They will be used on a continuing basis, starting with 10 indicators in 1994 and 20 in 1995, at which time the indicators will become mandatory. These cross-disciplinary indicators have significant research potential from the TQ perspective. They show the critical healthcare system processes that need to be managed and targeted for continuous quality improvement. Subsequent research questions and measures may be developed based on these valid indicators. Together, these efforts will create an accessible database of uniform quality measures in Joint Commission accredited hospitals.

The Agency for Health Care Policy and Research (AHCPR) was created by Congress in 1989 to address the issues of quality, appropriateness, effectiveness, and access in healthcare. This agency is a focal point for research on health services. Recently, it completed several congressionally mandated clinical practice guidelines. These guidelines are research-based multidisciplinary documents of client care management. At present, clinical practice guidelines exist for acute pain management, urinary incontinence, pressure ulcers, among others. Overall, Congress asked the AHCPR to complete 16 clinical practice guidelines. (These documents are available free of charge from the AHCPR Publications Clearinghouse, P.O. Box 8547, Silver Springs, MD 20907, 1-800-358-9295.) Each document includes a patient guide and a clinician guide. The application of these research-based guidelines to clinical practice shows how research can be utilized in day-to-day healthcare practice. There is little doubt that clinical practice guidelines will become the leading edge of practice and future clinical research. Integrating these guidelines into TQ systems research will be a challenging opportunity for researchers. An additional research emphasis will be dissemination research focused on ensuring adoption of these guidelines.

The Nursing Minimum Data Set (NMDS) provides an additional example of uniform data sets. NMDS consists of three broad categories: nursing care, patient or client demographics, and service elements. Together, these categories cover 16 elements, 10 of which are the same as those already being collected for the Uniform Hospital Discharge Data Set (UHDDS) (Werley et al., 1991).

Washington's Statewide Obstetrical Review and Quality System (StORQS) is another database. This statewide project focuses on gathering data elements and formulating indicators to monitor obstetrical care (Jones et al.,

1993). Other healthcare areas, and indeed other states, could follow Washington's methodology as a generic model to establish similar data systems.

The uniform databases discussed here are simply a representative sample of systems currently in place. Because the uniform data sets include essential elements of care, we can make conceptual links with related processes in healthcare systems. In turn, the processes we improve will direct our TQ research. The creation of uniform data sets, as well as the rapid technological changes in information management, will have an unprecedented impact on future quality research.

RESEARCH on TQ

The paucity of published research on the object of TQ demonstrates the need for increased investigation in this area. However, most studies on TQ are not represented as research. When a healthcare organization and its clinicians are faced with real-world problems and opportunities for improvement, they tend to take immediate action (Church Chason, 1993). Seldom do they have the luxury of resource availability, research sophistication, and a controlled environment, all of which would enhance the probability of research on TQ.

The American Quality Foundation and Ernst & Young have reported preliminary results on the International Quality Study (IQS) being conducted in Canada, Germany, Japan, and the United States (Anderson et al., 1991). The survey includes four industries: healthcare, banking, automotive, and computers. Objectives of the study were to (1) develop an inventory of various quality management practices, (2) discover the most effective management practices related to quality, (3) determine the influence of culture on the application of quality management practices, and (4) develop a global awareness of trends and directions. Preliminary findings indicate a strong relationship between cultural variables and TQ. This study represents a future trend—global as well as interdisciplinary interests in research on quality.

Yuhaz (1991) used a sample of executives (n = 1642) to study functional requirements for TQ. He surveyed them by telephone to determine needs, methodologies, and functional requirements for TQ implementation. He identified 57 TQ needs. Of those, he identified 14 as the major functional requirements. Listed in priority, they are as follows: team building, productivity improvement or work restructuring, an organization-wide plan for TQ, start-up operations and education, follow-through operations and education, leadership orientation to TQ, management development, merging of QA and Quality Improvement (QI), performance appraisal for TQ, physician

support, mission and communication reinforcement, board level development, and leadership and marketing communications. Yuhaz found that
79% of the healthcare organizations were not committed to a particular TQ
methodology. This type of research provides valuable national data about
TQ implementation and opens the door to other investigations. We could
study these 14 variables using different levels of analysis. Longitudinal
analysis, for example, would help us keep abreast of changes initiated
through these and other organizational variables in TQ implementations.

Al-Assaf and his colleagues have conducted a number of surveys in an
attempt to capture the attitudes and perceptions of various position holders
toward TQ. One national survey of 167 VA directors and QA professionals
explored the attitudes and perceptions of this group toward Total Quality
Improvement (TQI). Both groups had positive perceptions of the future of
TQI in healthcare. They also agreed on implementation methods and
impacts on other philosophies, objectives, and programs (Tindill et al.,
1993). A second survey by Al-Assaf et al. (1993) interviewed a sample of VA
Medical Center Chiefs of Staff (n = 167). Results indicated that they were
involved in TQ considerably, openly supporting it and offering their time
for implementation. A third study of CEOs and administrators in private
hospitals showed that they too were willing to be involved with TQ. Further
results showed a correlation between the length of time the institution was
involved with TQ and the managers' willingness to become involved. The
longer managers were involved with TQ, the less confident they were that
it was a long-term process that will continue to flourish during the next
decade (Al-Assaf and Huff, 1993). These less than optimistic findings
certainly call for further exploration. Al-Assaf and Doss (1993) studied
perceptions and attitudes in a sample of 35 administrators and 119 staff
members of a selected segment of the Oklahoma Mental Health System. In
this sample, management and staff were supportive of the TQ concept and
ready for its implementation.

INSTRUMENTATION RESEARCH

In order for research to keep pace with the rapidly developing science
of quality management, methodological studies are needed, especially in
the area of instrumentation. It is important that we use valid and reliable
instrumentation as we create a research-based body of knowledge on TQ.
The increase in qualitative studies will ultimately enrich the development of
valid and reliable instrumentation. Researchers may go back to the data
source, such as internal and external customers, to explore the essence of
researchable phenomena.

Most reports in the literature focus on the patient as the customer. In contrast, the work of Nelson et al. (1992) focuses on internal customers, namely physicians and staff. They established psychometric data for the Physician Judgment System (MDJS) and the Hospital Employee Judgment System (HEJS). The sophisticated methods they used to develop and test the scale provided evidence to support the reliability and validity of both instruments. The content of the instruments deals with perceptions of quality and has merit for future research.

As we develop instruments, we must include the critical items that relate to the variable we are studying. The research-based indicators currently being developed by the Joint Commission and the clinical practice guidelines being written by the AHCPR will help us identify these critical items. These documents and others will provide the basis for state-of-the-art instrument development. Both the Joint Commission indicators and the AHCPR clinical practice guidelines will help us create valid and reliable instrumentation to study structure, process, and outcome in healthcare organizations. These resources are very important contributions to the investigations of quality of care. Our major challenge is to integrate the substance of the guidelines and indicators into a research-based TQ system.

EPIDEMIOLOGICAL STUDIES

Research on quality should consider the merit of epidemiological study methods. Epidemiological methodologies are important in determining occurrence rates of adverse events, which in turn can provide assistance in discovering problem areas. Although a detailed discussion of these methods is beyond the scope of this chapter, an article by Everett (1993) provides further reading.

COST STUDIES

Cost containment and cost benefit analyses are other areas in which quality research needs to be focused. If we can link cost to quality at theoretical and practical levels, we will have made an important research contribution. A cost benefit study by Falconer et al. (1993) provides an example. In a controlled environment, they implemented a critical pathway method (CPM) for inpatient stroke rehabilitation. The results of the study neither substantiated nor refuted the theory that CPM can reduce cost and improve outcomes. This example emphasizes that scientific rigor must be used in testing new ideas and interventions. Where possible, the studies should be replicated in various circumstances and settings.

247

DEMONSTRATION PROJECTS

Major demonstration projects are very important to the rapidly evolving TQ field. Summaries of several notable projects will benefit our discussion of TQ research.

Berwick and his associates at the Harvard Community Health Plan (HCHP) initiated a demonstration project funded by the Hartford Foundation. Twenty-one healthcare providers from separate institutions were paired with quality experts in the industry. Each team was asked to solve a problem that faced the provider (Berwick et al., 1991). One successful team improved the patient transport system at Massachusetts General Hospital. Pre- and postintervention data dealt with incident reports, patient satisfaction, transportation staff turnover, and patient transfer turnaround time. All of these elements showed dramatic improvement (Sullivan and Frentzel, 1992).

Marszalek-Gaucher and Coffey (1991, 1993) report the experience of transforming the organizational culture at the University of Michigan Hospitals. Although their report is not research *per se*, many of the innovative TQ approaches and action steps lend themselves to the formulation of researchable questions.

A current major demonstration project, funded by the W.K. Kellogg Foundation, is directed toward improving quality in home care. The project has utilized scientific research approaches to accomplish its objectives of defining consumer-based outcome measures, developing systems to use the outcome measures, and incorporating the process into the Community Health Accreditation Program (Peters, 1992). As with the AHCPR project, selected elements of this project offer great potential for TQ research. When this project accomplishes its objectives, the results will form the basis for future research on quality improvement in home healthcare.

A Spanish model for TQ, reported by Ruiz et al. (1992), offers an example of an international demonstration project. Its pilot studies themselves provide useful research components. Overall, the system has achieved several objectives that have potential for related research (Ruiz et al., 1992):

- Patient uniform minimum data set
- Patient classification system
- Cost analysis framework
- Nosocomial infection control approach
- Standard questionnaires for providers and consumers
- Standard nursing quality indicators
- Introduction of TQ in medical curricula
- Implementation of TQ activities

This report could be considered a case study of TQ implementation in the Spanish healthcare system.

The literature provides a number of accounts of specific improvement processes, including patient fall prevention (Corbett and Pennypacker, 1992), lab turnaround time (Bluth et al., 1992), maintenance of patient skin integrity (Ward, 1992), and treatment of patients with hypertension (Waggoner, 1992). Each of these accounts deals with one or more of three major TQ components: the team and its CQI functioning, the detailed analysis of processes and specific problems within them, and the improvement process overall. They generally include charts, graphs, and clinical comparisons, but avoid in-depth statistical analysis. A common base of research certainly would benefit these types of TQ projects. In addition, we should consider planning research in conjunction with these improvement projects.

RESEARCH UTILIZATION

Research utilization is the application of research in clinical practice. To utilize research, clinicians usually explore, analyze, and synthesize relevant studies on the phenomenon of interest until their efforts translate into a selection of research-based processes or interventions. Here, outcome evaluation is imperative and may in itself become a clinical research study—as long as it uses sound research protocol. The evidence suggests the need to develop and strengthen clinical and organizational research-based practice.

The classic work entitled *Conduct and Utilization of Research in Nursing Project* (CURN), by Horsely and her associates in 1983, provides an example of research utilization to improve clinical practice. Although the project dealt with specific nurse-oriented patient care problems, its approach could be applicable to other disciplines or interdisciplinary TQ teams as well. Steps in the research utilization process are as follows (Horsely, 1983):

1. Identifying the change agents and organizing for action
2. Identifying problems
3. Identifying and assessing relevant research-based knowledge
4. Adapting and designing the research-based practice innovation
5. Conducting a trial and evaluation of the innovator
6. Deciding whether to adopt, modify, or reject the innovation
7. Developing the means to diffuse the innovation
8. Developing the mechanism to maintain the innovation

The foregoing steps easily parallel the processes inherent in TQ implementation and continuous improvement. It may be helpful to refer to this mechanism when developing a research-based application of TQ. Research utilization is different from actually conducting research. As in the CURN example, at times it may be appropriate, or even ideal, to use both.

RESEARCH AGENDA

The time has come for a national research agenda that addresses the current paradigm shift to TQ in healthcare. A national research agenda would focus and prioritize investigations on TQ in healthcare, impacting funding sources and future policy development. In addition, it would provide a much needed influence to improve leadership behaviors and organizational performance.

In the absence of such a national research agenda, we will discuss ideas and frameworks that merit consideration. Vuori (1989) developed one such framework. He presented it to the World Health Organization, and it was published subsequently in an international journal. Vuori's scheme of research topics follows.

Research Needs*

This [material] lists salient research issues and needs in quality assurance emerging from the above discussion. No attempt is made to set priorities. Research needs in quality assurance can be considered in the order in which one would develop a quality assurance scheme:

— concepts related to quality,
— epidemiology of quality,
— criteria and standards,
— methods of quality assurance,
— introduction of quality assurance,
— organization of quality assurance,
— improvement of quality,
— evaluation of the impact of quality assurance.

Concepts Related to Quality

— What is quality? Is it a multidimensional or unidimensional concept?
— If it is multidimensional:
　　— what are the dimensions;
　　— can the different dimensions, e.g., efficiency and accessibility, be weighted?
— Studies on the views of the parties concerned on what is quality.

---

*Reprinted from *Quality Assurance in Health Care,* Volume 1, No. 2/3, H. Vuori, "Research Needs in Quality Assurance," pp. 157–159, Copyright 1989, with kind permission from Pergamon Press Ltd, Headington Hill Hall, Oxford 0X3 0BW, UK.

— Studies on the relationship between:
  — quality and quantity,
  — quality and costs,
  — quality assurance and cost-containment,
  — quality assurance and technology assessment.

Epidemiology of Quality

— Studies on the basic questions of epidemiology (who, where and when):
  — who provides high/poor-quality services,
  — who receives high/poor-quality services,
  — where (in which setting) are high/poor-quality services being provided?
— Impact of the severity of disease on the quality of care.
— Does the quality of care of the same provider differ over time, health problems and care settings?
— Studies on factors influencing clinical decision-making.
— Studies on factors influencing:
  — provider satisfaction,
  — patient satisfaction.

Methods of Quality Assurance

— Validation of structural, process and outcome measures:
  — analysis of the relationship between structure and process, structure and outcome, and process and outcome;
  — studies on concordance between provider and patient views on the quality of care.
— Development of:
  — practicable outcome measures for different outcomes (e.g., physical, physiological and psychosocial);
  — better structural measures, including organizational and sociological variables (e.g. power structure and communication channels);
  — methods for the analysis of clinical decision-making;
  — algorithms for process analysis;
  — sampling methods to increase the cost-efficiency of quality assurance.
— Development of methods for the assessment of:
  — patient satisfaction;
  — psychomotor skills;
  — interpersonal skills and other aspects of the "art of care";
  — quality of special health services (e.g. nursing homes, physiotherapy and terminal care);
  — quality of care given by different provider groups (e.g. physiotherapists, nutritionists, psychologists and occupational therapists);
  — care given in connection with nonspecific health problems (e.g. headache, chest pain and back pain);
  — The quality of an entire healthcare system (as opposed to quality of care given by a provider).

— Improvement of medical records to serve better quality assurance.
— Studies on the contribution of diagnosis-related groups to quality assurance.
— Studies on patients as a source of information on the quality of care.

Criteria and Standards

— Studies on:
    — explicit vs. implicit criteria,
    — possibility of weighing criteria,
    — the costs of meeting criteria and standards.
— Development of:
    — criteria for elements of care vs criteria for the entire care strategy (e.g.
      conservative vs operative treatment),
    — methods of setting standards.

Introduction of Quality Assurance

— Studies on how to set a change agent in the medical environment.
— The impact of professional values on the acceptance of quality assurance.
— Studies on other factors influencing the acceptance of quality assurance.
— Case studies on successful and unsuccessful introduction of quality assurance.

Organization of Quality Assurance

— Studies on:
    — the impact of the sociopolitical climate on quality assurance;
    — the "politics of quality assurance" (power relations, etc.);
    — the impact of different sanctions and rewards;
    — the impact of public–private mix on quality assurance;
    — clinical management styles;
    — care strategies (e.g. operative vs conservative care) as determinants of the
      quality of care.
— Development of:
    — organizational models for different settings (particularly for hospitals and
      primary healthcare);
    — methods for involving consumers, decision-makers and administrators in
      quality assurance.

Improvement of Quality

—Evaluation of different methods for correcting observed qualitative deficiencies.
—Studies on the role of continuing education in the improvement of quality.

Evaluation of Quality Assurance

—Studies on the impact of the introduction of quality assurance on the actual
 quality of care and on the outcomes of care.

Vuori's framework has made a significant contribution to the body of knowledge that is shaping our national research agenda. At the same time, other ideas emerged. In 1989 Berwick reported that health services research might produce ideas that would guide the practices of healthcare managers, purchasers, and regulators. He also believed that regional and local policymakers were moving toward research-based decisions. Berwick's research agenda suggested the need to focus on four areas to develop effective healthcare in the 1990s—efficacy (knowing what works), appropriateness (doing what works), execution of care (doing well what works), and values (knowing what is right). Notably, each of these four areas for healthcare research reflects a key element of quality. Can we establish a relationship between a healthcare *research agenda* and a healthcare *quality agenda?* Perhaps the key elements of quality can provide a broad framework to guide TQ healthcare research in various social units of analysis.

Berwick himself explored the relationship between healthcare research and quality. In a discussion of unintended clinical variations and their treatment and control, he stated that "sound research might well be able to demonstrate the methods taught by Shewhart and others and could have a valuable role in assisting in the interpretation of clinical data and in guiding parsimonious medical intervention" (Berwick, 1991). To emphasize the importance of quality management research, he proposed the following questions:*

1. Can the proper use of statistical process control theory reduce waste, tampering, and iatrogenic complications in clinical settings, especially in intensive care units where continuous monitoring invites excessive intervention?
2. What is the capability of key clinical and support system work processes in hospitals and group practices? (The study of "process capability" is a formal, statistical undertaking in modern quality management.) Which processes tend to be in statistical control, and which tend not to be?
3. What is the epidemiology of process failures in healthcare systems? What are the most common root causes of failure? (The answers will of course vary widely among processes, institutions, and types of failure.)
4. What is the "cost of poor quality" (waste, rework, complexity, variation, inspection, and losses to patients, for example) in economic terms in healthcare processes? How can we better measure total costs in healthcare organizations?
5. Where are major loci of unnecessary complexity and of unintended variation in healthcare processes?

---

*Reproduced with permission from Berwick, D. M. (1991). "Controlling Variation in Healthcare: A Consultation from Walter Shewhart." *Medical Care,* 29(12):1124.

6. Where does suboptimization occur within healthcare organizations? Is it among healthcare organizations? Is it between healthcare and non-healthcare organizations? How can we better manage healthcare as a system, optimizing total performance? (These questions have technical, economic, and political dimensions, and all warrant attention.)

Overall, the initial agenda of inquiry might be this—Where does undesirable variation occur in healthcare? How much does it cost? What are its causes? How best can it be reduced?

Berwick also recognizes the need for a research agenda on quality in healthcare. Recently, he suggested (D.M. Berwick, personal communication, 1993) that the following areas should be included in such an agenda:

- Basic research in the science of quality
- Statistical application in the interpretation of variation
- Inquiry into institutional performance (such as leadership, organizational conflict, and group process) and physiological variables
- Demonstration models of quality
- Classic health service indicators (such as health status and the burden of illness in the community)

As the science of quality evolves, and more healthcare organizations implement TQ, ideas for a national research agenda will continue to be developed. Berwick's concept of a national research agenda deserves serious consideration. We can expect his voice to play a role in shaping the future of the science of quality in healthcare.

SUMMARY of the PRESENT and PROJECTIONS for the FUTURE

In this age of rapid healthcare reform and its accompanying macro and micro system changes in the delivery of care, forecasting the future of quality endeavors is somewhat presumptuous or very elusive at best. Current trends provide the safest foundation for any glimpse of the future. Throughout the world, economic, political, and social forces are in a constant state of flux. Value systems and philosophies are changing as well. In the present age, no one country, system, or healthcare organization stands alone. This trend toward globalization is likely to play an important part in the future of healthcare delivery and in shaping the level of quality afforded the consumer. We are reaching for an international consensus on the consumers' rights to quality healthcare and on professional standards. This may lead to international standards, indicators, and guidelines. If we want to advance the science of quality, we would be wise to pool the expertise of leaders across the world in the areas of research, education, and practice.

The ability to link international databases is finally a reality. Ultimately, these databases will include uniform data sets as well as information management systems. The international Health Service Information Management System (HSIM), which expedites rapid retrieval of major categories of information, is a prototype of the database of the future (Williamson et al., 1991). Access to international databases will improve the way we utilize and conduct research on quality. In turn, this will strengthen the research base for implementing TQ.

As information management technology and research expertise continue to develop, they will bring an increasingly scientific approach to TQ implementation. Yet, there is still a place for basic, applied, and evaluation research on TQ. We can expect to see more research-based publications, building a foundation of knowledge on the science of quality.

Based on empowerment, collaboration, and teamwork, the TQ leadership paradigm represents one of the most profound changes ever faced by traditional management in healthcare organizations. This type of leadership will allow healthcare organizations to tap their greatest resource—their human resource. Ultimately, the organizational milieu will be one that supports a mission that is quality patient care, not just in words, but also in fact.

Lest this analysis of the present take on a utopian flavor for the future, there are a couple of issues that we must face squarely. First, limited financial resources for healthcare could increase competition while decreasing service provisions, cooperation, and collaboration. To avoid this situation, and still control healthcare expenditures, we will need to develop new, consensual solutions to age old problems. Second, TQ is still a new concept to many members of the healthcare community. It is subject to many, often conflicting, interpretations. Some say that TQ is the only comprehensive management methodology that can guarantee the delivery of cost-effective, accessible, high-quality patient care, while ensuring the long-term financial survival of healthcare organizations. Others see TQ as a mere buzzword and suggest that "this too shall pass." To deliver a quality healthcare service in the future, we must reconcile both of these positions.

Clearly, we must develop a national research agenda for quality in healthcare. We can draw on our past experiences, our present analyses, and our future projections to create a research agenda and subsequent knowledge base that ensures high-quality, affordable, and accessible healthcare in the 21st century.

REFERENCES

Al-Assaf, A. F. and Doss, D. (1993). "Implementing Total Quality Management in Health Care: Attitudes of Mental Health Professionals." paper presented at 10th International Conference on Quality Assurance in Health Care, Maastricht, The Netherlands.

Al-Assaf, A. F. and Huff, L. (1993). Comparing Attitudes of Private and Public CEOs and QA Coordinators Regarding TQ Implementation, unpublished paper, University of Oklahoma.

Al-Assaf, A. F., Tindill, B. S., Curtis, K., Gentling, S., McCaffres, R., and Wheeler, J. (1993). "Perceptions of VA Chiefs of Staff on TQ Implementation." *American Journal of Medical Quality* (accepted for Fall 1993 publication).

Anderson, C. A., Cassidy, B., and Riverburgh. P. (1991). "Implementing Continuous Quality Improvement (CQI) in Hospitals: Lessons Learned from an International Quality Study." *Quality Assurance in Health Care,* 3(3):141–146.

Berwick, D. M. (1989). "Health Service Research and the Quality of Care." *Medical Care,* 27(8):763–771.

Berwick, D. M. (1991). "Controlling Variation in Healthcare: A Consultation from Walter Shewhart." *Medical Care,* 29(12):1212–1225.

Berwick, D. M., Godfrey, A. B., and Roessner, J. (1991). *Curing Health Care,* San Francisco: Jossey-Bass Publishers.

Bluth, E. I., Lambert, D. L., Lohmann, T. P., Franklin, D. N., Bourgeois, M., Kardinal, C. G., Delovisio, J. R., Williams, M. M., and Becker, A. S. (1992). "Improvement in 'Stat' Laboratory Turnaround Time." *Archives of Internal Medicine,* 152(4):837–840.

Burns, N. and Grove, S. K. (1993). *The Practice of Nursing Research,* 2nd edition, Philadelphia: W.B. Saunders.

Church Chason, C. (1993). *Strategy Management for Total Quality in Healthcare (Workshop),* Chason Associates, Inc. (CAI), 2350 Palm Lake Dr, Merritt Island, FL 32952.

Corbett, C. and Pennypacker, B. (1992). "Using a Quality Improvement Team to Reduce Patient Falls." *Journal of Healthcare Quality,* 14(15). 38–54.

Everett, W. D. (1993). "An Epidemiologic Approach to Quality Assurance in Hospitals." *Health Care Management Review,* 18(1):91–96.

Falconer, J. A., Roth, E. J., Sutin, J. A., Strasser, D. C., and Chang, R. W. (1993). "The Critical Path Method in Stroke Rehabilitation: Lessons from an Experiment in Cost Containment and Outcome Improvement." *Quality Review Bulletin,* 19(1):8–16.

Gaucher, E. J. and Coffey, R. J. (1993). *Total Quality in Healthcare: From Theory to Practice,* San Francisco: Jossey-Bass Publishers.

Herman, J. L., Morris, L. L., and Fitz-Gibbon, C. T. (1987). *Evaluation Handbook,* Newbury Park, Calif.: Sage.

Horsley, J. A., Crane, J., Crabtree, M. K., and Ward, D. J. (1983). *Using Research to Improve Nursing Practice: A Guide,* New York: Grune & Stratton.

Joint Commission (1992). *Accreditation Manual for Hospitals for 1993,* Oak Brook Terrace, Ill.: Joint Commission on Accreditation of Healthcare Organizations.

Jones, L., LoGerfo, J., Shy, K., Connell, F., Holt, V., Parrish, K., and McCandless, K. (1993). "StORQS: Washington's Statewide Obstetrical Review and Quality System: Overview and Provide Evaluation." *Quality Review Bulletin,* 19(4):110–118.

Marszalek-Gaucher, E. and Coffey, R. J. (1991). *Transforming Health Care Organizations,* San Francisco: Jossey-Bass.

Miller, D. C. (1991). *Handbook of Research Design and Social Measurement,* 4th edition, Newbury Park, Calif.: Sage Publications.

Nelson, E. C., Larson, C. D., Hays, R. D., Nelson, S. A., Ward, D., and Batalden, P. B. (1992). *Quality Review Bulletin,* 18(9):284–292.

Peters, D. (1992). "A New Look for Quality in Home Care." *Journal of Nursing Administration,* 22(11):21–26.

Rossi, P. N. and Freeman, H. E. (1989). *Evaluation,* 4th edition, Newbury Park, Calif.: Sage Publications.

Ruiz, U., Karmele, A., Buenoventura, R., Coll, J., Coronado, S., Rivero, A., and Rocillo, S. (1992). "Implementing Total Quality Management in the Spanish Health Care System." *Quality Assurance in Health Care,* (1):43–59.

Sullivan, N. and Frentzel, K. U. (1992). "A Patient Transport Pilot Quality Improvement Team." *Quality Review Bulletin,* 18(7):215–221.

Tindill, B. S., Al-Assaf, A. F., and Gentling, S. (1993). "Total Quality Improvement: A Study of Veterans Affairs Directors and Quality Assurance Coordinators." *American Journal of Medical Quality,* 8(2):45–52.

Vuori, H. (1989). "Research Needs in Quality Assurance." *Quality Assurance in Health Care,* 1(2/3):147–159.

Waggoner, D. M. (1992). "Applications of Continuous Quality Improvement Techniques to the Treatment of Patients with Hypertension." *Health Care Management Review,* 17(3):33–42.

Ward, S. S. (1992). "Quality Monitoring for Maintenance of Skin Integrity." *Journal of ET Nursing,* 19(3):91–94.

Werley, H. H., Devine, E. C., Zorn, C. R., Ryan, R., and Westra, B. L. (1991). "The Nursing Minimum Data Set: Abstraction Tool for Standardized, Comparable, Essential Data." *American Journal of Public Health,* 81(4):421–426.

Williamson, J. W., Reerink, E., Donabedian, A., Turner, C. W., and Christensen, A. (1991). "Health Science Information Management." *Quality Assurance in Health Care,* 3(2):95–114.

Yuhasz, L. S. (1991). "The Functional Requirements for TQ." *The Quality Leader,* 2(1):1–3.

PART V

CASE STUDY

12

TOTAL QUALITY within the VA HEALTHCARE SYSTEM: A CASE STUDY

Steven J. Gentling, MHA

John Morrison, MPH

"To care for him who shall have borne the battle and for his widow, and his orphan."

Abraham Lincoln, March 1865

Executive Order 5398, signed by President Herbert Hoover on July 21, 1930, established the Department of Veterans Affairs (VA). Its purpose was to provide America's veterans an assortment of benefits. One of three main organizational elements within the VA is the Veterans Health Administration (VHA). The purpose of the VHA is to provide American veterans with quality healthcare. Its commitment to Congress and the American taxpayer is to provide that quality care in the most effective and efficient means possible. In the decades following its inception, more demands have been placed on the VHA. Its role and responsibilities have been expanded, and today's VHA is vastly different than the VA of fifty years ago. It has become a very visible component of the U.S. healthcare system. Its mission has expanded to include healthcare education and medical research (Figure 12-1). With its 171 medical centers and 223 outpatient clinics, the VA has become the largest healthcare system in the United States. It employs 260,000 people, has an average daily census of 62,943 inpatients, treats more than 1 million patients a year, and has over 22 million outpatient visits annually. VA medical centers (VAMCs) and VA outpatient clinics (VAOPCs) are affiliated with 1246 healthcare educational institutions.

Figure 12-1.   Graphic representation of VHA mission.

In addition to providing healthcare to eligible veterans and serving as a vital component in healthcare education, the VA has also become one of the nation's largest medical research organizations. During the past ten years, the VA has funded 18,895 research projects involving approximately 8000 scientists.

This case study will examine the implementation of total quality (TQ) within the VA system. Specifically, we will follow the implementation of TQ at the VA Medical Center, Oklahoma City, Oklahoma, a 399-bed medical center affiliated with several leading healthcare educational institutions, including the University of Oklahoma. Along with providing inpatient care, the medical center operates an extensive outpatient clinic program. During fiscal year 1992, it saw 186,117 outpatient visits and an additional 18,042 through their satellite outpatient clinic in Lawton, Oklahoma, and Veteran State outpatient clinics in Ardmore and Clinton, Oklahoma.

The VAMC in Oklahoma City oversees an extensive research program, which currently includes 212 ongoing research projects involving 80 scientists. Several of these projects are conducted jointly between the VA and the University of Oklahoma. Although a majority of the funding is obtained through the VA system, a significant number of projects are funded through federal and state grants and private donations.

HISTORY of TQ IMPLEMENTATION in VHA

A number of years ago, VHA leaders realized that difficulties in the VA healthcare system mirrored major problems in the national healthcare system. They recognized that solving these problems would require an intense commitment, a specific focus, and the flexibility to deal with enormous changes. The healthcare system needed to become more efficient while maintaining high standards of quality care for veterans. As the largest healthcare provider in the country, it needed to take a leadership role in meeting this challenge. Implementing TQ within the VA system was determined to be the primary vehicle to meet this challenge, although this would not be an easy task. Traditionally, TQ has been associated with manufacturing and industry. Because of its numerous success stories in reducing waste and increasing efficiency and quality, TQ has become a commonly accepted process to enhance manufacturing. However, the processes involved in manufacturing are generally consistent and fairly predictable, which is why the statistical process of TQ is easy to use in decreasing variation. Healthcare, on the other hand, is quite different. Although processes and medical procedures do have some degree of predictability, no two patient medical cases are exactly alike. Because the very nature of healthcare demands flexibility in the treatment of patients, it is very difficult to control variation, one of the foundations of the TQ process. VHA leadership realized that TQ within the VHA healthcare system would differ from the TQ commonly associated with manufacturing. Although a movement toward this new philosophy and management system existed within healthcare, it was still too early for any healthcare organization to claim total integration and implementation of this revolutionary way of doing business. To some extent, the VHA has thus become a pioneer in merging TQ and healthcare.

Because of the numerous problems surfacing within the healthcare industry, major reforms within the near future are inevitable. These reforms can be expected to focus on providing quality care, while controlling costs. TQ is a science that has developed a reputation for doing just that. The VHA realized that working with the TQ principles, while at the same time remaining flexible, would allow the TQ process to be adapted to an ever-changing healthcare system.

Once the vision of implementing TQ throughout the VA system was established, the next step was to begin an implementation strategy. This implementation strategy had two critical elements. The first was to identify how the TQ process would be introduced and integrated into this large healthcare system. The second strategy was to establish facilitator roles during the embryonic stages of development. A letter identifying this vision and plan was sent to each of the 171 medical centers. It requested a

263

proposal from those interested in implementing TQ. Each proposal had to present reasons why their facility should be selected as one of the initial sites for TQ implementation. In addition, the letter explained that those selected would be responsible for some of the additional implementation costs and the mentoring of future implementation at other VHA sites. It was reasoned that the financial obligation and mentorship responsibility would facilitate the identification of those hospitals whose leaders were committed to the principles and philosophy of TQ. A panel was established to review the proposals and determine which sites would have the highest probability of succeeding while representing a diversity in size, mission, and geographic location. The medical centers chosen were located in Albany, NY; Albuquerque, NM; Big Spring, TX; Brooklyn, NY; Danville, IL; Indianapolis, IN; Lexington, KY; Loma Linda, CA; New York City, NY; Oklahoma City, OK; Prescott, AZ; San Francisco, CA; and Tuscaloosa, AL.

In April 1991, the VA Central Office, headquartered in Washington, D.C., advertised for "Request for Proposals" from quality management consulting firms interested in a contract to assist the VA in implementing TQ. After reviewing the proposals, it was determined that American Productivity & Quality Center (APQC) would best meet the needs of the VA. A contract was negotiated and awarded to APQC on July 5, 1991.

The proposal submitted by APQC essentially outlined a TQ implementation strategy in four phases. The first phase would involve the 13 pilot-site medical centers, 4 regional offices, the VA Central Office, and trainers from the Regional Medical Educational Centers (REMCs). (In 1972, the Department of Veterans Affairs (DVA) established seven strategically located REMCs and Continuing Education Centers (CECs) to provide education and training to VHA physicians, nurses, and other healthcare personnel.) Phase I of the implementation plan would last approximately one year. It would provide 96 consultant days and 30 training days to each of the pilot sites. During this time, a consultant would train a designated individual at each site. Training consisted of the tools of TQ and the techniques of an effective consultant, so that when the consultant dollars were expended, the designated individual would be able to assume the role of TQ expert and internal consultant. The second phase, which involved 24 hospitals, would be given half the number (48) of consultant days of the Phase I hospitals. The medical centers implementing TQ under Phases II, III, and IV would receive all their training from RMEC master trainers and internal consultants, certified under Phase I training. The third phase, to be launched in the third year, would involve 48 hospitals. Funding would be received for 24 consultant days. The fourth and final phase, involving 80 medical centers, would receive 10 consultant days. At this point, the VA would have a full cadre of trainers and internal consultants and the contract consultants will no longer be needed.

TQ would be integrated successfully throughout the VA by 1995 (as shown in Figure 12-2).

Shortly after the contract was awarded, the consultants made an initial visit to each of the 13 medical centers selected as Phase I sites. The purpose of these visits was to introduce the consultants to the organization, to introduce the organization to TQ, and to learn about each individual medical center, so that a TQ implementation plan could be developed to reflect the unique strengths and needs of each facility.

Quality management, whether it be labeled TQ, CQI, etc., has gained much popularity during the past decade. As a result, there is extensive literature to guide organizations through the transition from traditional management systems to participative management. However, as mentioned earlier, TQ in healthcare has just recently surfaced as a focused philosophy and process. Although many healthcare organizations have initiated implementations, few, if any, have reached the point where they can claim success in having a TQ organization. As a result, the consultants, although seasoned in assisting manufacturing organizations in implementing TQ, had little experience with TQ in healthcare organizations. In essence, when accepting the VA contract, they accepted a dual role. They would be *teachers* of TQ and *students* of TQ within healthcare. This became evident at the Phase I sites, where the consultants developed, through a learning process, the curriculum for Phases II, III, and IV.

TQ IMPLEMENTATION at VAMC, OKLAHOMA CITY, OKLAHOMA

TQ implementation was initiated at most of the Phase I sites in the late summer and early fall of 1991. The leadership of the VAMC, Oklahoma City had an introduction to TQ during a three-day management workshop in July 1991. This was the consultants' initial visit. Most of the workshop focused on TQ. It included a history, a discussion of top TQ leaders and their philosophies, an explanation of traditional benefits shared by TQ organizations, and an outline of the global TQ implementation plan for the VA.

A few months before the workshop, the medical center's CEO, Steven Gentling, hired a full-time TQ coordinator to act for him in implementing TQ. Eventually, this TQ coordinator would assume the role of an internal consultant. He also assembled an executive steering body for TQ initiatives. This group included seven members of the top management staff. At the time, the reasoning was that the committee needed to consist of those leaders who had the power to implement change and thus show the commitment of top management to this philosophy. It was later discovered that although this group was successful as a steering committee, it lacked

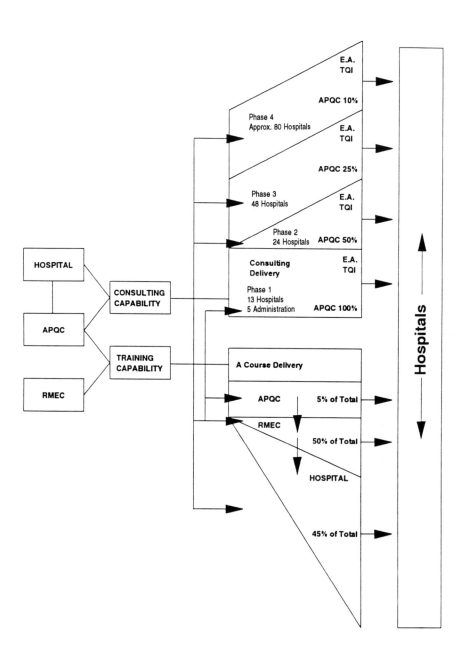

Figure 12-2.   Chart of APQC roll-out plan.

full support from the medical center staff because it was perceived as not truly representing the totality of the medical center. When the executive steering body became aware of these feelings, they elected to expand the membership to include the union president and three other members from various levels within the organization. The intent was to create a steering committee that further cut across organizational lines and more closely reflected the culture of the medical center. It became clear that the role of a TQ steering committee is to reflect the collective expertise and wisdom of every member of the staff. The present steering committee at the medical center is a better reflection of its culture. Employees at every level feel that they have representation, which is critical because this committee will undoubtedly institute change that will impact and involve them.

During this transition, the steering committee made another significant change—they changed their name from Executive Steering Committee to Medical Center Steering Committee (MCSC), reflecting a new composition and representation. This is a significant change not only because it is symbolic of TQ, but because it indicates the willingness and desire of top management to change in order to meet the needs of the total organization.

Initial Assessment

In October 1991, the medical center conducted an assessment of needs using the seven examination categories of the 1991 Malcolm Baldrige National Quality Award. These categories include leadership, information and analysis, strategic quality planning, human resource utilization, quality assurance of products and service, quality results, and customer satisfaction. The assessment team consisted of 29 staff members, mostly department heads and program officials from both administrative and clinical areas. Team members were selected based on their experience with one of the seven areas of the Malcolm Baldrige criteria.

As a result, seven teams were established. During this initial meeting, APQC conducted training on data collection and discussed various methods for obtaining the information needed to conduct the assessment. In addition, the meeting helped each team establish a strategy on how they were going to conduct their assessment. During the two months that followed the initial meeting, the teams conducted their assessment, gathered their information and data, and wrote up their findings. The information obtained in assessing the medical center consisted mostly of historical data, interviews, and surveys, both written and oral. Upon completion, the committee assembled for a one-day wrap-up in which each of the seven subcommittees presented its findings and recommendations for improvement. Through a nominal group process, the team then prioritized a list of 53 opportunities for improvement. Consolidation of this information resulted in a final report submitted to the MCSC in December 1991.

Recognizing the need to focus on priority processes, the MCSC, after receiving the final report, met to determine which of the 53 opportunities for improvement to focus on first. They established TQ process teams to analyze and implement corrective action for four of the top eight in the prioritized list of improvement opportunities that were identified in the assessment process: (1) improve availability of medical records; (2) decrease the amount of waiting time in the outpatient areas; (3) implement a reward, recognition, and performance evaluation system; and (4) formalize patient education. Although the assessment did not rate parking as a high priority relative to other items, the MCSC chose it as the fifth opportunity for improvement. This was done because of the high visibility of the parking issue and its impact on patients and staff. The MCSC selection criteria for choosing these opportunities centered on processes that were perceived as fairly simple and that could be improved fairly quickly. In time it became clear that these *perceptions* of these processes were not founded on fact. Some were much more complex than initially thought. As with anything new or radically different, it was important to ensure commitment from the medical center staff. One sure way of obtaining this commitment is to generate success stories.

The initial assessment tool showed that there was opportunity for improvement. However, the process was too lengthy, time consuming, and excessively complex, and not all employees had the opportunity to participate. As a result of feedback from the VAMC as well as other Phase I sites, VA Central Office worked closely with the consultants to revise the assessment process. In the end, it was replaced with a survey that still measures the medical center in the seven areas of the Malcolm Baldrige criteria. The survey is easier to use, less time consuming to administer, and consistent throughout the VA system. It provides comparative data which serves as a baseline for future analysis and, most important, gives all employees the opportunity to participate. The survey was recently administered at the VAMC, with a 45% rate of return.

Mission and Vision Statements

One of the initial TQ objectives of the MCSC was to develop a mission and vision statement. In discussing this issue and trying to determine what to convey, it was decided to seek the input from staff of the medical center. By inviting their input, the MCSC, in essence, took the first step in developing a culture in which everyone feels that his or her opinions and ideas are valued. A request for input was advertised through the TQ monthly newsletter, the medical center weekly bulletin, and the medical center electronic mail system.

Although the MCSC was overwhelmed with a large number of responses, those received were considered by the steering committee in the following statements:

Mission Statements

We are committed to serving eligible veterans of Oklahoma and surrounding states with compassionate and timely healthcare services within available resources, and we will be the principal advocate to ensure that each veteran receives the care and support earned in service to this country.

Vision Statements

We will be clearly recognized within the community and state as a vital component of healthcare, medical education, and research systems and the provider of efficient and effective service in each of these processes. We will meet or exceed the expectations of all the customers we serve including each other. We will achieve a level of national excellence in clinical and administrative healthcare arenas.

Since then, these statements have been used in every training program and at numerous meetings for all employees. They also are used in various medical center publications and reports. They have become the foundation of the new culture.

TQ Awareness Training

It was decided to provide all employees with awareness training. Initially, two versions of TQ awareness training existed, a four-hour session and a two-hour session. The difference was reflected primarily as more in-depth discussion centering on the tools and the quality gurus. The training sessions were conducted over a six-week period beginning in October 1991. Although everyone was welcome to attend either training session, management was encouraged to attend the four-hour session. Shortly after they began training, course critiques and other feedback mechanisms indicated that many of the participants did not feel the four-hour training needed to be that long. On the basis of this feedback, the long version was eventually discontinued. It also was important not to make the awareness training mandatory, but rather to encourage, coach, and sell the idea and employee participation. A 70% participation rate was enjoyed, which most would agree is a successful start. TQ awareness training has been made a permanent part of our new employee orientation at the VAMC, which ensures that all new employees joining the staff of the medical center have a good understanding of the TQ transition.

Forming Initial TQ Teams

The MCSC selected five opportunities for improvement and wrote draft charters (agreements or contracts). The charters were written in draft form to allow teams the opportunity to make changes as necessary. It was recognized that many times teams will be launched to improve complex processes of which the MCSC, in all likelihood, has limited knowledge. Because most teams consist of process experts, it is important that they have the flexibility to change their charters. This flexibility enables them to work more effectively when improving the processes identified for improvement.

The next step was to select and train facilitators and team leaders. Facilitators are nonparticipating team members. They do not become involved in improving the content of a specific process, but instead are responsible for maximizing the effectiveness of the TQ process. They keep the team on track, ensure participation of all members, and aid the team in identifying which statistical tools to use to improve their process. To select facilitators, eight staff members were identified who had good people skills, were respected within the medical center, and could remain objective in a team setting. To identify team leaders, the MCSC looked for individuals who were process experts with leadership and facilitator skills, and were either process owners or had a good degree of knowledge concerning the process with which they would be working. After these individuals were identified, the coordinator recruited them. Because the opportunities the MCSC chose were broad, organization-wide issues, they decided that advertising for volunteers would be the best method for obtaining membership on these initial teams. MCSC began an advertising campaign that included placing notices on bulletin boards, in the medical center weekly bulletin, and the monthly TQ newsletter. They requested that individuals contact the team leader if they were interested in participating as a team member on one of the initial TQ teams. Drafts of the team charters were placed in several places throughout the medical center, along with the name and phone number of the team leader. Following the designated window of opportunity for volunteers, each team leader prepared a list, noting his or her recommended team membership, and presented it to the MCSC. In turn, the MCSC approved the teams and established training dates.

The initial training for team members was conducted in late January 1992. A three-day course was specifically designed for team leaders and facilitators. The MCSC, the five team leaders, and the eight facilitators attended. Although this training was valuable in helping to establish a firm foundation for the implementation of TQ, many of the members felt that it needed some revision. As a result, members of the steering committee began working on a revised team member course. Medical center staff presentations on communication and team building were incorporated into the training. In mid-April 1992, the five teams participated in the revised three-day team member training session, consisting of four hours of enhancing communication skills, eight hours of team building skills, and ten hours of quality tools. The last two hours of the third day were devoted to the first team meetings, in which they agreed on their operational ground rules, reviewed their draft charters, and established agendas for their second meeting.

Upon completion of each TQ training class, feedback was provided through course critiques in order to improve the effectiveness of the training. As a result of the critiques, it became clear that many of the participants in the initial training were unhappy with the course content and its structure. Because of the amount of material covered in a short time, many believed TQ to be too complex and confusing. Through constant feedback, the training was redesigned to where most participants now believe that TQ is not unnecessarily complex. As a result, they feel comfortable and, in many cases, excited about forming TQ teams to improve processes.

OUTCOMES

Most of the teams meet for an hour once a week. In addition to the weekly meeting, the team members often devote one to three hours per week collecting data if historical data are unavailable. However, many of the teams find the data they seek through the medical center's centralized computer system. It takes most teams approximately six months to devise an action to present to the MCSC. However, there have been some exceptions. The Reward and Recognition Team has been meeting for eleven months and, from all indications, will probably continue to meet for at least six more months. The systems they are attempting to improve are very broad and deeply entrenched within the culture of the medical center. Another facet of the team's mission has increased the complexity of what they are attempting to do—every staff member of the medical center is a customer of the systems they are working to improve.

These teams have been successful in identifying problems and inefficiencies in the system. The Patient Education Team was the first team to present an action plan to the MCSC. The team consisted of a physician, a pharmacist, a dietitian, a social worker, and three nurses. In analyzing the patient education system, they discovered that, although some excellent patient education programs exist, the presentations are sporadic and often lack consistency and uniformity. They also identified areas that had no formal patient education programs. Studying this problem in greater depth, they soon discovered that this problem was common to healthcare in general. The U.S. healthcare system focuses on tertiary rather than preventive care.

271

After formulating their findings, the Patient Education Team developed an improvement plan that established the foundation for a formal patient education program. This included the restructuring of the Patient Education Committee already in place. Unfortunately, due to circumstances outside their control, the improvement was ineffective. It is noteworthy that the more time this team spent together, the more committed its members became to their task and to the team. When given the choice, most of the TQ team members elected to become members of the newly structured Patient Education Committee. The Gantt chart which follows is a time chart of the patient education action plan (Figure 12-3).

Although most teams will consist of the process owners or those who have the power to implement changes recommended by a team, there will be times, for a variety of reasons, when this will not be possible. This can be frustrating for the team. Because of the complexity of healthcare processes and the number of people who have partial ownership of processes, this will not be an uncommon occurrence. For example, the medical center launched a team to look at the amount of time patients wait in the Urology Clinic before being seen by a physician. The team verified that a problem did exist and was able to identify several reasons why. However, the team also discovered that it was not in the position to resolve most of the problems. Because the medical center is affiliated with and serves as a teaching facility for the University of Oklahoma Medical School, many of its processes have dual ownership. This relationship often makes it difficult to implement change.

This became painfully obvious when the team submitted their action plan to the steering committee for approval. It was decided that the best approach for resolving this issue would be to have the team present their findings and recommendations to the physicians who had significant ownership and control. With the support and leadership of the Chief of Staff, who is a member of the MCSC, the team's recommendations for approval will likely be implemented.

Although all the teams are instituting changes to improving efficiency and quality, one team in particular deserves mention, because they are dealing more with changing the culture than a work process. When the MCSC established the charter for the Reward and Recognition Team, they were essentially thinking of a team that would review the monetary award and recognition system as it applies to the performance evaluation process. They wanted to determine if giving employees monetary awards based on their performance rating was effective. If it was not, they wanted to devise a more effective way of rewarding and recognizing those individuals who go above and beyond what is called for in their performance plans. This team, like most of the cross-functional teams, is composed of members from

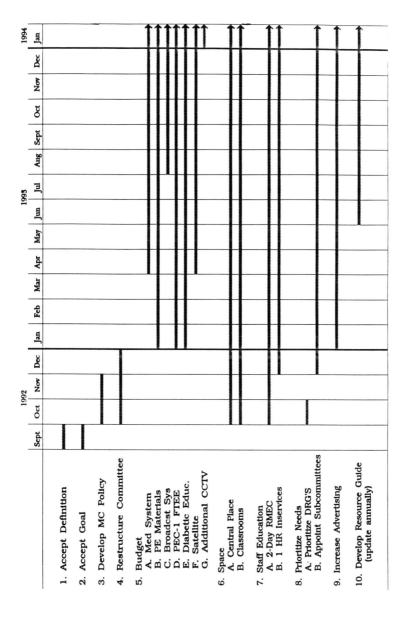

Figure 12-3.   Schedule for implementation of patient education recommendations.

various levels within the medical center, both clinical and administrative. After the team gained a good understanding of the existing system, they concluded that they could be more effective by expanding their charter to include reviewing the performance and evaluation system. Although some members of the MCSC opposed this team's suggestion, most supported it, and the MCSC approved the expanded charter. In keeping with the philosophy of empowerment, the MCSC wrote the original charter in draft form. In this manner, a team can suggest changes in scope and, when appropriate, these can be incorporated into the charter. There are several reasons for this philosophy—it enhances the commitment of the team members; it gives the team a sense of empowerment; and, in most cases, the team will be comprised of the experts in the process. It stands to reason that those who are the process experts can best determine the scope of what it is they should be evaluating.

The team distributed surveys to medical center staff to gather and analyze data on the existing award and recognition system and performance and evaluation system. The intent of the survey was to gain a better understanding of employee feelings and concerns about these systems. Of the 1500 that were distributed, 396 were returned. The results of the survey were not surprising and perhaps would be reflected similarly in other large bureaucracies. However, the results were not all negative. The majority of respondents indicated that they believed their performance standards were realistic and achievable. The survey also revealed that the majority believed their standards to be realistic and that their supervisor followed the standards in judging their performance.

Essentially, respondents indicated that they perceived the current system (in which a supervisor determines performance ratings and is responsible for distribution of reward and recognition dollars) as unfair and full of favoritism. Historically, supervisors have elected to distribute reward and recognition dollars in conjunction with high performance ratings. Based on the results of the survey, the first proposed action plan of the team recommended disconnecting the performance evaluation system from the award and recognition system. Instead of giving out rewards once a year based on the employee's evaluation, the team recommended recognition during the course of the year for special acts and contributions. Once again, the members of the MCSC had significant discussions, the majority of which focused on the timing of the recommended changes as opposed to the actual change. However, the MCSC is continuously improving and learning that, whenever possible, it is important they totally support the TQ teams, especially when those teams obtain data that represent the thoughts and feelings of the staff of the medical center.

The Reward, Recognition, and Performance Evaluation Team realizes they have only scratched the surface. The medical center is a traditional bureaucratic organization that historically has rewarded individual competitive behavior. The team understands that the current performance and evaluation system rewards individuals for "keeping the boss happy," which often means the supervisor is viewed as the customer. In reality, our boss is more of a supplier than a customer. The team's next big task will be to create an evaluation system that promotes teamwork. Here, an individual's behavior will be judged based on his or her ability and willingness to be a team player. This type of evaluation system will focus less on personal accomplishments and more on how individual work and actions impact teams and the medical center overall. The team will develop a system where feedback concerning customer requirements and satisfaction comes from the customer and not the supplier.

The MCSC has launched several other cross-functional teams since its initial establishment of TQ teams in April 1992. However, because cross-functional teams look at large issues, they will need more time to make a significant effect on changing the culture during the early phases of TQ implementation. After all, broad processes usually involve a large number of people, which means that the processes are not specific to any one person or group. Therefore, they usually do not involve the specific work process of individuals, and even if they do, not to the extent that a work group has the power to change the process. These processes are divided into two levels. A Level I process involves all medical center staff. Level II processes are subdivided and controlled by two or more departments. A third type of process also exists at the medical center and is called Level III. It is more specific and is controlled by one department. Teams that address Level I or Level II problems or opportunities for improvement are launched and chartered by the MCSC. The MCSC is in the process of establishing Service Steering Committees (SSC) to launch teams that are department (service) specific. The medical center has a total of 35 services. To date, 11 SSCs have been established and trained. The MCSC and the SSC have identical functions. The major difference is the scope of the processes with which they work.

Just as the MCSC is responsible for acting as a steering body for implementing TQ at the medical center level, the SSC acts as a steering body for implementing TQ at the service level (as shown in Figure 12-4). There is one major difference between these two committees. It is at the service level that employees will become specifically involved in improving their individual work processes. The service level is also where a more rapid change in culture can be effected. When employees are given an opportunity to change and improve their work processes and environment, they

ORGANIZING FOR TOTAL QUALITY IMPROVEMENT

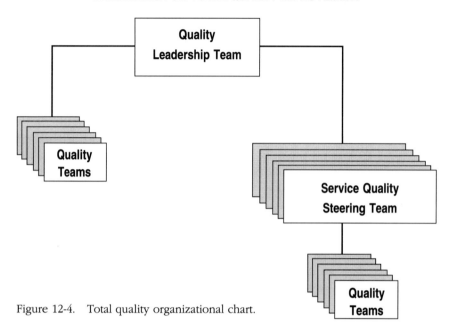

Figure 12-4.   Total quality organizational chart.

begin to feel a sense of ownership and empowerment, which leads to a change in perception. Of course, a key ingredient to changing a culture is "empowerment."

Recently the MCSC began forming steering committees at the department level, even though improvements are already occurring in processes and even culture. Notably, some department steering committees have elected to launch teams to address cultural issues before launching teams to consider improving work processes. For example, the Environmental Health Service will involve its 70 employees in selecting new uniforms. The Dietetics Service has launched a team to develop criteria for hiring full-time employees. As stated earlier, the majority of services have launched Reward and Recognition teams, where traditionally the supervisor alone determined reward and recognition. Some SSCs have launched teams to improve work processes. For example, the Social Work Steering Committee established teams to review social work coverage. As a result, they developed a plan to increase social work coverage in the outpatient clinic, general surgery, medicine, and rehabilitation medicine. The Laboratory Service Steering Committee launched several teams to look at the time it takes to process specimens and lab results. These are only a few of the many different types of teams being established by the SSCs.

CELEBRATING SUCCESS,
COMMUNICATION, and PERSISTENCE

There have been many attempts in the past to enhance the effectiveness and efficiency of management systems and work processes. Although a few were somewhat effective, the majority had little, if any, long-term impact. These various endeavors are often referred to as "programs of the decade." Initially, many of the medical center staff were somewhat indifferent to TQ. As usual, many viewed it as the "program of the decade." A number of staff are still essentially indifferent. This is natural and should be expected. After all, it is difficult for people to commit time and energy to something if they are uncertain of the outcome. This is especially true in healthcare, where time is often in short supply. Even so, methods have been found to encourage commitment. The strategy is simple: share and celebrate TQ success (regardless of the size of the success), communicate, and never give up (persistence).

After launching the initial teams at the medical center, it was recognized that some individuals felt uncomfortable about communicating their activities with the rest of the staff. A few teams were very insistent about not discussing team business with nonteam members. After examining this problem, it began to make sense. The culture is not fully conducive to free and open communication, despite the fact that numerous forms of communication exist within the system (e.g., newsletters, all-employee meetings, countless staff and committee meetings, bulletin boards, etc.). In many ways communication is discouraged. This is especially true when dealing with territorial or turf issues. In large bureaucracies it is common for individuals (especially managers) to feel ownership over the areas they control or manage. As a result, they feel that they should make any decision concerning their area of supervision or "ownership." This kind of thinking leads to communication barriers; instead of one system working together as a team, many subsystems exist, working independently and not communicating with each other. Reinforcement of individual competitive behavior was another inhibitor of communication and contributor to turf issues. We do not feel comfortable communicating up the chain of command unless it involves communicating something that will make us look good. We are taught not to communicate unless we can communicate success. Many teams chose not to communicate until they had something positive to communicate. As the culture changes, communication should become more effective and flow more openly.

It is important to communicate TQ endeavors and success stories whenever possible. TQ updates are presented at the director's monthly staff meeting, which is conducted by the director to update all levels of management on current events. Updates are also presented at all-employee meetings, which are held six times each year. The monthly TQ newsletter serves two purposes—keeping the staff updated on team progress and providing a tool for aiding culture change. This newsletter also discusses the benefits of TQ, future expectations, and how those expectations can be met.

Celebrating TQ success stories is important, regardless of the size of the success. All teams will improve the processes they are working on. However, that does not imply that the team has not been successful. The fact that a group of experts gets together and forms a team to look at a process to determine if an opportunity for improvement exists is a success in itself. Newsletters and storyboards are some of the methods used at the medical center to celebrate TQ success stories. A storyboard is a poster board that displays a team's history. It begins with a brief statement explaining the purpose or mission of the team. The methods the team used to understand and analyze the process are then described. The final document is the team's action plan for improving the process. As a general rule, we also include an 8 × 10 color photograph of the team members along with their names at the end of the story.

Other mechanisms used at the medical center include such rewards as the MCSC treating teams to breakfast. Currently, a certificate of appreciation is being designed which will be presented at an all-employee meeting to a team that has reached a milestone or success.

Persistence is a vital ingredient to ensuring success in implementing TQ. Initially, many on the MCSC falsely believed that the TQ transition could be accomplished quickly. However, that was based on viewing TQ as merely a statistical tool. It was falsely assumed that most people would embrace the opportunity to get together with their fellow workers to improve the processes in which they worked. However, there is more to TQ than just statistical tools. Implementing teams to use the TQ tools for improving processes is quick and easy. The hard part is dealing with the fact that TQ is also a change in culture. No organization can change its culture over night. It takes patience, time, and most of all, persistence.

CONCLUSION

Although the transition to TQ at the VA Medical Center in Oklahoma City is still in its infancy (18 months), change is beginning to occur. Greater flexibility is available in changing processes. Channels of communication are beginning to open. However, much still has to be accomplished before the medical center can truly be considered a TQ organization. The next major step is to develop and administer a supervisory program designed to assist supervisors in their transition from managers to leaders. As most TQ experts agree, middle management is the toughest segment of the organization to change. Top management at the medical center is totally committed to and even excited about the possibilities of TQ. However, understandably, mid-level management is apprehensive and feels somewhat threatened. The goal is to develop a TQ supervisory program that will help them feel good about TQ and at the same time aid them in going through the transition. This training will focus on getting people to change their work ethics or philosophies. Changing the culture will require changing the structure of the organization. Changing the organizational chart will not be sufficient. Change must also occur in the power structure—the relationship between levels within the organization. Changing this relationship will open channels of communication, change perceptions concerning ownership, and eventually dissolve individual turfs.

Supervisors will be expected to participate in changing this traditionally autocratic and bureaucratic system to a participative management system. In order to do this successfully, the role of the supervisory staff will need to move from managers to team leaders. As team leaders, they will learn how to facilitate their teams, helping them to identify opportunities for improvement. They will learn how to use the TQ process to improve quality and efficiency, while decreasing waste. They will learn to share decision-making responsibilities and how to coach their teams effectively, so that each team can make its own decisions. One of the major goals is for the members of each team to collectively feel a sense of ownership over what they do. Historically, management has held this ownership because management has been responsible for making all final decisions. This mentality has discouraged committed participation from many of the staff. Apparently, this reluctance to share decisions explains why they have not yet formed TQ teams to improve their processes.

In the spring of 1993, the medical center is scheduled (at the time of this writing) to conduct a two-day training session for all of its 127 staff members in supervisory roles. The objective of this orientation is to instill within the supervisors the understanding that TQ is not just a fad that will eventually disappear. Ultimately, it is a philosophy and management system that will change every element of their organization. It is a new way of doing business. It will allow us to take off our blinders and become a learning organization that embraces change and opportunities for improvement. It will teach us that efficiency and quality can exist in the same environment. However, the most important objective is that the supervisors understand that the implementation of TQ within the medical center, as well as the entire healthcare system, *must* happen. Our healthcare system is out of control, and we can no longer afford to ignore its problems. If we are to meet the demands of the American public, change is absolutely essential. TQ will be the means for implementing that change.

The format for the two-day TQ supervisory orientation was still in the planning phases at the time of this writing. Essentially, it will consist of presentations, discussions, and workshops dealing with the history of the U.S. economy in comparison with its competitors, a historical overview of TQ, and a discussion of how our global competitors have used TQ to learn how to compete effectively with U.S. industries. Current economic problems facing U.S. industries, including healthcare, will be discussed, as well as the enormous spending problems confronting the federal government.

As a part of this orientation, the first TQ forum will be conducted. Here, the leadership—the director, associate director, chief of staff, and 35 department heads—will begin planning a TQ implementation strategy that will involve every department at every level. These leadership forums, which will occur every two weeks, will become a permanent part of our system. They will allow department heads to start working together as a team. Department heads will become a support network, sharing their success stories and discussing problems in an open nonthreatening environment. Communication will flow freely. The goal is for all of the 127 managers to become team leaders, internal consultants, facilitators, and TQ process experts.

In addition to the two-day orientation and the TQ leadership forum, all of the leaders will attend a four-day TQ training session, which will be offered six times during the summer of 1993. The training will include one day of group dynamics and skills in building teams, one day of tools training, one day of facilitator training, and one day of practical exercises and case studies.

Although still in its infancy, the TQ program at the VA Medical Center in Oklahoma City is ambitious and totally committed to the concept and principles of TQ. TQ will provide the medical center with the opportunity to become the best it can be. Their goal, which they believe to be conservative, is to successfully implement TQ by mid-1996.

ANNOTATED BIBLIOGRAPHY

Douglas W. Stewart, DO

AHA Division of Quality Resources (1992). "The Role of Hospital Leadership in the Continuous Improvement of Patient Care Quality." *Journal for Healthcare Quality,* 14(5):8–15.

The message conveyed to health industry leaders in this article is very clear and prescriptive. Organizations should be motivated internally to adopt the CQI philosophy. Leaders of organizations must take the most active role in the study and implementation of CQI. The process of implementation requires a long-term investment, is different for every organizational culture, and must be comprehensive.

Before describing the steps that hospital leaders should take in implementing CQI, the article answers several questions to justify the substantial effort required to effect such an organizational change. What is CQI? Why change our traditional QA program? What have we learned from traditional QA? What can CQI bring to traditional QA? The explanations are simple and to the point. Although not exhaustive, the answers to these questions are worth reading because they represent cogent responses to common concerns about CQI.

The recommended steps to assure organizationwide implementation and action constitute the greatest contribution of this article. The major approaches of the three main quality gurus are combined and summarized for the hospital leader. There is even a table for comparison of Deming's 14 steps, Juran's 10-step plan, and Crosby's 14-step process. This section is essential reading for the healthcare organization leader seeking practical advice along the road to long-term process improvement in healthcare.

Al-Assaf, A., Tindell, B., and Gentling, S. (1993). "VA Directors and QA Coordinators Attitudes towards TQM Planning and Implementation." *Journal for Healthcare Quality,* (accepted for publication).

Attitudes and practices of leaders of organizations are critical determinants of the effective implementation of TQ in an industry. The authors of this article provide an outstanding sample of a method of measurement (survey) utilized in TQ. The focus also rests on the importance of attitudes and beliefs during the continuous process of transforming the culture of an organization. Finally, this aspect of TQ is always subject to improvement, so that turning TQ on itself may be expected to yield useful information planning.

Batalden, P. (1991). "Organizationwide Quality Improvement in Health Care." *Topics in Health Records Management,* 11:1–12.

This article represents another comprehensive review of quality improvement that touches on the evolution of quality control and provides a complete definitions of terms and an explanation of the fundamental principles behind OQI. Dr. Batalden is the leader of the Quality Resource Group at Hospital Corporation of America (HCA). He has a wealth of experience as a physician leader in the implementation and cultivation of quality improvement in healthcare.

The brief historical perspective of quality improvement reviews the key events and people. The beginning of the quality revolution in post World War II Japan, for example, began when General Douglas MacArthur invited Dr. W. Edwards Deming to travel to Japan and teach statistical process control to Japanese engineers. The results of the next three decades of application firmly established Japanese production processes as world leading.

The article is especially helpful in addressing the setting in which the quality improvement techniques are utilized. Batalden describes the linking of OQI methods and organizational environment. The reader is better able to appreciate the importance of the policy framework and organizational structure in relation to the organizationwide dynamics of change.

Finally, the author draws on the work of Dr. Donald Berwick to enable QA professionals to gain insight into their traditional roles and how their duties may radically change in leading their organizations in the continuous process of OQI. The list of references for this section, as for the rest of the article, is very good.

Berwick, D. M. (1988). "Continuous Improvement as an Ideal in Health Care." *New England Journal of Medicine,* 320:53-56.

Berwick's now classic "The Theory of Bad Apples" article begins with an example of two work environments. One system relies on a foreman who inspects the work in progress in order to detect and take action against a worker whose performance does not pass inspection. The second workplace is characterized by workers who, under the guidance of their foreman, look for opportunities for improvement in their activities. In the latter setting, the foreman seeks to lead the workers in a quest for mutual development and process improvement. This foreman also directs attention toward the group average, rather than the workers ranked at the bottom, for efficiency or effectiveness. The reader is then asked in which environment he or she would rather work. This important dichotomy is reinforced throughout the article.

Dr. Berwick first established the distinction between quality assurance (QA) and quality improvement (QI) for the healthcare industry with this important article. He describes inspection as "at best inefficient, at worst a formula for failure" and, in any case, a tremendous waste of resources. The article represents the first exposure of many healthcare workers, especially physicians, to the Theory of Continuous Improvement and *kaizen*. The logical alternative to quality by inspection involves proactive measures (prevention) and correct identification of root causes of problems. The improvement process is directed toward the group average, not the outlier, and toward learning, not excuses or defense. Berwick writes, "The Theory of Continuous Improvement works because of the immense, irresistible quantitative power derived from shifting the entire curve of production upward even slightly, as compared with a focus on trimming the tails."

Bisognano, M. (1993). "Continuous Quality Improvement in Health Care." *Managed Care Quarterly*, 1:53–54.

A distinction is made in healthcare organizations between service quality and clinical quality. This essay relates that this dichotomy is antithetical to the unifying framework of CQI. The brief paper is valuable for its discussion of top management participation and key steps in implementation. The author is vice president of the Juran Institute.

Casalou, R. F. (1991). "Total Quality Management in Health Care." *Hospital and Health Services Administration*, 36:134–146.

The article is a comprehensive review of the TQ principles taught by Dr. W. Edwards Deming and applied to the health service industry. This analysis will prove to be invaluable for leaders, as well as frontline workers, in healthcare. Some healthcare workers experience difficulty in applying TQ to their contributions to hospital or clinic organizations. There is a need for many different ways to introduce this paradigm so that the many and varied personal characteristics of learning may be accommodated. Casalou does a great service to those working to spread this thought revolution throughout their respective organizations. Instead of reading *The Deming Management Method* by Mary Walton (a very fine book to begin the study of TQ), many people in healthcare will turn directly to this article for a concise overview of TQ according to Deming. Each of the 14 points (or principles) receives explanation, with ample references for further study. Healthcare service industry examples are utilized for demonstration.

In addition to the superb analysis of Deming's 14 principles, the author devotes additional attention to implementation of TQ. This brief, final section is also quite helpful. There is a discussion of planning for TQ, addressing resistance to change, using quality consultants or outside trainers, and turning the TQ process on itself in order to continuously improve implementation.

Chaufournier, R. and St. Andre, C. (1993). "Total Quality Management in an Academic Health Center." *Quality Progress,* 26:63–66.

This case study describes the model used to bring about the implementation of TQ in the unique healthcare setting of an academic health center (George Washington University Medical Center [GWUMC] in Washington, D.C.). The article is well written and demonstrates the value of the case study method in learning TQ. The authors describe the first three years of organizational transformation. Strategic planning for and the establishment of a quality improvement structure receive much deserved attention in this article. Instead of developing a new model for process improvement, GWUMC borrowed from Hospital Corporation of America (HCA) both their vice president for quality (Paul Batalden, M.D.) and a process improvement strategy he originated. Dr. Batalden was effectively utilized as an external consultant and trainer. FOCUS-PDCA, the basic team process improvement model developed by Batalden, has proven to be as successful for GWUMC as it has for HCA.

The process of education and training in TQ philosophy at this academic health center reinforced the axiom that the best way to learn something is to teach it. Senior management became proficient in quality control tools and team-building skills. These top managers subsequently served as principal faculty for the training of all managers.

Gillem, T. (1988). "Deming's 14 Points and Hospital Quality: Responding to the Consumer's Demand for the Best Value in Health Care." *Journal of Nursing Quality Assurance,* 2:70–78.

Gillem provides a very informative interpretation of Dr. Deming's 14 points for CQI. The perspective of the health service industry is carried throughout the article as the paradigm shift required to understand that this philosophy represents a significant reorientation for a hospital. The author provides a tremendous educational tool for TQ training in healthcare settings. The bulk of the article reviews Deming's 14 points, with examples drawn from hospital administration. Mr. Gillem was a quality director at Hospital Corporation of America when the article was published. He called upon the expertise of Paul Batalden, M.D., and the use of Deming's management methods by the HCA in 400 hospitals around the world.

In addition to the valuable translation of Deming's 14 points, Gillem explains the differences between quality assurance and quality improvement. Implementation of TQ in many healthcare organizations represents the "transformation from the current practice of attempting to assure quality to actually measuring and improving the quality of care."

Green, D. (1991). "Quality Improvement versus Quality Assurance?" *Topics in Health Records Management,* 11:58–70.

TQ advocates have long contended that an early organizationwide improvement might be experienced by abolishing QA. Deborah Green counters this argument, implying that QA should not be abandoned because it has a use in implementing TQ in an organization. The use of measurement in conjunction with improvement and correction methods establishes common ground between the two quality processes. Green also provides a useful table for the comparison of key aspects of QI and QA. Further analysis of the strengths of QA and QI leads the author to suggest a way to employ the valuable differences between the two models. Ultimately, the implementation of QI does not preclude the use of QA. Traditional QA programs may admirably serve as a foundation for the comprehensive, organizationwide quality improvement transformation. This premise is supported in great detail by two tables within the article and multiple lists within the text.

Kaluzny, A., McLaughlin, C., and Simpson, K. (1992). "Applying Total Quality Management Concepts to Public Health Organizations." *Public Health Reports,* 107:257–264.

These authors, from the Cecil G. Sheps Center for Health Services Research at the University of North Carolina, provide an overview of TQ directed toward an audience from the public sector. The distinction is clearly drawn between the traditional QA role and the organizationwide process of TQ. The recommendations for implementation and application of TQ—in public health agencies take the form of ten prescriptive steps to meet anticipated challenges. These actions are directed toward the leadership of public health practice. The article should be of great help to those of us in the public health community to "examine the potential of TQ within [the public health agency] organizational framework."

Laffel, G. and Blumenthal, D. (1992). "The Case for Using Industrial Quality Management Science in Health Care Organizations." *Journal of the American Medical Association,* 262:2869–2872.

Traditionally, the healthcare system has evaluated the quality of healthcare it delivers by measuring performance, comparing the performance against a standard, and improving performance when standards are not met. This article argues that current practices of healthcare quality assessment limit endeavors to improve quality. Modern quality science, a discipline in which statistical methods are used to assist decisions concerning product quality and production processes, is presented as an alternative to the traditional approach to evaluating healthcare quality. With the application of modern industrial quality control principles to healthcare organizations, advances in the quality of care and service are possible. These principles include redefining quality as a continuous effort by all members of an organization to meet the needs and expectations of the customer; measuring quality while recognizing that variation is inherent in any process and is the result of many possible causes (rather than a single person or some other isolated cause); and improving quality by (1) managerial support for CQI, (2) focusing on processes rather than workers, (3) eliminating unnecessary variation, and (4) revising strategies for personnel management.

This article is frequently cited in the healthcare quality management literature. It serves (along with Berwick's "The Theory of Continuous Improvement" article) as an outstanding introduction to the quality revolution in the healthcare industry. It is not specific to the hospital setting and in this regard promotes application of this process to medical groups, professional schools, and public health organizations.

Masters, F. and Schmele, J. (1991). "Total Quality Management: An Idea Whose Time Has Come." *Journal of Nursing Quality Assurance,* 5:7–16.

This article reviews TQ in broad terms and is written primarily for nursing professionals. The authors briefly describe some of the quality gurus, with an emphasis on the philosophy of W. Edwards Deming, Ph.D. The relationship of TQ to the traditional QA program is examined with a bias toward TQ. There are several helpful points raised in a section on TQ implementation in a healthcare organization. Finally, the article includes a very useful list of references from nonhealthcare, as well as healthcare, sources.

The reader may find this article helpful only after first studying texts and other review articles on TQ, as the comprehensive nature of the TQ philosophy is not apparent in this article. Only with some prior understanding of the history and theory behind TQ can the student benefit from the useful points raised in this article.

McEachern, J. E., Schiff, L., and Cogan, O. (1992). "How to Start a Direct Patient Care Team." *Quality Review Bulletin,* 18:191–200.

Hospital Corporation of America has been a leader in CQI implementation in healthcare for more than a decade. These authors, all from HCA, provide a substantial "how to" article for the improvement of direct patient care processes. The paper offers a great example of teamwork and process improvement for CQI training purposes. By sharing this case study and process in such detail (flowcharts, tables, and diagrams are well utilized throughout the article), readers may also be able to replicate the process in their own organizations.

Meisenheimer, C. (1991). "The Consumer: Silent or Intimate Player in the Quality Revolution." *Holistic Nursing Practice,* 5:39–50.

In the healthcare industry, patients constitute one of the main groups of external customers. Healthcare professionals are recognizing that they are a service industry and that assumptions regarding consumers can be made. The practitioner provides expert information on health, but the task of valuation of quality of care falls on the patient. Quality care is partially defined as the degree of customer satisfaction elicited by the technical aspects of care, coupled with the influence of the interpersonal relationship. "Because the standards have been easier to define and more data have been more readily available, more attention has been given to the technical aspects of care than to the neglect of the interpersonal relationship." The author focuses on customer satisfaction as a measurable outcome of quality care. She explores customer satisfaction characteristics and their subtle determinants.

This article serves to help those engaged in the healthcare industry gain a valuable, new perspective on the customer. A new view of patients as customers is essential for the paradigm shift required from TQ. Clinicians would be well served by reading this article.

Merry, M. (1990). "Total Quality Management for Physicians: Translating the New Paradigm." *Quality Review Bulletin*, March:101–105.

An outstanding introduction to TQ for physicians and other health service providers, this commentary helps the reader to reposition or gain a new perspective. Dr. Merry avoids explaining the history of the evolution of TQ and concentrates on drawing contrasts between traditional healthcare management and TQ. In this way, the new paradigm is translated into real terms for the clinician using real-world examples. As such, the use of statistical control of processes is interpreted as simply applied epidemiology

Merry continues to elaborate on the complex paradigm shift required to bring about physician understanding and leadership by discussing forces influencing the acceptance of TQ. Resistance to change, intense competition, rapidly changing environments, and the unstable organizational structure inherent in the hospital are all addressed in simple terms. In order to acknowledge and then overcome these obstacles, Dr. Merry advises that physician support, education, and active participation "must be framed in terms and metaphors that are supportive of, rather than threatening to, physicians' current perceptions of their needs." He proceeds to list four fundamental needs of the clinician that lead to "appropriately empowering the physician participants."

Oberle, J. (1990). "Quality Gurus: The Men and Their Message." *Training*, January:47–50.

While this essay is not from the healthcare management literature, the discussion of the philosophies espoused by the three main quality leaders is still relevant. This paper briefly traces the evolution of the careers of these leaders since 1979–80. This time period spans the creation of the Crosby Quality College and the Juran Institute (1979). The U.S. awakening to Dr. Deming dates back to the airing of the NBC *White Paper,* "If Japan Can Do It...Why Can't We?" with Bill Moyers in 1980. The information is far from biographical, but is sufficient to lay the groundwork for further study.

Similarities in the three approaches are emphasized, rather than highlighting the differences. For example, "None of the experts offers a quick fix to heal years of mismanagement." They all assign responsibility for failure to top management and misguided leadership. All three gurus embrace basically the same fundamental message—commitment. In conclusion, the author quotes an AT&T manager who compares following a quality expert to selecting a religion. "Does it matter what church you go to as long as you do the right thing?" This essay is very useful in comparing and contrasting the philosophies of these great men in a nonindustry-specific format.

Peters, D. (1992). "A New Look for Quality in Home Care." *Journal of Nursing Administration,* 22:21–26.

This brief article provides another well-constructed comparison of quality assurance and quality improvement. The specific setting is home healthcare. The author provides very convincing rationale to support proactive quality management rather than auditing for negative factors that may escape detection of etiology. Dr. Peters also discusses individual and organizational values in relation to defining quality. Dr. Stephen Covey is cited in this article which touches on an aspect of TQ philosophy left undiscussed by other experts. Covey's approach to self-development (or *personal* continuous quality improvement) has many parallels to organizationwide quality improvement. Important values discussed in the article include empowerment, caring, and cooperation.

This clear and concise article has important information on the application of TQ to home health agencies, community-based care for the developmentally disabled, or hospice care. There is a refreshing discourse on values wherein Peters elaborates on outcome as a quality measure and provides examples of these measures.

INDEX

A

Academic Health Center, 284
Access, 3
Accreditation, 7, 15, 76–77, 184–185, 210, 239, 244, see also Joint Commission on Accreditation of Healthcare Organizations
of community health organizations, 81
standards for hospitals, 4–5
ACHE, see American College of Healthcare Executives
Ackoff, T. L., 69
ACS, see American College of Surgeons
Administrative cross-functional teams, 104
Affinity charts, 99
Agency for Health Care Policy and Research (AHCPR), 224, 225, 232, 244, 247
Agenda, for implementing direct patient care team, 107, 109, 114
AHA, see American Hospital Association
Aharony, I., 215
AHCPR, see Agency for Health Care Policy and Research
Al-Assaf, A. F., 246, 281
AMA, see American Medical Association
Ambulatory care, 18
American College of Healthcare Executives (ACHE), 187
American College of Surgeons (ACS), 4, 15
American Hospital Association (AHA), 187, 281
American Hospital Association Directory, 130
American Medical Association (AMA), Principles of Medical Ethics, 187

American Medical Records Association, 218, 219
American Nurses' Association Code for Nurses, 187
American Productivity & Quality Center (APQC), 264
American Quality Foundation, 245
American Society for Quality Control (ASQC), 162
Anderson, C. A., 245
Andrews, S. L., 213, 217
APACHE II, 232
Applied research, 242
Appraisal costs, 163–164, 165
APQC, see American Productivity & Quality Center
ASQC, see American Society for Quality Control
Authority, 196
Avery, A., 5
Awareness training, 269–271

B

Bader, B., 234
Balance sheet, 139
Bar graph, 136
Basic research, 242
Batalden, P. B., 60, 211, 213, 282
Bednar, D. A., 214
Belasco, J. A., 200, 201, 202, 203
Beloff, J., 214
Benefit, defined, 63
Berger, S., 212
Bernardi v. Community Hospital Association, 185–186

289

The Textbook of Total Quality in Healthcare

Huff, L., 246
Hungler, B. P., 99

I

ICFs, see Intermediate Care Facilities
IHS, see Indian Health Service
Implementation of total quality, 91–122,
    281–282
  cultural change and, 94–96
  evaluating quality, 99–100
  executive level commitment, 93–94
  how to start a direct patient care team,
      103–122
    materials and methods, 105–112
    sample results for chest pain team,
      115–121
    sample results for HIV team, 112–115
  organizing quality, 98–99
  planning for, 96–98
Indian Health Service, 24
Individual outcomes, in home care, 86–87
Individual responsibility, 29
Industrial quality management science
    (IQMS), 209 210, 285–286
  in healthcare organizations, 40–50
    personnel management, 48–49
    quality, defining, 43–44
    quality, improving, 44–49
    quality, measuring, 44
    quality of care, theory and practice,
      41–43
  for physicians, 51–59
Information management, see Data
    management
Innovativeness, OQI and, 69
In Search of Excellence in Home Care
    project, 81, 83, 86, 87, 89
Inspection, continuous improvement and,
    37
Inspector General v. Greece, 183–184
Institute of Medicine (IOM), 224, 231
Instrumentation Research, 246–247
Insurance, 15–16, 17, 21, 177, see also
    Medicaid; Medicare
Interagency outcomes, in home care, 88–89
Interdisciplinarity, 94
Intermediate Care Facilities (ICFs), 20
Internal customers, 97
  data management and, 123; see also Data
    management

International Quality Study (IQS), 245
InterStudy, 226
Interview, 130, 131, 267
Intra-agency outcomes, in home care,
    87–88
IOM, see Institute of Medicine
IQMS, see Industrial quality management
    science
IQS, see International Quality Study
Ishikawa, K., 62
Ishikawa diagram, 148–149, see also Cause-
    and-effect diagram
  for brainstorming session, 53
  OQI and, 67

J

Japan
  cultural fit with TQ, 197
  history of QI, 60, 62
  origin of TQ, 3, 5–6
  Theory of Continuous Improvement in,
    33–35
Jaques, E., 56
JCAH, see Joint Commission on Accredita-
    tion of Hospitals
JCAHO, see Joint Commission on
    Accreditation of Healthcare
    Organizations
Jenks, S. F., 233
Jennings, B. M., 225
Job descriptions, 195
Joint Commission on Accreditation of
    Healthcare Organizations, 15, 210,
    211, 221, 223, 244, 247
  Agenda for Change, 10, 76
  position on QI, 75–79
  ten-step model for monitoring and
    evaluation, 91
Joint Commission on Accreditation of
    Hospitals, 7, 8, 10, 184, 223
  Agenda for Change, 224, 233
  historical background, 4–5
Jonas, S., 13
Jones, L., 244
Judicial system, role in shaping healthcare
    quality, 173–174
  ethics and, 174–175
  liability, 184–186
  licensure, 182–184
  physician peer review, 180–182

Juran, J. M., 29, 30, 33, 35, 56, 60, 62, 96,
144, 213

K

Kaiser Permanente, 15–16, 23
Kaizen, 34–35, 283
Kaluzny, A. D., 91, 212, 285
Keil, O., 214
Key quality characteristics (KQCs), in
implementing direct patient care
team, 111–112
Kovner, A.R., 15
KQCs, see Key quality characteristics

L

Laffel, G., 40, 215, 216, 285
Laws, see Government regulation of
healthcare; Legislation; specific
legislation
Leadership, 29, 45, 62, 267, 270, 281
continuous improvement and, 35
OQI and , 66, 68
transformational, 200
Leebov, W., 91, 97, 98, 126
Legislation, see also Government
regulation of healthcare; specific
legislation
COBRA, 179
ethics and, 174–175, 187–188
HCQI, 176–178
judicial involvement in determining
quality, 179–187
liability, 184–186
licensure, 182–184
physician peer review, 180–182
role in shaping healthcare quality,
173–174
Stark laws, 178–179
Lezzoni, L. I., 232
Licensing, of physicians, 173, 177, 180,
182–184
Licensing boards, 177, 180
LoGerfo, J. P., 223
Logs, 133, 134
Lohr, K. N., 225
Longo, D., 232
Longo, D. R., 124
Lorenz, M. C., 144
Luff, H. S., 223

M

MacArthur, Douglas, 5, 60
Mail survey, 130–131
Malcolm Balrige criteria, 267, 268
Malcolm Balrige National Quality Award, 267
Malpractice lawsuits, 9, 10, 21
Managed care, 22
Managed fee-for-service, 22
Management, 6–7
commitment of, in implementing TQ,
93–94, 99
continuous improvement and, 36
OQI and, 68–69
of personnel, 48–49
VAMC, 265
Management information systems, 227
Management philosophies, total quality
and, 191–205
managing the process through change to
TQ, 202–205
organizational cultures, 192–193
TQ and corporate culture, 196–199
transforming organizations to TQ,
199–202
use of power in organizations, 193–196
pluralistic, 194–195
structured, 195–196
unitary, 193–194
Manager, ethics and, 174, 187–188
Managing cultural transformation, 199–205
Manufacturing industries, 5–7, 213–215
Marine Hospital Service, 14
Markson, L. E., 224, 226, 232, 233
Marszalek-Gaucher, E., 200, 248
Maslow's hierarchy of needs, 57–58
Masters, F., 286
Matrix, 139
McEachern, J. E., 103, 286
McLaughlin, C. P., 212, 285
MCSC, see Medical Center Steering
Committee
MDJS, see Physician Judgment System
Measurement of quality, 30
home care and, 86–89
Medicaid, 7, 17, 18, 20, 184–185
Medical Center Steering Committee (MCSC),
267, 268, 269, 270, 271, 272, 274,
275, 276
Medical education, historical background,
4, 13, 14–15
Medical liability lawsuits, 9, 10

OQI, 60–74
for physicians, 51–59
research and, 239–257
strengths of, 219
VA healthcare system, case study,
261–280
Total quality management (TQM), 239, see
also Total quality
TQ, see Total quality
TQM, see Total quality management
Training, 47, 49–50, 202, 204, 269–271, see
also Education
continuous improvement and, 36
cost and, 163
QI and, 47
Tree diagram, 99
Trend chart, 139–140, 141
Trust building, 94, 95
Tyler, R. D., 219

U

UHDDS, see Uniform Hospital Discharge
Data Set
Undisciplinarity, 94
Uniform Hospital Discharge Data Set
(UHDDS), 244
Unitary organization, 193–194
United States
cultural fit with TQ, 197, see also Cultural
transformation
history of TQ in manufacturing, 3, 6–7,
213–215
IQMS in, 210
United States healthcare system
historical background
1600s–1850s, 13–16
1950s–1990s, 16–25
VA, see Veterans Administration
healthcare system
U.S. Department of Health and Human
Services (DHHS), 177, 231–232
home care and, 81
U.S. Public Health Service, 14, 24, 224,
231

V

VAMCs, see Veterans Administration
Medical Centers
Vance, M., 81, 83

VAOPCs, see Veterans Administration
outpatient clinics
Variance analysis, 169
Variation
control charts to monitor, 145–148
elimination of unnecessary, 47–48
in measuring quality, 44
Veterans Administration, 281
Veterans Administration healthcare system
case study in implementing TQ, 261–280
communication, 277–278
forming teams, 270–271
history of, 263–265
initial assessment, 267–268
mission and vision statements, 268–269
outcomes, 271–277
success of, 277–278
TQ awareness training, 269
Veterans Administration Medical Centers
(VAMCs), 261
case study in implementing TQ, see
Veterans Administration healthcare
system
sample questionnaire, 153–156
Veterans Administration Outpatient Clinics
(VAOPCs), 261, 262
Veterans Health Administration (VHA), 261
VHA, see Veterans Health Administration
Vision, 200–201, 202, 240, 263
statement, 268–269
Volkwein, F., 192
Vuori, H., 250, 253

W

Waggoner, D. M., 249
Ward, S. S., 249
Weighted voting technique, 138–139, 140
Weinstein, S., 56
Werley, H. H., 244
Wilensky, G. R., 233
Williams, S. J., 16
Williamson, J. W., 255
Williamson, R. G., 211, 216
Worthman, L., 232

Y

Yuhasz, L. S., 245, 246

Z

Zero defect, 30, 53